The Nature and Grounds of Political Obligation in the Hindu State

NEW EDITION

The Nature and Grounds of Political Obligation in the Hindu State

Originally published in 1935 as a part of the series:
Regional & Sociological Studies (Mainly Indian) edited by
N.A. Thoothi, D.Phil. (Oxon), with a Foreword by Prof. P.A. Wadia, M.A.

J.J. ANJARIA

Preface to the New Edition

SHAILENDRA J. ANJARIA

Introduction to the New Edition

ULKA ANJARIA

ACADEMIC FOUNDATION
NEW DELHI

New Edition published in 2012
by

ACADEMIC FOUNDATION
4772-73 / 23 Bharat Ram Road, (23 Ansari Road),
Darya Ganj, New Delhi - 110 002 (India).
Phones : 23245001 / 02 / 03 / 04.
Fax : +91-11-23245005.
E-mail : books@academicfoundation.com
www.academicfoundation.com

Originally published in 1935
by Longmans, Green and Co. Ltd., Calcutta.

Cataloging in Publication Data–DK
Courtesy: D.K. Agencies (P) Ltd. <Docinfo@dkagencies.com>

Anjaria, J. J. (Jashwantrai Jayantilal), 1908-1970.
The nature and grounds of political obligation in the Hindu state / J.J. Anjaria. – New ed.
p. cm.
Includes bibliographical references.
Includes index.
ISBN 13: 9788171889273
ISBN 10: 8171889271

1. Hinduism and state–India. 2. Hinduism and politics–India. 3. Political obligation. 4. India–Politics and government–To 997. I. Title.

DDC 320.011 23

Typeset by Italics India, New Delhi.
Printed and bound in India.

Contents

Chapter II

Chapter III

Preface to the New Edition

Shailendra J. Anjaria*

I am privileged to see published for today's readers this new edition of a work by my late father J.J. Anjaria, written in 1935. He passed away in 1970 at the age of 61, leaving unfulfilled a good part of his aspiration to live the experience of India developing as a stable, variegated modern state with an economic system that can meet the needs and aspirations of all parts of society. This work was written when my father was a student of political science, before he became an economist; and is fascinating for its revelation of how a profound knowledge of the values and culture of the Indian ancients and Western scholars on the subject of political obligation can frame the thinking of a future professional economist. I hope readers will appreciate this as a sample of the work of a generation that came before mine which has helped carve out the basic shape of today's India.

I am profoundly grateful to Deena Khatkhate and the late Anand Chandavarkar, my father's friends and colleagues first at the Reserve Bank of India and later at the International Monetary Fund, who for long gently persisted in encouraging me, while I still worked at the IMF, to ensure that this somewhat forgotten work is freshly resurfaced. Last year I resettled in India at the end of an enthralling IMF career that culminated in my serving

* Shailendra J. Anjaria, Mumbai, December 2011.

as Secretary of the IMF. Since then, my top priority has been to bring out this edition without further delay.

I owe my deep thanks to Rituraj Kapila, who proved invaluable in guiding the Academic Foundation's republication of this work without further delay. That my daughter Ulka, without ever having known her grandfather in person, outlines in her introduction the connections between this work and today's academy, is for me, a priceless bonus.

Introduction to the New Edition

Ulka Anjaria*

"[T]hey are to be understood with reference to their age."

— J.J. Anjaria, *The Nature and Grounds of Political Obligation in the Hindu State,* p. 292

J.J. Anjaria's 1935 book, *The Nature and Grounds of Political Obligation in the Hindu State*, tackles a crucial set of problems for a colonized nation on the cusp of sovereignty: Who are we? What makes us unique? What are our indigenous traditions? What did we look like before British colonization and what will we look like in its wake?

For Anjaria, trained in his early years in political science and later switching to economics, considering the possibilities for India's national culture entailed interrogating the relevance of ancient political philosophy—in particular the role of political obligation—for India's modern future. He conducts this inquiry by means of a careful exegesis of the political philosophy embedded in ancient texts, focusing on, among others, the *Mahābhārata*,

* Ulka Anjaria is Assistant Professor of English at Brandeis University, Waltham, USA. She researches and teaches on Indian literature and film, and has published in, among others, Economic and Political Weekly, Novel: A Forum for Fiction, Journal of South Asian Popular Culture and Biblio. Her monograph, *Realism in the Twentieth-Century Indian Novel: Colonial Difference and Literary Form*, is forthcoming.

Kauṭilya's *Arthaśāstra*, the *Manu-smṛiti*, the Purāṇas, the Buddhist *Dīgha Nikāya* and Jataka tales, and Jain scriptures such as the *Nitivākyāmrita*. He combs these texts for any philosophical insights that might be useful for a modern state that seeks both to ensure that its citizenry flourishes under modern ideals, and also carries forward India's own cultural and political heritage.

Anjaria's innovation is to challenge the assumption that because there were no strictly political works in ancient India, the culture lacked a political philosophy altogether. He extracts a theory of political obligation from texts that many would consider works of religion, rather than politics—works which, contrary to the presumptions of the discipline, consider man "essentially a spiritual being" (37). Yet rather than bracketing their religious purpose in order to distill a secular theory out of them, he considers their ultimate spiritual goal—the achievement of *dharma*—as central to their political philosophy. What he ends up with is a conclusion that will please the contemporary anthropologist: the idea that in ancient India "political obligation is not merely political in a narrow sense; because of its association with *Dharma*, it becomes religious or spiritual" (279). To understand the political rationality of this pre-modern time, he suggests, one must become fluent in cultural and religious concepts, which seem to have nothing to do with politics at all. This is a lucid instance of what, even today, is seen as a radical intellectual practice—of crossing long-held disciplinary boundaries in order to discover nuanced theoretical formations in unlikely places.

Anjaria unearths a set of ideas about kingship, authority and ideal citizenry that for the most part do not lend themselves to democratic interpretation. Rather, they suggest, among other things, that monarchical authority had divine backing, that physical force was justified to keep a citizenry in order, and that individual enlightenment was more important than the social good. These, Anjaria concludes, are at heart anti-democratic values. He thus argues against the views of some of his intellectual contemporaries, including D.R. Bhandarkar, who suggested that ancient India offered "inspiring examples of early democracy" (Verma, 2010: 17), and S. Radhakrishnan, who suggested that women in ancient India held an "exalted" position (225). Anjaria recommends that such scholarship, even in its eagerness to endorse the Hindu past, must nevertheless subject the texts to rigorous scrutiny. By framing his argument as a rejoinder to this nationalist impulse, Anjaria establishes himself in opposition to Fanon's indigenous intellectual, who forges a national culture by "discover[ing] [with the greatest delight] that there was nothing to be ashamed of in the past, but rather dignity, glory, and solemnity" (210). Anjaria contests the claim that Indians should unthinkingly valorize their past merely because it is theirs. The work thus stands as a critical reassessment of not only ancient Indian political philosophy, but the very contemporary inclination to resurrect a past without consideration of its continued relevance for the national future.

The book thus exhibits a crucial ambivalence between the triumphant march into a modern future that characterizes the more vanguardist proponents of planning in 1930s and 1940s India, and the kind of cultural essentialism that turns its back on modernity altogether. The ambivalent cultural and intellectual life of early twentieth-century India is fairly easy to identify in literary works such as those of Tagore or Premchand, or even in the self-consciously experimental ethics of Gandhi—all of which are formally attuned to ambivalence. For Anjaria, however, influenced by social scientific positivism in his approach to intellectual history, the ambivalence is contained beneath the surface of the text. It appears at moments, for instance in his clear frustration with the most anti-democratic elements of ancient India such as slavery and the oppression of women and lower castes—a frustration which reveals his personal stakes in his arguments despite what remains for the most part an objective tone. Such moments serve as provocative symptoms of how deeply colonialism's "double consciousness" was felt even in the social sciences. By tracing the intellectual's internal battle between the powerful sway of European ideals of liberalism, democracy and progress on one hand, and an immanent and partially formed sense of nationalist spirit on the other, the text offers another instantiation of how fraught the experience of colonial modernity in fact was.

The book is thus not merely a call for the reform of indigenous institutions, nor what the Editor calls "a more or less secular revaluation [of the Hindu Polity] in terms of volition, freedom of personality, and democracy" (25). Rather, it textualizes the conditions of intellectual ambivalence under which India's nation-builders were working. N.A. Thoothi's General Introduction to the Series along with P.A. Wadia's Foreword both draw the reader's attention to the forward-thinking spirit of the age, with Thoothi citing his teacher and an early sociologist at Bombay University, Patrick Geddes, whose "great dream... was to build the City Beautiful, the New Jerusalem, as he called it" (24). Thoothi strives to perpetuate Geddes's modernist desire "to survey, to build and to rebuild" (24)—and Anjaria himself sometimes takes that tone, especially towards the end of the book, when he promises that "The *Dharma-rājya* of the future cannot be created on the foundation of an iniquitous social order... In the State we build up, there shall not be a slave buried alive beneath the foundation... We have not merely to visualise our ideal polity; we have to live it" (299). However, underlying these moments of exultancy is a deep ambivalence that underlies the whole project of considering the encounter between the 'West' and the 'East'. This emerges in the text as a sensibility that is more akin to what Sudipta Kaviraj describes as the "unhappy consciousness" of intellectuals such as Bankimchandra Chattopadhyay than the triumphalist rhetoric of Geddes. It sheds new light on Anjaria's careful sifting through the traditions of the past to ensure that nothing of value gets left behind—a methodology which at times appears fruitlessly painstaking, with Anjaria evaluating minute differences in philosophy of the most important texts only to find, very often, no noteworthy differences to speak of. Here the social scientist's eye seems overlain by the archaeologist's, rendering him unwilling to let any potentially valuable detail go unobserved, in the hope that it will later contribute to the completion of a larger puzzle. I read this impassioned care as an unarticulated appeal to preserve the nuance and richness of ancient thought from being overwhelmed by the admittedly more charismatic rhetoric of modernization and progress.

These questions and the equivocation with which he necessarily faced them were not merely academic for Anjaria, but central to the unfolding of his own life. He was born in Bhuj, the capital of the princely state of Kutch, in 1908. His father was a school teacher and his mother died when he was young. The family disposed of very modest means, but because Anjaria performed remarkably well in school, he was offered a full scholarship for advanced studies in Bombay, where he completed his B.A. and M.A. degrees. He went on to secure his M.Sc. in Economics at the London School of Economics. As an academic and then later as a policy maker and adviser to the Indian government and the International Monetary Fund, he lived variously in Bombay, Delhi, London and Washington D.C. until his retirement and premature death in 1970.

The range of social contexts he encountered in the course of his travels—from the relatively isolated princedom of Kutch (Mehta, 2005: 75) to the world's most important metropoles—was not a unique experience in the early twentieth century; however, it remained, to use Ashis Nandy's term, an "ambiguous" one. The journey from village to city has become an oft-repeated trope in Indian literature of the early twentieth century, in part because it had such an affective resonance in forming India's unique modernity. It is difficult to forget the image, for instance, of Satyajit Ray's Apu, toying, while on the train for Calcutta, with a small globe that he had been unable to fit in his suitcase. The vision of the young man holding a globe as the train—a classic icon of modernity—pulls in to Sealdah Station is emblematic for the possibilities offered by migration to the cosmopolitan city and beyond. Underlying this image, however, is a profound ambiguity—not only for who is left behind, but regarding what the city even means, and whether it promotes or in fact frustrates self-growth. The city in its own constitutive heterogeneity—what in another context has been called a mix of 'foreign form' and 'indigenous content'[1]—frustrates both colonialist and nationalist narratives, which operate along a strict dichotomy between the native and the colonial. Indeed, for most modernizers, the city was the essential site of India's national modernity. In this way, for Apu and so many other migrants, the city is in fact an unanswerable question. How do we begin to delineate the multiple selves and journeys that comprise these variegated itineraries of the modern?

Because we have very few of Anjaria's personal writings or statements on such questions, we know little of his views on these travels and trajectories. What we do see throughout his published works is the determination to remain unswayed by the more charismatic registers of nationalist rhetoric for which modernity and the west are inherently problematic. As a social scientist and economist, he was committed to values not because they were British or Indian but because they would contribute to a better Indian society and, later on, a stronger economy. In some ways, then, his perspective was staunchly disinterested. But the diversity of his writings, and specifically the excruciating form of this less well-known work, do raise the question of what underlay this demeanor. Why was he so interested in unearthing the political philosophy embedded in various ancient Indian texts if his ultimate goal was only to debunk them, or to point out their irrelevance to modern India? The indecipherability of this question should not be dismissed, but preserved. Clearly Anjaria's sense of self, as with so many others of his education and class in colonial India, was constituted by a reality "in which many different subject positions and even nonbourgeois, nonindividualistic practices of subjectivity intersect" (Chakrabarty, 2000: 144). These do not cohere to provide some sort of seamless whole, but often contradict one another, producing a multivalent subject that emerges precisely from the different kinds of experiences and perspectives that intellectuals under colonialism were compelled to inhabit, all at once.

1. This is how Meenakshi Mukherjee describes the early Indian novel, but the same can be said for urban life in the former colonies as well (18).

What this work teaches us, therefore, is that truly decolonial thinking does not necessarily entail a dismantling of colonial binaries, but should direct attention to how these binaries are continually deployed to reshape the subjectivity of the colonized, and how in this repeated deployment their precariousness is revealed. Thus, when at times Anjaria makes use of a binaristic differentiation of Indian and European political values, this does not indicate Anjaria's simplistic understanding of the world. If anything, his personal, linguistic, and cultural fluency in both western and Indian contexts—and within India, in both small towns and big cities—reveals that his was a much more cosmopolitan consciousness than his occasionally dichotomous rhetoric conveys. Today's readers will certainly question the textual basis of his ancient sources, which limit him by definition to Brahminical, male, and politically sanctioned perspectives. Likewise, they might worry that the picture he paints of political authority in ancient India conforms to Orientalist images of authoritarian despots (Said, 1978: 203). And they might contest his relatively surface-level picture of European political thought, pointing to a wide range of perspectives that deserve their own in-depth study. These may be valid criticisms. But when these choices are considered as part of the very problem he is seeking to address, Anjaria can be re-read as offering a fascinating account, both in what he writes and also in the parallel unfolding of his text-as-knowledge, of how the operation of dichotomous thought is not a form of censorship, but what Foucault would call an "incitement to discourse" (17). This book is part of the discourse incited by colonized thinking. It is, like many other valuable texts of the time, both a product and a radical recalibration of such thinking in service of a modern India.

Works Cited

Chakrabarty, Dipesh (2000). *Provincializing Europe: Postcolonial Thought and Historical Difference.* Princeton: Princeton University Press.

Fanon, Frantz (1965). *The Wretched of the Earth.* Trans. Richard Philcox. New York: Grove Press.

Foucault, Michel (1978). *The History of Sexuality,* Volume I. Trans. Robert Hurley. New York: Pantheon.

Kaviraj, Sudipta (1995). *The Unhappy Consciousness: Bankimchandra Chattopadhyay and the Formation of Nationalist Discourse in India.* Delhi: Oxford University Press.

Mehta, Lyla (2005). *The Politics and Poetics of Water: The Naturalisation of Scarcity in Western India.* Hyderabad: Orient Longman.

Mukherjee, Meenakshi (1985). *Realism and Reality: The Novel and Society in India.* New Delhi: Oxford University Press.

Nandy, Ashis (2001). *An Ambiguous Journey to the City: The Village and Other Odd Ruins of the Self in the Indian Imagination.* New Delhi: Oxford University Press.

Said, Edward (1978). *Orientalism.* New York: Pantheon.

Verma, S.K. (2010). *Political History of Ancient India.* Delhi: Global Media.

General Introduction to the Series

This series of monographs embodies the results of researches conducted by students working under my direction in the Bombay University School of Economics and Sociology, and by myself. The studies bear upon problems of human life in its various aspects—regional, economic, institutional, cultural and philosophical with view to advance constructive suggestions concerning the complicated problems that confront us at the present day.

Such an undertaking necessitates the treatment of facts and ideas in a scientic spirit and manner. Only patient investigation can yield results that prove valuable for the guidance of life. Every problem has its practical bearings. Hence, to understand a problem we must study it with reference to its past as well as its present, in order that we may be enabled to estimate its future. Vague and unscientific endeavours and conclusions are worse than useless; for they not merely vitiate human effort but frustrate purpose and aspiration, and paralyse our hope to shape the future.

And, in our own days, there is an urgent need for the kind of inquiries that the present series proposes to undertake and pursue. We are in the midst of an 'omnipresent anarchy of values'; consequently, we are in a drift which bids fair to sweep the world to disaster. If equilibrium be regained and maintained, there must be a clear adequate understanding of the fundamental facts, purposes, values and difficulties of human life. The humble aim of this series is to study and understand the various aspects of the human problem, and discover and formulate, or may be, rediscover and reformulate, a scheme of values that may become the basis of a more equitable and stable human order. One of our objects is to prevent loose thinking which is at the root of so much disharmony in the world of human relationships. It is the hope of Science that a disinterested pursuit of truth will rally human beings round the banner of its eternal values; humanity might thus be brought together by recognising the common affinities and life-values underneath the seeming differences arising from regional and historical causes.

The problems of human life being various, the methods of approach are also many: philosophical, scientific and practical. In the series herewith presented, all these methods have been employed. There is a common purpose running through the labours of individual writers, however divided they may be on specific issues and details, however varied and even contradictory may be their conclusions. That purpose is to present the human problem in all its aspects carefully analysed and discussed.

Our ambition is to build up a body of systematic knowledge, at once scientific and of practical utility, which might help in the reconstruction of the future, and to organise a school of thought with an 'ethos' and a 'quest' uniquely its own. However partially the ambition and hope may be realised, we feel sure that what we are doing is worth doing, and that it is high time it should be undertaken by some of us in India.

The great dream of the Editor's teacher, Sir Patrick Geddes, was to build the City Beautiful, the New Jerusalem, as he called it. He is no more amongst us to dream, to survey, to build and to rebuild. But it is our hope and purpose that the master's wishes should be fulfilled, however fragmentarily and inadequately, by the humble efforts of those who have inherited a little the light of his spirit, and felt the urge of his indomitable will to strive, to labour, to plan and to achieve.

— N.A. Thoothi
School of Economics and Sociology,
University of Bombay,
March 1935

Editor's Note*

This, the second of the Studies in Hindu Polity in this series, was undertaken by Mr. J.J. Anjaria, who worked on it under my guidance during 1929-32, at the Bombay University School of Economics and Sociology.

In the first of the Studies on Hindu Polity in this series, Professor Pratapagiri has taken a review of Hindu Polity on the widest possible canvas, evaluated the same and suggested lines of construction in terms of Spiritual Values. In the present work Mr. Anjaria attacks a specific issue of Hindu Polity, namely the Problem of Political Obligation, goes into its details, synthesises them in terms of the universal principle of Dharma, and suggests a more or less secular revaluation in terms of volition, freedom of personality, and democracy.

Such revaluation, according to Mr. Anjaria, need not be through a wholesale rejection of past tradition and heritage which contain precious elements worthy enough to serve in the reconstruction of the future. The elements are the essential ingredients of our culture. Therefore Mr. Anjaria pleads for the upkeep and nurture of this central core of Hindu culture and civilisation, and sees ontogenetic and phylogenetic possibilities in this conception, loyalty to which, he assures us, should remove discrepancies between the actual and the ideal in any age, and enable us to reject ideas and institutions which have lost their

---

* As published in the original 1935 edition of J.J. Anjaria's book which is a part of the series: Regional & Sociological Studies (Mainly Indian), edited by N.A. Thoothi, D.Phil (Oxon).

meaning and have ceased to be instruments of life; such loyalties may thus help man to avoid errors of the past, satisfy man's creative spirit, and relate old and new loyalties in a central principle underlying the universe—a principle that has through all the vicissitudes of ages, kept up the culture and civilisation of our forefathers. If we judge the services of Dharma as a whole, we must keep it next to our bosom, even as we try to keep Love within us; if we judge Dharma piece-meal (even as we do the gospel of Love) and find it wanting, we do so at our peril.

For, the problem is really not so simple as it is assumed to be; and, it really does not admit of being posed in terms of 'man failing Dharma' or 'Dharma failing man'. 'Dharma' and 'man' are not abstract terms or entities. Man lives in a region, lives on it, draws not only his material but, to an extent unsuspected by most of us, his spiritual sustenance from it, is inevitably affected by it and in turn affects it, is moulded by it and in turn moulds it. We cannot, indeed we must not, think of man apart from the region in which he lives, any more than we can afford to think of a tree apart from the soil in which it is rooted. And, what is Dharma but the way, method and ritual of living? Therefore how can it be considered, for any practical purpose, without reference to the community of men which devised it and to the region to which the community belonged? It should follow of necessity that if man adheres to and lives by the Dharma of his region, there would be no conflicts between ideal and practice. Whence, then, do the conflicts arise? Whence is it that Dharma becomes unsuited to the necessities of life, and that sometimes Dharma and life have nothing to do with each other, that the claims of God and Caesar are not only separate but totally inconsistent? It is because the Dharma professed or attempted to be practised in a region is not always the Dharma of the region. Dharma gets imposed just as political suzerainty gets imposed on regions and folks. And it also happens, when there is no question of political or spiritual domination, that, for whatever reason, spiritual progress fails to keep pace with material progress either because material progress, prosperity and consequent sense of absolute security overshadow and finally drive into background the spiritual resources on which they are reared (cf. the history of modern Europe), or because (which may really amount to the same) the folk may thoughtlessly or carelessly or indifferently continue to rely on and employ instruments, methods, ways, of spiritual progress which, owing to passage of time, rate of progress, vicissitudes of history, may have lost their ancient significance and their creative and fulfillng potency.

The conflict, therefore, can only be envisaged in the right perspective if we analyse it regionally and historically as suggested above.

Mr. Anjaria's method, his analysis and synthesis, his conclusions and valuations are admirable; they are of great value and complete for the purpose of his inquiry. But it is our belief that for a more concrete realisation of the problems of polity, a regional interpretation is necessary in addition to and parallel with the historical which Mr. Anjaria has employed here. We put forward this suggestion with the more confidence since Mr. Anjaria is inclined to accept and be guided by a pluralistic and secular bias.

— N.A. Thoothi

Foreword

If it is man's privilege to look before and after, at no time in the history of the civilised world has the need for looking before and after been so urgently imperative as in these post-war years when expediency and opportunism seem to be the only governing factors in our lawmaking bodies on the one hand and in our foreign offices on the other. The extent to which we shall look "before" us, shall have a vision of the kingdom and shall work for it, will depend on our ability to look "behind" us, on our powers of interpretation of the past under the urge of a genuine desire to understand it. The work which is now in the reader's hands is an attempt to understand and interpret the Hindu conception of the grounds of Political Obligation: it is not simply descriptive, a bare record collected out of documents; it aims at correlating the particular problem to the rest of Hindu life and the objectified purposes of the Hindu soul. I feel sure its value will be judged not simply by the accuracy of its documentation, but by the earnestness of the desire to understand, to correlate and to interpret, which is manifest throughout its pages. May it contribute its own little mite to the process of awakening in this land of ours which, while it draws on its own ancient heritage, is full of the promise of leading a groping humanity out of the mire and confusion of a planless existence!

— P.A. Wadia

Preface

The aim of this short study has been explained in the Introduction. It remains to add here how conscious I am of the ramifications of the problem of political obligation. To anyone who is aware of the recent writings on the subject, it would be evident that an adequate understanding of the problem requires an investigation into geographical, economic, religious, and in the broadest sense, cultural foundations of the Polity. The present study may only be regarded as a starting point of such further investigations. In so far as it represents an attempt systematically to analyse the relevant data and to interpret them as a whole in the light of a central conception, it is hoped, it justifies itself.

This work was submitted to the University of Bombay for the M.A. Degree in 1932. I am under a deep obligation to Dr. Thoothi, the Editor of the present series, who, as supervisor of my studies at the University, has always helped me with suggestions and criticisms. It has been his conviction that the keynote of ancient Indian culture is the concept of Dharma—the stumbling-block of writers only superficially acquainted with the essential basis of Indian thought. My interest in political theory I owe to Prof. Wadia, whose student I had the privilege to be. His insistence that institutions are but instrumental to life has had a great meaning for me. He has placed me under a further debt of gratitude by writing the Foreword. It is a pleasure also to acknowledge the great help I have received from frequent discussions with my friend and some time teacher, Prof. R. Pratapagiri, M.A. Nothing more needs to be said about this here, since the result of his own research on the subject appears as a separate volume in this series. My thanks are also due to my friend, Mr. C.L. Gheevala, M.A. for kindly going through some of the proof and helping in the preparation of the Index.

And finally, I am thankful to the University of Bombay for having made a substantial grant towards the cost of publishing this book.

— J.J. Anjaria

Introduction

The aim of this Thesis is to search out and examine the nature and grounds of political obligation as visualised by Hindu thinkers. The impulse to association is fundamental in man and life in society necessitates conformity to certain rules of conduct. Even in primitive societies we find a rudimentary organisation which supplies and maintains with the help of custom and taboo a norm of conduct for members. Man is dependent on society for his very origin and upbringing. Life, even on a purely biological level, presupposes some social organisation. Every man is thus a member of a community. The higher the plane on which he wishes to live, the more intimate and varied become his contacts with his fellowmen. And every community needs an organisation of some sort, an organisation to regulate, co-ordinate and harmonise the various activities of man in society. Thus men, by nature 'political' beings, are necessarily citizens of a State.[1] Here, then, is a problem for the thinker. What is the relation of the State to its members? Why do men obey the State? In other words, what is the nature of political obligation and on what grounds is it based?

Philosophers have thought on this problem from early times. It was this problem which Plato and Aristotle attempted to solve. It is this problem which Hegel, Green and Bosanquet have attempted to solve. The solutions of the problem bear indelible stamps of the varying conditions of the times. Theories do not hang like castles in the air. They have their roots in the characteristic facts and signs of the times. It may, indeed, be admitted that theories

---

1. cf. McKechnie: *The State and the Individual*, pp. 1-3.

mould facts to a great extent. There is certainly an interaction between the two. It cannot be gainsaid, however, that the necessary data for the thinker have to be taken from facts. Thus, particular theories must be related to the whole cultural environment of the times, if they are to be properly understood.

The State is a phenomenon of universal occurrence, but its forms have varied from time to time and from place to place. Political theory has similarly evolved through various stages. There is thus a close relation between political theory and history. As the conditions of the problem vary from age to age, so the solutions must necessarily vary with them. Yet we should not lose sight of the fundamental unity of the problem itself. The ultimate problem before all the peoples of the world is one. We might call it the search after Reality. This one problem is offered, as it were, for solution to different peoples in different settings. The solutions, therefore, are bound to differ. Each gets a glimpse of Truth from a particular angle of vision. But Truth is many-sided. The solutions might seem to be different, perhaps even contradictory. In reality, they are but different aspects of the same Truth. It is by co-ordinating them that the whole Truth can be realised, not by spurning some and exalting others. Behind the diversity of solutions, there is an underlying unity. In fact, this diversity itself makes for a rich harmony. The State, we must not forget, is founded on facts which gather round human nature. Therein lies the unity of the problem.[2] Only there are different pathways, different avenues of approach to the problem. The Greeks viewed their problem in the setting of the city-state, and produced their theory of the State. This theory has great elements of value even to the present day. It would not be too much to say that modern political theory is, in fact, the Greek theory, amplified and restated so as to explain modern conditions. Rome's contribution to the problem lies in her law, and in her emphasis on the brotherhood of mankind. The ancient Indians, too, have their own contribution to make to the solution of the problem. We do not, indeed, expect

---

2. cf. Barker's remarks on the relation of history and political theory in *The Study of Political Science and its Relation to Cognate Studies*, pp. 17-19.

the same sort of developments in India as in ancient Greece and Rome. Now and then we might come across similarities. More often, perhaps, there may be divergence. These similarities as well as divergences have a meaning for the ultimate solution.

Our task is to find out how ancient Hindu thinkers viewed their problem. We have to see what political obligation meant to them, and how they explained it in ethical terms. "The central problem of political philosophy and the chief aim of political action is," as Vaughan points out, "to secure the right relation between the individual and the State".[3] The problem before us is to see what sort of relation between the individual and the State was sought to be established as the right relation by the Hindu thinkers of old. We must also try to understand on what grounds the loyalty of the individual to the State was explained by them.

It must be pointed out here that our concern is essentially with the ideal. We propose to study the Hindu 'Idea' or the Hindu 'Ideal' of the State. The actual may fall short of the ideal; but the actual can easily be understood if the ideal has been thoroughly grasped. To understand and criticise the actual may not be without value. Such a study, however, has at best but tentative validity. The actual might soon develop into something nobler; and so the criticism made with reference to its earlier stage would no longer be applicable after the new developments. To study and to evaluate the ideal is to be on surer grounds. For, the actual is but the partial manifestation of the ideal. If the ideal is found to be fundamentally sound, the actual has only to reach up to it. If, however, the ideal itself is defective, the actual must necessarily be so. In a word, the real nature of a thing is not what it is at any given point of time. It is what it has in it to be. That is why we propose to study the Hindu conception or the Hindu ideal of the State.

Similarly, as regards the grounds for political obligation, it is the ideal that concerns us. Our question is: why according to ancient Hindu thinkers the State claims and deserves the allegiance

3. *Studies in the History of Political Philosophy*, I, p. 2.

of its members; why, that is to say, the individual *ought* to obey the State. Ours is not an enquiry as to why in any particular instance the individual actually obeys the law of the State. Psychology tells us that a variety of motives enters into every one of man's decisions. Not only that; a study of human nature in politics reveals how non-rational aspects of human nature influence man's political life. Sir Henry Maine maintains that obedience to authority is based upon habit.[4] In actual practice, it is well-known, men obey orders without scrutiny out of sheer inertness. They do not stop to reason out why the law should be obeyed. There may be a vague perception of the utility of rendering obedience; perhaps, the consequences of disobedience, vaguely apprehended, might secure obedience; or again, the law might be obeyed out of sheer habit. "The State as it was and is", as has well been said, "finds the root of allegiance in all the complex facts of human nature".[5] Thus, it is not difficult to see that obedience to the Hindu State must have been rendered in each case out of a variety of motives or perhaps even without raising the question of justification.

All the same, man is a rational being. He reflects upon his conduct. He tries to correlate means and ends. The question why he *should* obey the State does, therefore, occur to him. And it has to be answered in terms of reason. Obedience to authority *is*, thus, explicable in rational terms. And this exactly is the nature of our problem. We seek to know on what grounds, ideally, in the eyes of our ancient thinkers, obedience to the State would be justified.

A word might here be said regarding a peculiarity of the political thought of our ancients. The early scholars in the field of Indology were, it seems, very much impressed with the profundity of Indian thought in the realm of metaphysics. From this, they seem to have concluded that philosophy was the only field which the Indian genius could explore. Max Muller and Bloomfield, Janet

4. It may be added here that habit itself is often the result of repeatedly doing a thing with the clear perception of its value on rational grounds.

5. Laski: *Grammar of Politics*, p. 22.

and Dunning, all express the view more or less to the effect that in the field of politics Indian thought is a blank; and that, therefore, India has no contribution to make to the development of the political thought of the world. This view has been challenged by various Indian scholars, who have recently applied themselves to the study of Indology. It is not necessary here to go into the details of various arguments advanced by them. It is obvious that no civilisation can flourish except on sound material bases. However high a tree shoots up, its roots must need be in earth. How, then, could Indian culture have been exclusively spiritual? And, in the realm of politics, the profound sayings of Bhīsma on his bed of arrows, the teachings of Kauṭilya and of Śukra and the maxims of policy laid down by various *Dharmaśāstra* and *Arthaśāstra* authors supply a wealth of material for the student.

The charge that India has nothing to offer to the political thought of the world has a meaning for us. It brings home to us how difficult it is to appreciate India's achievements in this direction without taking into consideration certain special characteristics of her political speculation. These characteristics are the result of the attitude to life, which determines the approach of ancient Hindu thinkers to various problems.

It must be unhesitatingly admitted that the Hindu mind has always had a peculiar fascination for pondering over the nature of the eternal principle of the universe, which must be the Reality behind the constantly changing, transitory phenomena of this world. The fundamental idea underlying all Hindu thought seems to be that man is essentially a spiritual being.[6] The real victories of man must, in this view, lie in the field of the beyond and the hereafter. The greater, therefore, the freedom for the mind—or the soul—to ponder over the things of the spirit, the better for the ultimate end of life. This attitude is inevitably reflected in the Hindu scheme of learning. The first subject for study is the sacred works of the sages. Other 'sciences' (Vidyās) are, indeed, not to be neglected. Vārtā and Daṇḍanīti are to be studied along

6. cf. *Creative Unity by Tagore,* p. 107.

with Ānvīkshakī and Trayī. It is remarkable, however, that even Vārtā and Daṇḍanītī are influenced by and implicitly accept certain truths from Ānvīkshakī and Trayī. The *Arthaśāstra* of Kauṭilya, for instance, which is only too often regarded as secular and is in that respect contrasted with the *Dharmaśāstras*, accepts as sacrosanct the division of society into four Varṇas and the division of the individual's life into four Āśramas. Kauṭilya further lays down that the performance of one's duties, as determined by the Varnāśrama scheme, leads to infinite bliss (ānantya). The high estimation in which Danḍanīti is held by Hindu thinkers is due to the fact that it is conceived of as the guarantee of the maintenance of *Dharma*. The study of the various sciences and arts would, then, be of value only as related to the ultimate goal of life. The emphasis all along is on the final consummation. The problems of life here are certainly not ignored. They are, however, of secondary importance.

It is probably this peculiar way of looking at things that explains the absence of specialised studies of sciences like Economics, Politics and Sociology. To the ancient Hindu thinkers, the problems of life were undifferentiated. They, therefore, discuss social, economic, political and religious topics all together, without drawing a clear line between them.

Thus, a study of political theory as such was never undertaken by the ancient thinkers of our land. The solution of our problem as to the nature and grounds of political obligation has to be worked out from the various maxims of policy and rules of statecraft that they lay down in great detail. Certain norms of conduct are laid down by them as being conducive to the *summum bonum*. At every step, life is regulated. For blind impulse, there is no scope at all. Perhaps, it may be said with justice that these regulations leave little scope for individual initiative. Such a thorough-going attempt to regulate life can, however, be understood in the light of the Hindu view of life. It would be easier to concentrate on matters spiritual, if one's life, in its various aspects, were lived in accordance with well-defined rules. This would relieve the individual of the trouble of thinking out for himself and determining the correct rule of conduct in matters of daily life. There would thus be greater scope for his energies to be directed to the thinking out of deeper problems. This, however, is but a tentative suggestion. What interests us here more particularly is the fact that there are ample data for a study of the attitude of Hindu thinkers to vital problems in Politics. Only, these data have to be interpreted, so as to give us a theory. The approach of Hindu authors to the problem of government is intensely practical. Hence, all that they give us is a host of practical maxims of statecraft. It is from these that we have to make out the Hindu ideal of the State, and also the Hindu explanation of political obligation. In other words, the solution of our problem is to be found by interpreting and working out the logical consequences of these maxims. This work, thus, is an attempt to interpret the practical rules of policy laid down by Hindu thinkers in the interests of good government and to develop out of them their view of political obligation.

It is hardly necessary to indicate the value of such a study. Our culture-contact with the West has raised new and important problems for us. Our social and cultural ideals are being reshaped. India is passing through a period of Renaissance. The different parts of the world are becoming more and more closely related. India cannot keep herself aloof from this world-current. The stage of more or less unconscious social evolution is past. We must now have well-planned, consciously shaped and directed social development. In view of all this, a study of our ancient political ideals even within the limits of our problem is bound to be of value. History, indeed, does not repeat itself. We do not turn to the past to get a ready-made solution of our present problems. You can never step into the same current twice, it has been said. So also, the present problem can hardly be an exact replica of the past. Yet, it is desirable that we look back to the past. It is necessary to evaluate our past attainments. More necessary, perhaps, is it to take note of our past errors. It is by thus looking at the past that we can hope to look forward.

The question why the individual ought to obey the State has been differently answered by different thinkers of the West. Some have explained political obligation in terms of force or the fear of force. Others have sought to justify the duty of obedience to the State on the basis of divine right. According to some, the authority of the State is founded on a contract, while others develop the organic theory of the State. It may be possible to trace some of these theories—not, indeed, in exactly the same form—in Hindu thought. The first four chapters of this book are devoted to the analysis and explanation of these conceptions in Hindu thought. Their implications are worked out and they are compared with those of the Western theories.

It is interesting to note that we find the germs of different theories, at first sight irreconcilable, in one and the same work. The question thus arises: do these works, then, only contradict themselves? How else can ideas of divine right and contract, for example, be found side by side in the same work? This peculiar feature of Hindu thought has certainly misled some scholars. Taking a random quotation from Manu or Kauṭilya, it is possible to maintain that the Hindu authors give us a particular theory of the State. Thus, it has been asserted that the relations between the ruler and the ruled in ancient India were regarded as at bottom contractual. It is possible to point out similarly passages which inculcate the duty of unquestioning obedience on the part of the subjects. On the other hand, some scholars have laid emphasis on what seems to them a recognition of 'the right to rebellion' or 'the right to tyrannicide'. Bewildering as these diverse explanations are, they are not really contradictions, if examined with reference to the Hindu conception of *Dharma.* These different theories have all to be related to the central conception of *Dharma.* It is only in the light of this conception that the real nature of the Hindu State and the ultimate explanation of political obligation can be understood. And this forms the subject matter of the last four chapters. An attempt has been made, in the course of these chapters, to bring out the various implications of *Dharma* relevant to our purpose and also to note the defects of the Hindu theory so arrived at.

It may finally be mentioned here that this work represents probably the first attempt at a study of the problem of ancient Indian Polity along these lines. Different scholars have, indeed, carried on extensive studies in this field. They are certainly of immense value to the student of Indian political thought. However, these studies are in the main of a descriptive and analytical nature. Many of them, again, take up only some aspects of Ancient Indian Polity, more or less at random. The value of such studies is undeniable. However, the time has now come when more attention should be paid to the theoretical basis of these various problems, of which a descriptive study has already been made by different scholars. The present work is an humble attempt in that direction. lt is not enough merely to enumerate the various duties of the king or of the subjects. It is not enough merely to say that here and there, a certain political theory seems to have been implied. It is necessary to go deeper to understand the exact significance of all that is said about the problem of political obligation and to find out the theoretical basis of the various practical rules and maxims. Then only could we get a proper perspective of the problem of political obligation as viewed by our ancient thinkers: and then only could we see how far their solution is adequate or otherwise.

CHAPTER I

THE DIVINE RIGHT THEORY IN HINDU POLITICAL THOUGHT

The conception of the divinity of kings seems to have been common to all early peoples. "The earliest known religion," says Hocart, "is a belief in the divinity of kings."[1] In ancient Egypt, the king was regarded as an embodiment of certain gods. The Sumerian city-kings were looked upon as similarly divine. Hammurabi was identified with the sun-god in Babylon and also among the Hittites.[2] The wielder of authority thus seems to have been generally regarded as divine by early peoples; and this divine halo round the king may have secured to him the obedience of his people. At any rate, of all the theories that explain the origin of the State, the oldest, we are told, is the one which attributes it mediately or immediately to God or to some superhuman power.[3] We shall, then, see if we have the conception of the king's divinity in our early literature also.

The earliest document which throws some light on the social and political life in India is the *Ṛig-veda*. The *Ṛig-veda*, 'the Veda of verses' (rik) consists chiefly of verses in praise of various gods. It may well be called 'the book of psalms.'[4] In this work, therefore, we cannot, indeed, expect to find much of political thought. However, the hymns of the *Ṛig-veda* do give us glimpses into the life, customs, manners, ideas, and ideals of the early Indo-

---

1. *Kingship*, p. 7.
2. *Ibid.*, pp. 7-20.
3. Garner: *Introduction to Political Science*, p. 87.
4. Macdonell: *History of Sanskrit Literature*, p. 30.

Aryans. Incidentally, the work throws light on their conception of kingship. In one of these hymns,[5] the royal sage, Trasadasyu, applies to himself the title 'demi-god' (ardhadevatā). Vague as this suggestion is, Dr. Ghoshal points out that the passage may be taken as hinting at the divine or the semi-divine position of the king.[6] There is another hymn in the *Rig-veda*, which also may well be taken to be attributing some sort of divinity to the king. The hymn is dedicated to a Rājā and it prays for benedictions from various gods:

> "May Indra, gratified by the perpetual oblation, firmly establish this (prince); may Soma, may Brahmanaspati address him as their votary."
>
> "May the royal Varuna, the divine Brihaspati, may Indra and Agni ever give stability to thy kingdom."
>
> "...... May Indra render thy subject people payers of their taxes."[7]

This does not, indeed, explicitly speak of the king as divine; but it invokes the gods to lend their support to the authority of the king. And when Indra is supposed to be at the back of the king, making the subjects pay their taxes, we can certainly regard the king's position as divine. These, however, are but vague references.

In the *Atharva-veda*, the idea of the king's divinity is suggested more definitely. In one place, the king is associated with Indra with the words:

> "I unite with thee (i.e. the king) Indra who has supremacy, through whom one conquers and is not (himself) conquered, who shall instal thee as sole ruler of the people, and as chief of the human kings."[8]

The king is here regarded as being installed, and then maintained in supremacy, by Indra. In another hymn, the king is identified with Indra. The hymn is meant to be the charm for a king, on the eve of battle; it describes an oblation to Mitra and Varuna, who are invoked to help the king:

---

5. *Rig-Veda*, IV, 42, 8-9.
6. *Hindu Political Theories*, p. 2o.
7. *Rig-Veda*, X, Anuvaka 12, hymn 22 (Wilson's Translation).
8. *Atharva-Veda*, IV, 22 (Bloomfield's Translation).

> "With inspiration follow ye this strong hero; cling close, ye friends, to Indra (the king) who conquers villages, conquers cattle, has the thunderbolt in his arm, overcomes the host arrayed (against him), crushing it with might."[9]

The Taittirīya Samhitā, in one place,[10] explaining the rite of making offerings to the gods, Indra and Bṛihaspati, states that the Rājanya is connected with Indra, while Bṛihaspati is the priestly power. The *Śatapatha Brāhmaṇa* repeatedly identifies the king with Indra.[11] Besides such references, we get in the same work a passage, where the authority of the king is justified on the ground of his divinity. In reply to the remarkable question, why the king, who is one, rules over the subjects, who are many, it is stated that he, the Rājanya, is the visible representative of Prajāpati; hence, while being one, he rules over many.[12]

In this simple statement, we have the first direct enunciation of the theory of the king's divine right. The king rules and commands obedience because he is the representative of the supreme Creator. In obeying the king, the people really obey Prajāpati. Our early literature thus not merely gives us vague hints about the divinity of the king; it goes further. Here, in the *Śatapatha Brāhmaṇa,* the king's divinity is offered definitely as an explanation and a justification of his authority.

From this Vedic literature, when we turn to the *Dharmasūtras,* we find that these aim at a discussion of the various problems of life. The discussion does not, indeed, assume the character of a system; the ideas of the *Dharmasūtras* are no more than a series of hints, rules and regulations on different topics. What we must note, however, is that these concern themselves with the problems of life in society in all their variety. It is here that social relations are discussed, apart from the sacrificial and ceremonial details, characterising the *Brāhmaṇas.* At the basis of this discussion lies the conception of a unified social order, with the clear classification

---

9. *Atharva-Veda,* VI, 97.

10. ii. 4, 13; *vide* Ghoshal: *op. cit.,* p. 21.

11. V, I, 3, 4; V, 2, 5, 3; V, I, I, II.

12. *Śata. Br.,* V, 2, 5, 14.

into four classes and the formulation of the four stages of life, each with prescribed duties. It is as an incident in this comprehensive scheme of *Dharma* that the duties of the king are laid down. We would expect to find, in these works, a clear presentation of the theory of the king's divinity. But our expectation does not come true. These authors do not give us direct dissertations about the divinity of the king. They do not take up the hints about this doctrine from the earlier literature. We should, however, not hasten to conclude from their silence on this point that they either disapproved, or had no idea of the doctrine. The reason is, our ancient sages and law-givers never attempted the formulation of theories as such. Their main concern was to prescribe rules of conduct for definite occasions. It is only from these that their general attitude has to be made out. When, therefore, we find that a particular idea is not taken up or developed by them, we must admit the possibility that perhaps they took it for granted. We would, then, hesitate to accept the conclusion that evidently this doctrine was thought to be too colourless to form the basis of the king's authority.[13] It must also be noted here that the *Dharmasūtras* certainly lay great stress on the importance of the king's office. The king and the Brāhmaṇa are conceived to be the guardians of the moral order of the world (dvau loke dhṛitavratau rājā brāhmaṇascha bahuśrutaḥ). "On them", says Gautama,[14] "depends the existence of the fourfold human race, of internally conscious beings, of those which move on feet and on wings, and of those which creep, (as well as) the protection of offspring and the prevention of the confusion of the castes and of the sacred law." The full significance of this statement will be brought out later.[15] It would be enough to point out at this stage that the king is here conceived of as the protector of *Dharma*. His is a lofty role, and his duties and responsibilities in this capacity give him a position which is almost divine in nature. As he is the sustainer of eternal *Dharma*, a peculiar sanctity hedges round him. However, there is

13. Ghoshal: *Hindu Political Theories*, p. 37.

14. VIII, 1-3 (Biihler).

15. See *Infra*, Ch. V.

evidently no attempt in the *Dharmasūtras* explicitly to justify the king's authority on the basis of his divinity.

The *Arthaśāstra* of Kauṭilya[16] opens the discussion of the nature of kingly authority by envisaging a condition of affairs in which kingship—and that means any political authority—is absent. In the absence of the ruler, it is said, people were subject to all the evils of anarchy, which are summed up in the picturesque phrase, 'matsvanyāya.' As a remedy, people are said to have made Manu, the son of the Sun-god, their first king. They allotted to him one-sixth of their grains and one-tenth of merchandise as his dues. "Fed by this payment," the text goes on to say, "kings took upon themselves the responsibility of maintaining the safety and security of their subjects." ... "It is the king," we are told, "in whom the duties of Indra (the rewarder) and Yama (the punisher) are blended and he is a visible dispenser of punishments and rewards (heḍa-prasāda); whoever disregards kings will be visited with divine punishments also. Hence kings shall never be despised."

Rather confusing as the wording of this passage is, its significance, on the whole, is unmistakable. The author is here offering a justification for the authority of the king. The office of kingship, he says, is indispensable for the preservation of order in society. The life of man, in the absence of this office, is one where might is right and the weaker but goes to the wall. So great is the importance of the king's function as the preserver of order in society that even men in the Vānaprastha stage feel themselves bound to contribute their quota to the State. This passage, according to Jayaswal, is the monarchists' version of the Arājaka Theory of Social Contract.[17] Some other scholars have also taken this to imply the contractual basis of the State.[18] How far such a view is justified need not be discussed here.[19] There is not the slightest doubt, however, that Kauṭilya definitely invests

16. *Vide Bk.* 1, Ch. 13.
17. *Hindu Polity*, Part I, p. 173.
18. Vide P.N. Banerjea: *Public Administration in Ancient India*, p. 37 and D.R. Bhandarkar: *Carmichael Lectures*, p. 119.
19. See, however, Ch. II, *Infra*.

the king with divinity. "It is the king in whom the duties of both Indra and Yama are blended." This means that the divinity of the king is the result of the similarity of his functions with those of the gods. It is not, however, on this ground alone that Kauṭilya postulates the idea of the king's divinity. There is, it seems, the authority of the gods at the back of the royal authority. A violation of the king's command does not merely bring in its train the penalty meted out by the law of the State. There is also a divine punishment for such an offence. "Whoever disregards kings will be visited with divine punishments also." In other words, a breach of the king's command is not only a crime but also a sin.

The Kauṭiliyan theory of kingship, then, can be looked upon as postulating the divinity of the king in a variety of ways. Firstly, Manu, who is selected as the first king, is taken to be the son of Vaivasvata (i.e. the Sun-god). As such, he is not on a level of equality with other men. He is superhuman and has already a halo of divinity about him. Secondly, the king is said to be similar to Yama and Indra in respect of his functions. And finally, the authority of the king is regarded as having a divine sanction at its back. The divinity of the king is thus established in respect of his origin and his functions and is strengthened by the divine sanction behind his authority. Kauṭilya does not specify here whether a king, who rules unrighteously, should also be looked upon as having this divine right. He only draws the general conclusion that "kings shall never be despised." This does not mean merely that he should not be slighted in his personal capacity; for it is the office of kingship that is deified here. As Kauṭilya himself puts it, "the treacherous opponents of sovereignty would be thus silenced." In short, kingship is an office that invests its holder with divinity and this divinity must be obeyed or else divine punishment would be the result.

We shall now pass on to consider the evidence from the *Mahābhārata.* In the Rājadharmaśasana Parva of the Śānti Parva are described in detail the duties of the king. The Pāṇḍavas have won; theirs is 'the sovereignty of the earth' as the reward for victory. But Yudhishṭhira is inconsolable. The admonitions of Arjuna and Bhima, of Nakula and Sahadeva,[20] are all to no effect. It is ultimately the venerable grandfather—Bhīsma—on his bed of arrows, who is consulted. Gifted with divine vision, possessed of penetrating insight, able to behold "as distinctly as a fruit in hand all that is past, all that is future and all that is present," Bhīsma describes "all the duties laid down in the Vedas and the Vedāntas" (Ch. LV, 2o). In this solemn association, the *Mahābhārata* sets the discussion of royal duties. Yudhishṭhira puts to Bhīsma a very significant question. The problem of obedience to authority seems to him to be an enigma. He is anxious to know how it is that one man—viz. the king—who resembles others in birth and death, feels joy and sorrow even as others—nay, has all the attributes of a man in common with others—how it is that he "governs the rest of the world." "There must be," as Yudhishṭhira adds, "some mighty reason for all this because it is seen that the whole world bows to him as to a god."[21] The problem which is raised here is the problem of the basis of the sovereign authority. The important question is: why do men obey the State? It is the fundamental problem for political thought. In reply, Bhīsma expounds the principle of the divinity of the king.

"At first," we are told, "there was no sovereignty (rājyam), no king (rājā), no punishment (daṇḍa) and no punisher (dāṇḍikaḥ); all used to protect one another by means of Dharma." This blessed state could not, however, last long. Error possessed men's hearts (tatastān moha āviśat). They lost their sense of propriety; confusion arose. The Vedas disappeared. *Dharma* perished. Such a state of anarchy proved intolerable to the gods. They sought the help of the Divine Grandfather—Brahmā. The latter composed a comprehensive treatise on the subject,[22] and then approached Vishṇu requesting him "to point out that one among men who

20. See chapters VIII, XI and XIII.

21. *Śānti Parva,* Ch. LIX.

22. The treatise has been called a *Nīti-śāstra* (Vide Adhyāya 58, Verse 77 in the Nirnayasāgara Press Edition of the *Mahābhārata,* N.N. Dutt has translated the passage a little too freely. He omits the word *Nīti-śāstra*) and the contents of the work given in the text show how comprehensive is the scope of this 'Science' according to our authors. There is no attempt to isolate a particular aspect of the problem and to study it alone analytically.

deserves to reign supreme over the rest." Veṇa's son, Pṛithu, ultimately becomes the first king, having promised to maintain the duly-prescribed *Dharma.*

The first king, then, was appointed by Vishṇu at the request of the gods.[23] Secondly, he was descended from Vishṇu—"this great declaration of the Śruti is known among men that Pṛithu is the eighth from Vishṇu."[24] Thirdly, he was crowned by Vishṇu and the gods, with Indra as their leader.[25] Further, we are told, "the eternal Vishṇu himself, confirmed his power (sthāpanam akarot), telling him, 'no one, O king, shall excel you.'"[26] Nay, "the divine Vishṇu entered the body of that king," and that is the reason "why the entire universe adored Prithu who was the greatest of kings."[27]

The *Mahābhārata,* thus, explains the king's authority in terms of his divinity. The king is divinely ordained to rule. Descended as he is from Vishṇu, created at the request of the gods, blessed by Vishṇu—nay, representing Vishṇu himself in his person—the king's divine right is beyond question. No wonder, "the learned say, there is no difference between a god and a king."[28]

It may be pointed out here that although the text speaks specifically of Pṛithu, it lays down the principle of the divinity of the king as such. It takes it for granted that the divinity of Pṛithu could be passed on to—or could as well be attributed to—other kings as well. What the *Mahābhārata* aims at is the justification of the authority of the king—in general—as Yudhishṭhira's question shows. A close examination of the whole passage in question shows that it is not the person of this or that king that is sought to be deified but the office of kingship itself. "What other cause can

23. *Śānti Parva,* LIX, 87-88.
24. *Ibid.,* LIX, 112.
25. *Ibid.,* LIX, 115-12o.
26. *Ibid.,* 127.
27. *Ibid.,* 128.
28. *Ibid.,* 145.

there be," it is said, "for which men obey one person, save the divinity of the monarch?"[29]

The principle of the divine right of the king is further explained in reply to Yudhishṭhira's pointed question, "Why have the Brāhmaṇas declared that the king, the ruler of men, is a god?"[30]

It is stated in this connexion that the preservation of the social order in the path of righteousness depends on the king's office. In the absence of this office, "men would sink in utter darkness and meet with destruction;" "the strong would by force misappropriate the property of the weak;" "morality and the three Vedas would disappear;" "there would be inter-mixture of castes and famine would devastate the kingdom." The nature of his functions is thus said to constitute one more point in favour of his divine right. "Who is there," runs the text, "who will not worship him on whose existence depends the existence of the people and by whose destruction the people are destroyed?" Then follows the identification of the king's functions with those of various gods. "The king," it is said, "puts on five different forms according to five different occasions. He becomes Agni, Āditya, Mṛityu, Vaiśravaṇa and Yama."

The *Mahābhārata* thus emphasizes the divinity of the king from various points of view and concludes that obedience is due to him because of his divinity: "No one should obey the king by taking him to be a man; for he is in sooth a great god in human form."[31]

We pass on to the *Manu-smṛiti.* It gives us a brief but definite statement of the theory of the king's divinity.[32] The importance of the kingly office is brought out, as in the *Mahābhārata,* by

29. *Śānti Parva,* LIX, 151. Such a direct statement as this is, we hope, quite sufficient to show how mistaken is the view of Dr. Bhandarkar that "No school of Hindu Polity or law does either acknowledge the king's rule by divine right or consider his person as divine." (*Some Aspects of Ancient Indian Polity,* pp. 161-3). Narada, as we shall see later, goes even further, for, he says, 'a ruler, though worthless, must be constantly worshipped by subjects"!. (XVIII, 22.)

30. *Ibid.,* Ch. LXVIII.

31. cf. "The king is Indra; the king is Yama; the king is Dharma;" *Śānti Parva,* LXXII, 25.

32. VII, 1-13.

visualising the state of affairs in the absence of that office. The king's office, is, in a word, the sole guarantee of the maintenance of *Dharma*; and we might say, therefore, that this creates round the king a peculiar halo of sanctity. But that is not all. According to the *Manu-smṛiti*, the king was created by the Lord, when he saw creatures disappearing in all directions through fear, in the absence of the king. Further the king was created out of "the eternal particles of Indra, of Yama, of the Wind, of the Sun, of Fire, of Varuṇa, of the Moon, and of Kubera." It is because he was thus formed out of divine particles that "he surpassed all created beings in lustre." Again, the king, we are told, resembles these gods in respect of certain attributes. "Like the Sun, he burns eyes and hearts; nor can anybody on earth gaze at him." He resembles Fire,—nay, he surpasses Fire; for, "Fire burns one man only, if he carelessly approaches it," while, "the fire of the king's anger consumes the whole family together with its cattle and its hoard of property." We see, then, that the king is divine; firstly, because he is a creation of the Lord; secondly, because he embodies the essence of various gods, and thirdly because he possesses some of the attributes of these gods. To such a person, the people must render obedience. As the text explicitly puts it, "Even an infant king should not be despised (from the idea) that he is a mere mortal; for he is a great deity in human form."[33] Thus the *Manu-smṛiti* comes to the same conclusion as the *Mahābhārata*.[34]

The theory of the king's divine right may well be said to be more fully developed and worked out with greater clearness in the *Manu-smṛiti* and the *Mahābhārata* than in the *Arthaśāstra* of Kauṭilya. The main distinction lies in the fact that the former works speak of the creation of the king by Divine Will, while the *Arthaśāstra* does not mention this point. How do we account for this difference? The theories in the *Mahābhārata* and in the *Manu-smṛiti* were formulated, according to Dr. Ghoshal, "with the deliberate object of counteracting the tendencies inherent in the older ideas of the king's origin"—in particular, the Buddhist theory

33. *Manu*: VII, 8.

34. cf. *Śānti Parva*, LXVIII, 40.

of contract, which tended to strengthen the old familiar conception that the king was an official paid by the subjects for the duty of protection.[35] This may have been so.[36] The Brahmanical writers would probably prefer to lay greater emphasis on the conception of the king's divinity, which was already present in earlier literature, in view of the tendency of the Buddhist works to seek the origin of kingship in some sort of popular agreement, involving no divine intervention. (cf. mahajanasammato ti mahasammato).[37] Perhaps, also the necessity of sanctifying the rule of low-born Dravidian kings of the Buddhist period may have necessitated a greater emphasis on the king's divinity.[38] There is not in these works, however, a "sudden change of ideas about the rights of kings," as Dr. Shama Sastri would have us believe; for, as we have seen, the ideas about the king's divinity may be seen developing from early times.

The *Nārada-smṛiti* is another of the *Dharmaśāstras* justifying the subjects' duty of obedience, *inter alia*, on the ground of the king's divinty. "The kings," says the Smṛiti, "endowed with immense power appear (variously) in the five different forms of Agni, Indra, Soma, Yama, and Kubera."[39] The king and the Brāhmaṇa are

35. *Hindu Political Theories*, p. 125.

36. We say "this may have been so," because of the uncertainty of dates and also because, as we have already seen, we cannot be sure, if, in any given case, the author did not take for granted what he did not expressly refer to. As to the uncertainty of dates the difficulty is obvious. There are differences of opinion, for instance, as regards the date of Kauṭilya. Shama Sastri tries to prove that the traditional date of Kauṭilya—viz. 321-296 B.C.—may well be accepted as correct in spite of the arguments in favour of a later date advanced by Jolly, Schmidt, and Winternitz. Dr. Keith feels that Kauṭilya cannot be identified with Chāṇakya, the minister of king Chandragupta; for, the *Arthaśāstra*, he thinks, has in view a polity of small size and not an Empire, such as Chandragupta's was. (Vide his *Hist. of Sans.* Lit. p. 459). This objection has been sought to be met by Dr. Krishnaswami Iyengar (in his introduction to Dikshitar's *Hindu Administrative Institutions*) and also by K.V.R. Aiyangar (vide his *Some Aspects of Ancient Indian Polity*). Dr. Ghoshal also thinks that the advocates of the later date have not yet made out their case successfully (p. 15). The task of relating the theory of Kauṭilya to the rest of our literature is thus beset with obvious difficulties.

37. Refer, however, to our next chapter for a discussion of the Buddhist Theory.

38. Shama Sastri: *Evolution of Indian Polity*, p. 146.

39. Nārada, XVIII, 26.

declared to be the sustainers of the whole world and as such they are never to be rebuked or advised.[40] This sanctity of the king is said to be a sufficient justification for all that he does. "Whatever a king does is right, that is a settled rule; because the protection of the world is entrusted to him and on account of his majesty and benignity towards living creatures."[41] Nārada thus preaches the duty of the subjects to submit to the king's commands without demur. And to this end, he makes use of the law of Karma. "A ruler," he says, "has purchased his subjects through the practice of austerities; therefore, the king is their lord; for that reason, his bidding must be obeyed."[42] According to Nārada, then, the obedience of the subjects to the king is based, firstly, on the perception of the utility and importance of kingly duties, secondly, on the divinity of the king and thirdly, on the strength of the king's austerities, according to the law of Karma. The theory, as enunciated here, would seem to sanctify even misrule; for, it is laid down that "whatever a king does is right" and that "as a husband, though feeble, must be constantly worshipped by his wife, so a ruler though worthless must be constantly worshipped by his subjects."[43] We must not conclude, however, that Nārada is out to deify the worst tyrant. He enjoins the king to discharge his duties properly as the protector of *Dharma* and lays down spiritual penalties for default. His tone, however, may on the whole be said to be more authoritarian than that of the other *Dharmaśāstra* authors, for he seems to be over-emphasizing the duty of submission to the king on the part of the subjects. We would thus agree with Dr. Ghoshal, who remarks that in the *Nārada-smṛiti* we see the culmination of the Hindu doctrines of submission and obedience.[44] We must add, however, that this is due to Nārada's reference to the claim of the king on the loyalty of the subjects in virtue of his austerities in a previous birth. So far as the doctrine of

40. *Ibid.*, XV, 20 and XVII, 12.

41. *Ibid.*, XVIII, 21.

42. *Nārada*, XVIII, 25.

43. *Ibid.* XVIII, 22.

44. *Hindu Political Theories*, p. 186.

the divine right of the king is concerned, it is in the *Mahābhārata* and the *Manu-smṛiti* that we find its culmination. It is these works which emphasize the divinity of the king in a variety of ways and it is in these works, again, that the obedience of the subjects is regarded as based definitely on divine right.

In the *Nīti-śāstras* and in the Purāṇas we get but repetitions of the statements occurring in the *Mahābhārata* and the *Manu-smṛiti.* There is little freshness or originality about them. The *Nītisāra* of Kāmaṇḍaka is but a pale reflection of the *Arthaśāstra* of Kauṭilya. It just compares the king to Prajāpati in respect of his functions[45] and refers to the king as "the lord, the auspicious one, wielding the sceptre, through whose might the world follows the eternal path." More than this the work has nothing to say as regards the theory of the king's divine right.

The Purāṇas, again, justify the king's authority on the basis of his divinity. The *Agni Purāṇa* conceives of the king as assuming the forms of nine deities according to the nature of his functions. The king, we are told, is like the sun, because he can be gazed at only with difficulty on account of his lustre; he is like the moon in as much as he is the object of gratification to the people through his sight; he is the god of wind since he sweeps the world with his spies; he is Manu, Vaivasvata, because of his punishing crimes; he is Fire, when he burns the evil-minded; Kubera, when he gives away wealth to the twice-born; and Varuṇa, since he showers wealth. He is the Earth as he sustains the world by his forbearance; and he is the god, Hari, because he protects people by exercising his powers of enthusiasm, counsel and the like.[46] At the same time, the *Agni Purāṇa* enjoins the king to forego all pleasures and live only for the wellbeing of his charge.[47] The divinity of the king, suggested in the passage above, is more or less metaphorical, in as much as the king is said to be merely assuming different forms on different occasions. In the *Brihaddharma Purāṇa,* we get a more definite statement of the theory of the king's divinity.

45. I, II.

46. *Agni Purāṇa,* CCXXV, 17-20. (M.N. Dutt's translation).

47. *Ibid.*, CCXXIII.

The king, according to this work, was created by the Lord, by taking lordship from Indra, power from Agni, cruelty from Yama, prosperity from the moon, riches from the god of wealth and steadiness from Vishṇu.[48] In the *Matsya Purāṇa* also, it is said that the king was created by the Brāhmaṇa.[49] The *Bhāgavata Purāṇa* lays down that even a sinful monarch should not be disregarded by the people, for every monarch embodies the vigour of Lokapalas or the protectors of the universe.[50] It is evident that these Purāṇas borrow their ideas from the *Mahābhārata* or the *Manu-smṛiti.*

When we come to the *Śukra-nīti-śāra,* we seem to breathe a purer air. There is a certain originality in the approach of this work to many problems. Opening with a discussion of the supreme importance of the *Nīti-śāstra,* the work goes on to explain the functions of the king. And then it is said: "The king is made out of the Permanent elements of Indra, Vayu, Yama, the Sun, Fire, Varuna, the Moon and Kubera, and is the lord of both moveable and immovable worlds."[51] The king, further, resembles these gods because of his similar functions.[52] The king is thus divine. But divine right does not seem to form the main basis of political allegiance, according to Śukra. Like Nārada, he explains the secret of the king's power as due to "his deeds in the previous birth," as well as to his 'penance.' The author, it must be noted, recognises that there are differences of character and capacity among kings. Thus, a king may be sāttvika, rājasika or tāmasika.[53] Such recognition may have been the result of the author's observation of the conditions around him. He is thus led to make a clear distinction between a virtuous king and a king who is otherwise.[54] The former alone is declared to be a part of the

48. Quoted by Ghoshal, p. 184.
49. Vide B. Prasad: *Theory of Government,* p. 197.
50. IV, 13-23; referred to by B. Prasad: *op. cit.*, p. 199.
51. *Śukra,* I, 141-142.
52. *Ibid.*, I, 143-151.
53. *Śukra,* I, 57-58.
54. Ibid., I, 39-40.

gods; the latter, a part of the demons.[55] Herein lies the distinctive character of Śukra's contribution. For the first time, we have here a bold attempt to apply the conception of divinity to virtuous rulers only. In this respect, Śukra presents a pleasant contrast to Nārada, according to whom, even a "worthless king must be constantly worshipped by his subjects." A study of the various injunctions of Śukra to the king shows how the author vividly realised the need of keeping the subjects satisfied.[56] It seems also that he was quite aware of the fact that a particular king may behave in a way far from godlike. Śukra is not an apologist for tyranny. He knows that there are often enough kings who consider the robbing of others' wealth the greatest virtue. Such kings can certainly not be free from sin. As our author trenchantly observes, "If there accrue no sin to a king, robbers also should be absolved from sin."[57] When emphasizing the need for discipline, Śukra recalls several instances of kings who were ruined because of the lack of discipline. Śukra, then, it would seem, definitely discountenances the doctrine of the divine right of the king as applied to wicked rulers. To him, only the righteous king is divine. "The gods ruin and cast down a king who is not a Protector."[58] We would, however, point out here that it is difficult, if not impossible, to reconcile this attitude with his view that "the king is the lord of the earth because of his deeds in the previous birth as well as of penance."[59] If once we accept the proposition that the king is what he is because of his Karma and his Tapas, we lose the right of raising the question as to the proper or improper exercise of his power. The logical conclusion in such a case would be that which Nārada comes to—viz. that even a worthless king must be obeyed. Such a position is alien to Śukra's political system. He even points out that "the king is honoured because of his qualities." "It is not birth that makes a king. He is not respected so much because of his ancestry, as for

---

55. *Ibid.*, I, 139-140.
56. See I, 133, 134, 165 ff. 260 ff.
57. *Śukra*; V, 67-69.
58. *Ibid.*; 217-18 ff., 287-90. etc.
59. *Śukra*, I, 39-40.

his prowess, strength and valour."[60] Śukra thus dwells on the duties of the king rather than on his privileges. And yet we shall be sadly mistaken if we take this to imply that Śukra meant deliberately to depart from the traditional view of the king's authority. As a matter of fact, he whole-heartedly accepts the conception of kingship as the guarantee for the preservation of *Dharma.* Thus the king he regards as the maker of the age. It is the fear of the king's punishment which makes people perform their duties. To the king who fosters *Dharma,* even the gods give honour. What, then, to say of human beings?[61] The king, although endowed with good qualities, may be without subjects but the latter must not live without a king.[62] Evidently, the king's office is of supreme importance because of its association with *Dharma.* On the whole, the *Śukra-nīti-sāra* places more emphasis on the duty of the king to rule justly, but that, as we shall see later, is an attempt to explain the king's Svadharma. There is no fundamental departure from the time-honoured conception of the nature of the king's duties. All that we may say here is that Śukra's is an attempt to follow the traditional theory and to emphasize, at the same time, certain points which required particular insistence during his time.

We may finally notice the version of the theory of the king's divinity in the *Nītivākyāmṛita* of the Jain author, Somadevasuri.[63] In this work, the king is said to be divine on the ground that he assumes the forms of the Creator (Brahmā), the Preserver (Vishṇu) and the destroyer (Śiva). This would seem to be but a metaphorical way of describing the functions of the king. The author, however, insists that the king is always to be looked upon as a deity. A weak king should not be despised nor should a wicked king be opposed. If the king, who is a god, we are told, goes wrong, it can only be explained as the result of the Kali Age.

---

60. *Ibid.,* I, 363-364.
61. *Ibid.,* 43-49.
62. Ibid., 186-188.
63. Vide Ghoshal, pp. 202-203.

The above survey shows that the conception of the king's divinity has been handed down to us from early times; and we find interesting reminiscences of the same even in modern times. This may be seen, for instance, in the fact that in the *Madhyalila,* even the Moslem king of Bengal is addressed as a part of Vishnu.[64] It is obvious considering the evidence brought forward above that the theory of the divine right of the king has an important place in the history of Hindu political thought. Jayaswal, however, asserts that the statement of the theory of the king's divinity in the *Manu-smṛiti* represents but a solitary attempt "never approved or adopted by a single subsequent law-book."[65] It is not difficult to see that such a view is clearly unfounded. The general trend of the various statements of the theory noted above is, beyond question, to offer a justification for the authority of the king. In the *Mahābhārata* and in the *Manu-smṛiti,* the divine right theory is offered as an important argument to inculcate the duty of the subjects to obey the king. In the *Nārada-smṛiti* and in the *Śukra-nīti-sāra,* the theory is to be found alongside with the view that the king's authority is based on his austerities. There is thus a difference in emphasis as among various authors. Manu, for instance, would assert that "one should not transgress even that law which the king makes with reference to his favourites nor his orders which inflict pain on those in disfavour."[66]

Nārada also similarly emphasizes the duty of the subjects to yield unquestioning obedience. Śukra, on the other hand, as we have seen, places greater emphasis on the king's duty to rule righteously. Granting these differences of emphasis, it must be said that the Divine Right Theory has an important place in Hindu thought as one of the justifications for political allegiance.

It would be proper to emphasize here that the divinity of the king has been postulated to justify his authority. In other words, it is certainly an explanation for political allegiance. Some of our scholars, however, seem evidently to have lost sight of this

64. *Ibid.*, p. 172.

65. *Hindu Polity,* Part II, pp. 202-203.

66. VII, 13.

point. Prof. B.K. Sarkar,[67] for instance, looks upon this theory as merely a metaphorical expression of the king's majesty—that is, of the State. The king, he points out, is not "a vicar of god" as understood by medieval Western philosophers. "The divinity which hedges round the monarch," he tells us, "is the glory and importance of the functions that he has to perform as Svamin." The metaphor of the king's divinity, according to the author, "is meant only to bring to the forefront the supreme character of Bodin's 'majestas' as an abstract attribute in civil society." The author clearly ignores the point we have been making. The divinity of the king is in some cases, as noted above, taken to be the result of a parallelism between his functions and those of the gods. Such a statement may, indeed, be looked upon as metaphorical. Let us, however, not forget that even this metaphor is utilised by our authors to serve as a plea for the king's right to rule. Again, this metaphorical statement often occurs together with the view that the king was created by the Lord himself. Shall we call this a metaphor too? A study of such statements on the whole shows that the Hindu thinkers do not really distinguish between the king's divinity as the result of his divine creation and as a result of his godlike functions. The king, in Hindu thought, it must also be noted, is not the Vicar of God; but he is the sustainer of the eternal *Dharma.* A slight disturbance in this order upsets even the gods. In this sense, the king may be looked upon as fulfilling God's purpose, and therefore having the right divine to command obedience. In brief, then, Prof. B.K. Sarkar's attempt to underrate the importance of this theory by equating it with Bodin's 'majestas' must be pronounced to be far-fetched.

It must also be noted here that it is Śukra alone who clearly distinguishes between a good ruler and a wicked one, the former being a part of the gods and the latter of the demons. Taking his cue probably from this statement Dr. Bhandarkar maintains that a king is a Naradeva only so long as he is virtuous and ceases to be so the moment he goes to the bad.[68] May we only

67. *Political Institutions and Theories of the Hindus,* pp. 179-180.

68. *Carmichael Lectures,* p. 130.

ask: who determines whether the king has 'gone to the bad' and has therefore forfeited his claim to the allegiance of the people? In other words, we have to understand clearly the significance of such a statement. Dr. Bhandarkar evidently implies that the king's divinity is merely a metaphor, meant to exalt a *good* ruler. Prof. P.N. Banerjea is also of the same opinion; for, he observes, "only a righteous king was regarded as divine."[69] Based as these generalisations are on the above-mentioned dictum of Śukra, they cannot be held to apply to the earlier authors. The conception of the king's divinity is so deeply ingrained in ancient thought that some of our ancient thinkers maintain that even a wicked king must be obeyed. It is an unwarranted exaggeration, therefore, to say that "the bed-rock of Hindu Political Philosophy is furnished by the differentiation of the king as 'a part of the gods' from the king as 'a part of the demons.'"[70]

To sum up, the Hindu thinkers, it must be said, propound the theory of the king's divinity definitely to justify his authority. The statements of the theory do, indeed, take different forms. Sometimes, the king may be regarded as created by the Lord. In some cases, he may be compared to various gods because of the similarity of his functions to theirs. Sometimes, again, his authority may be represented as having a divine sanction at its back. Often, too, these different aspects of the theory may be found side by side in the same work. It is not necessary for us to distinguish between these inasmuch as the aim of them all is to invest the king with a divine right and so to offer a justification for his authority.[71]

---

69. *Public Administration in Ancient India,* p. 71.

70. cf. *Pol. Instns. and Theories of the Hindus,* p. 180.

71. The question whether the king was a Devata or a Naradevata, which has been discussed by P.N. Banerjea (*Public Admin. in Ancient India,* p. 71). Dr. Bhandarkar, (*Carmichael Lectures,* 1918, pp. 126-127) and by Dikshitar (*Hindu Administrative Institutions,* p. 61) is not germane to our discussion. We need not make any fine distinction between a Devata and a Naradevata. Even if the king is to be looked upon as a Naradevata and not a Devata as these scholars maintain, there is a divinity attributed to him by the mere fact that the term Devata is associated with him. And, as we have remarked above, when the epithet—Devata or Naradevata—is employed so as to justify his authority, we have a divine right theory indeed.

However, the nature of this divine right has to be clearly understood. We have to see how far the king's divinity makes him irresponsible. And here we find that the divinity of the king is constantly associated with his duty to preserve *Dharma.* His divinity is quite compatible with his subjection to *Dharma*—nay, we may even say that his subjection to *Dharma* serves really to bring out his divinity all the more clearly. The monarch is not above *Dharma*; for "Dharma is the king of kings." The concept of *Dharma* implies that the king is governed in his whole conduct by definite rules. His duties are all determined by *Dharma.* The principles of the polity are laid down by *Dharma.* What the king should do under certain circumstances and with what administrative machinery he should govern the people—all this is determined in the light of *Dharma.* Thus, there are numerous restrictions on the arbitrary exercise of his power. Or, rather, the channel of the exercise of kingly authority is clearly determined according to the injunctions of the sacred works. In the *Arthaśāstra,* there is an injunction, requiring the king to identify himself with the good of his subjects. "Of a king," it is said, "the religious vow is his readiness to action satisfactory discharge of, his duties is his performance of sacrifice; ...... In the happiness of his subjects lies his happiness; in their welfare, his welfare; whatever pleases himself, he shall not consider as good, but whatever pleases his subjects he shall consider as good."[72] According to the *Mahābhārata,* "the subjects should arm themselves for killing that king who does not protect them, who simply plunders their riches, who confounds all distinctions, who is incapable of taking their lead, who is without mercy and most sinful...... that king who tells his people that he is their protector but who does not or is unable to really protect them, should be killed......"[73] Manu's insistence on the king's divinity does not prevent him from recognising that "the king who through folly rashly oppresses his kingdom, will, together with his relatives, ere long be deprived of his life and of his kingdom."[74] We see,

72. *Arthaśāstra,* Bk. I, ch. 19.

73. *Anuśāsana Parva*: LXI, 52-53,

74. VII, 111-112.

then, that the king cannot claim the right divine to go wrong. On closer scrutiny, we find that the difference between the works like the *Mahābhārata*, the *Manu-smṛiti* and the Purāṇas, on the one hand, and the *Śukra-nīti-sāra*, on the other, is not as great or fundamental as it seems at first sight. The latter makes an explicit distinction between virtuous kings and wicked kings and speaks of the virtuous kings only as divine. The earlier thinkers postulate the divinity of all kings, by the mere fact of the occupation of the throne. It is the office of the king that is deified by them. The king as king is said to be divine; and, as such the subjects are enjoined to obey him. Sometimes, even, there is too great a stress on the duty of the subjects to obey the king. When, however, these authors come to discuss the duties of the king, they lay down various rules that he must observe, the principles by which he must conduct the affairs of the State and also dangers which he must avoid. These dangers are sometimes spiritual penalties and sometimes those of provoking the subjects into a rebellion. By means of these warnings, the king is enjoined to fulfil duly his function of protection. We conclude, then, that while the theory of the divine right of the king is expounded as a justification of the king's authority and as the basis of the subjects' duty to render obedience, the Hindu thinkers admit the possibility and seem to recognise even the advisability in extreme cases of deposing, abandoning or putting to death a wicked monarch. The king's divinity is not a charter for license. To put the whole position in a nutshell, from the point of view of the subjects, the king is indeed a great deity never to be slighted; the king on his part is at the same time subject to *Dharma*.[75]

Let us now see how far the Hindu theory is comparable to the European theory of the divine right of the king.

The conception of divinity as characterising political authority can be traced back to early Greek thought. The Pythagoreans applied their naturalistic principles to political phenomena and some of them developed a definite theory of politics. The essence

---

75. How far kingship in ancient India could be said to be an absolutism is discussed in Ch. VII infra.

of that theory was the divine right of wisdom to rule, and its practical outcome was a belief in monarchy of the theocratic type.[76] The Sophist Protagoras conceived the State "as an ordinance of God rather than as a creation of men."[77] The Greeks looked upon their city-state as an end in itself, through which alone, they as citizens acquired their real significance. To them, the State was divine in nature and not primarily the handiwork of man.[78]

With the Romans began, in practice, a clear distinction between divine and civil authority but they closely followed Greek thought and made slight, if any, advance on it.[79] The first effect of Christianity was "to bring not peace but a sword," to set up an irreconcilable feud between the spiritual and the civil power, between the Church and the State.[80] As a result of this feud, the question of the divine or the non-divine origin of political power came to be actively discussed. The maxim that what was Caesar's must be rendered unto Caesar and what was God's unto God was difficult to apply in practice with success. The temporal power of the Church went on increasing, so much so that it became a civic organisation, promulgating laws and enforcing obedience to them by military coercion. The day came when a Pope claimed to be "absolute master of all princes, who were bound to kiss his feet, and whom he could depose at will, by releasing their subjects from the oath of fealty."[81] The claims of the king, on the other side, were equally exaggerated in order to minimise the importance of the Pope. Frederick II, for instance, called himself "the Vicar of God on earth, the reformer of the age, a new Elijah discomfiting the priests of Baal," and denounced the Pope as "Pharisee anointed with the oil of iniquity; ...... a false Vicar of

---

76. Barker: *Greek Political Theory: Plato and Predecessors,* p. 48.
77. *Ibid.*, p. 63.
78. Willoughby: *The Nature of the State,* p. 43.
79. *Ibid.*, p. 45.
80. Vaughan: *Hist. of Pol. Phil.*, Vol. I, p. 9.
81. Mac Iver: *The Modern State,* p.119 and Dunning: *Pol. Theories, Ancient and Medieval,* p. 176.

God."[82] In the controversy between the Church and the State, it was the common ground of the disputants that the Papacy and the Empire were both divinely ordained. The point of controversy was the relation of these two jurisdictions to one another.[83] The champions of the Church also conceded the divine origin—at least the mediately divine origin—of the State, while the advocates of secular governments laid stress on the immediately divine origin of the State.[84]

The issue was at last decided by the Reformation. Although the Reformation was primarily a religious movement, it profoundly influenced social and political ideas. The secular governments of Europe saw their opportunity and allied themselves with the Reformers in repudiating the authority of the Pope. An obvious practical consequence was the further exaltation of the power and dignity of these monarchs.[85] By the teaching of the Reformers, the dignity of the rulers was based on the most explicit assertion of God's sanction.[86]

The doctrine of the king's divinity thus came into prominence as a result of the Reformation. The point to note here is that it assumed importance as a shield against the authority of the Church. In this form, then, it was not primarily a doctrine attempting to explain or justify political allegiance. It was not, so far, an explanation of the relations between the ruler and the ruled. Once, however, the monarchs learnt to employ the doctrine of their divinity, they were not slow to work out its implications in this direction also. In the sixteenth and seventeenth centuries, the theory was advanced as offering a resistance to the growing ideas of popular sovereignty.[87] In the hands of James I, Filmer and Bousset, the theory of the king's divine right became the justification of

82. Pollock: *Hist. of the Science of Politics*, p. 35.

83. *Ibid.*

84. Gierke: *Political Theories of the Middle Age*, pp. 30-31.

85. Dunning: *Pol. Theories—from Luther to Montesquieu*, p. 5.

86. *Ibid.*

87. Leacock: *Elements of Political Science*, p. 31.

his authority to rule and to demand the unquestioning obedience of the subjects.

The conception of the king's divinity has thus a long tradition behind it in Europe. It is, however, after the Reformation in the main that it is turned into a doctrine justifying the authority of the king.[88] In the Middle Ages, as we have seen, the doctrine was advocated just to prop up the authority of the king as against that of the Church.[89]

In the works of James I, the theory of the divine right of kings finds its characteristic expression. The royal philosopher was evidently out to justify absolutism. In his treatise entitled 'The True Law of Free Monarchy,' he maintains[90] that "kings are justly called gods: for they exercise a manner of resemblance of divine power on earth." He then points out how the king resembles God, in a manner that reminds us of the comparisons instituted by Hindu authors between the functions of the king and of the gods. "God," says James, "hath power to create or destroy, make or unmake at His pleasure, to give life or to send death, to judge all and to be accountable to none. And the like power have kings." Not only is there this similarity between the power of God and that of the king; but the kings are "God's lieutenants on earth" and "are called gods by God himself." It is thus the duty of the subjects to obey royal commands. The subjects have no right, asserts James, to question the validity of such orders. "As it is atheism and blasphemy," he declared in a speech in the Star Chamber Court in 1616, "to dispute what God can do, so it is presumption and high contempt in a subject to dispute what a king can do or to say that a king cannot do this or that." James I could certainly not have been ignorant of the fact that kings often go wrong, that often enough they are vicious

---

88. Acton: *History of Freedom*, p. 47.

89. In some cases, it seems, the deification of the monarch was meant to indicate the nature of his relation to his subjects. Vide Gierke: *Political Theories of the Middle Age*, pp. 34-35.

90. The quotations are taken from *Political thought in England: From Bacon to Halifax*, Chapter I, by G.P. Gooch.

and tyrannical. Even in such a contingency, however, the subjects have no right to call them to account. "The wickedness of the king," he asserts, "can never make them that are ordained to be judged by him to become his judges." Nay, a wicked king is also to be regarded as sent out by God as a plague on people's sins! Realising this, all that the subjects must do is to devote themselves to "patience, earnest prayer and amendment of their lives." These are "the only lawful means to move God to relieve them of that heavy curse." There is thus no remedy with the subjects directly to check a tyrant. In the words of James I, "Better it is to live in a Commonwealth where nothing is lawful than where all things are lawful to all men."[91] The royal philosopher explores every avenue to see that his absolutist doctrine leaves not the slightest possibility for the subjects to question his authority. "If princes," he declares, "command anything which the subjects may not perform because it is contrary to the laws of God or nature or impossible, subjects are bound to undergo punishments without either resistance or reviling and so yield a passive obedience where they cannot exhibit an active one." These words speak for themselves and it is not necessary to comment on them here.

In Filmer's *Patriarcha*, we get another exposition of the theory of the king's divine right.[92] Filmer rejects the idea that mankind was originally free. The origin of government, he maintains, was not a surrender of natural rights but an enlargement of the microcosm of the family. The king is, therefore, the father of the people. This does not, however, mean that there is a tie of kindred—a bond of affection—which binds the king and the people together. As Filmer puts it, "The father governs by his own will, not by the laws and wills of his sons and servants." We need not here discuss the fallacy involved in regarding the nature of the State as in essence the same as that of the family.[93] It is

---

91. Quoted by Dunning: *Political Theories from Luther to Montesquieu*, p. 216. cf. Laski: *The Foundations of Sovereignty and other Essays*, pp. 301 ff.

92. See Dunning: *op. cit.*, pp. 254-259 and Gooch: *Political Thought in England*, pp. 161-164.

93. See, however, Willoughby: *The Nature of the State*, pp. 20-22.

enough to keep in view the fact that Filmer traces the absolute authority of the king from God through Adam and posterity. The rule of the king is "the law of God" and therefore it "hath no superior power to limit it." The divine right of the king is, in a word, not to be questioned by the people.

The theory of the king's divine right involves, according to Dr. Figgis,[94] four component elements. They are: firstly, that "monarchy is a divinely ordained institution;" secondly, that "hereditary right is indefeasible;" thirdly, that "kings are accountable to God alone;" and fourthly, that "non-resistance and passive obedience are enjoined by God." The exposition of the theory by James I can easily be analysed into these four component parts.

It is obvious that the Hindu and European theories have some elements in common. The Hindu thinkers, like their European compeers, evince a partiality for monarchy and to them, too, it is almost "a divinely ordained institution." Hereditary right, again, is implicit in all their discussion.[95] There is thus a resemblance between the Western and Hindu theories, so far as these two elements of the doctrine are concerned. There is, however, no parallel in Hindu thought to the extravagant claims made by James I. According to the *Mahābhārata*, the *Manu-samhita*, the *Arthaśāstra* as well as the later works, the king is indeed accountable to God. The nemesis of misrule is spiritual downfall, sin and hell. At the same time, the king was not considered to be so much above the rest of humanity as to go unscathed for all his wickedness in this world. In cases of gross misrule, the subjects would be justified in deposing the king. The *Manu-smṛiti* and the *Nārada-smṛiti* enjoin the subjects not to despise or disobey even a weak or wicked king. They do not, however, suggest in the manner of James that

---

94. Vide: Gooch. *op. cit.*, p. 14.

95. Even in Vedic times, the kingship was normally hereditary (*Camb. History of India*, Vol. I, p. 94); in the period of the *Brāhmaṇas*, the hereditary character of the monarchy is clearly apparent. (*Ibid.*, p. 130.) In the epic times, "the order of succession," says Sidhanta, (*Heroic Age of India*, p. 176), "is generally according to primogeniture, and it is only in exceptional cases that the eldest son is passed over."

wicked kings are sent by gods as penalty for the people's sins.[96] They do not suggest "patient suffering and amelioration of their lives" as the only remedy "to move god to remove that heavy curse." In short, "non-resistance and passive obedience" are not enjoined by them.

It must be admitted all the same that our ancient thinkers very much dreaded the state of anarchy which in their eyes was the only alternative to kingly rule. In their enthusiasm to exalt the importance of the king's office, they fail to distinguish clearly, except in the solitary instance of Śukra noted above, between a good and a bad king. In other words, the theory of the king's divinity is not itself so framed as to be inapplicable to bad rulers. On the other hand, all stress is laid on the divinity of the king at one stage of the discussion; and only later on, they go on to indicate what seem to be modifications or limitations of this attitude. All that they then lay down is that, in the last resort, when the king definitely proves to be a wicked tyrant, not amenable to the checks and restraints of *Dharma*, when not only does he not protect them but literally crushes them down with oppression—only in such a contingency—the people might depose or destroy him. There is evidently no constitutional check on the king. There is nothing to prevent him from going wrong—except the words of counsel and expostulations of the ministers and the Brāhmaṇas. And these are not binding on him. Herein lies the distinct weakness in the position of our authors. Although they do not enjoin passive obedience to the king, the only remedy that the subjects have against the king is the reserve power of rebellion.

It is relevant to take into account here the tendency of the Hindu mind to exaggeration.[97] Our authors, further, always aimed at laying down maxims as guides to practical conduct. Theory as such had no interest for them. Hence, they were prone to lay

96. It must be admitted, however, that the Hindu thinkers do have a very low opinion about human nature; for, they are never tired of repeating that in the absence of the fear of Daṇḍa, the people would never follow their duties.

97. cf. B. Prasad: *Theory of Government*, p. 2.
Also Monier Williams' remarks in his *Buddhism* and Aurobindo Ghose: *Renaissance in India*, pp. 21 ff.

undue emphasis on one aspect of their teachings at one time and on another at another time. It is only by keeping in mind this feature of ancient Indian thought that we can understand and reconcile their statements, some seeming to inculcate abject submission on the part of the subjects, others justifying popular revolt under certain circumstances.

On the whole, then, we may conclude that the Hindu theory of the divine right of the king is similar to the European theory only to a limited extent. The similarity lies in attributing a peculiar sanctity to the king and regarding it as the basis of political allegiance. The Hindu theory, however, is compatible with the king's subjection to *Dharma*; rather, the Hindu theory is properly to be understood in the light of the conception of *Dharma* with all its implications.

As an explanation for political obligation, the theory of divine right is evidently untenable. It does not, really speaking, seek to relate political obligation to the moral nature of man. It appeals not to reason but to faith. It asks us to take it for granted that the king is a divinity and that a divinity is 'ipso facto' entitled to be obeyed. To an atheist or to an agnostic, the theory has no meaning at all.[98] But even granting that all power is from God, we do not see how we can be sure that any particular power is divinely appointed. The theory may perhaps seem to be satisfactory in what Comte would call the "theological" stage. In the modern age, it is quite beside the mark. An institution can be justified only in view of the purpose it serves. It claims our loyalty in so far as it fulfils and fosters a definite social purpose. And the State does not stand in any different category apart from other institutions in this respect. The theory of the king's divine right is but another way of classifying the people as "natural" rulers and "natural" slaves. Law, according to this theory, would be a command backed indeed by divine sanction but in no way expressing the will of the subjects. If we accent the doctrine, it is inconceivable how people could ever feel themselves the authors of the law they are called upon to obey. There is certainly a peculiar majesty

98. Willoughby: *The Nature of the State*, p. 51.

about the State because of its functions and the extent of power it wields. This majesty, however, is not the reason why people should obey a particular political authority. It is rather the result of the obedience rendered to it by the people. The power of the State with all its majesty is due really to the fact that its end has a great significance for the life of man. The divine right theory can be taken to be true only in the sense in which Hume takes it. "As it is impossible for the human race," he says, "to subsist at least in any comfortable or secure state, without the protection of government, this institution must certainly have been instituted by that beneficent Being, who means the good of His creatures."[99] Or, if the theory meant only that the Creator implanted in the breast of man the instinct for order and the impulse which manifests itself in political organisation, it becomes acceptable.[100] We must add, however, that the Creator has also implanted in man a sense of justice and a sense of loyalty to ideals which must be the touchstone of every institution. The theory of the divine right of the king—or any government in fact—cannot be accepted as the valid ground for obedience to it. We are only too apt to imagine that the existing institutions are something sacrosanct; we often imagine that they are necessary in themselves, perhaps even apart from the purpose they fulfil. That is why, as Lord Acton would put it, "the history of institutions is often a history of deceptions and illusions."[101] The acceptance of the king's divinity involves what Prof. Laski would call "the paralysis of will." What we must emphasize rather is the fact that the State is a fellowship of men for the enrichment of the common life.[102] It wins our loyalty only in so far as it attempts to realise its end. Compulsory though its membership is, its moral character is not essentially different from that of any other association. And further, it must always be remembered that the State acts through its agents, who are by no means infallible. Hence, the actions of Government always

---

99. Quoted by Garner: *Introduction to Political Science*, p. 90.

100. Willoughby: *The Nature of the State*, p. 52.

101. Acton: *History of Freedom and other Essays*, p. 2.

102. Laski: *Grammar of Politics*, p. 37.

need a perpetual vigilance on the part of the citizen-body, which in the last resort must always be prepared to withdraw its moral support to an actual Government. The dangers of obedience to authority must, in other words, be constantly guarded against; for, a failure on this score is bound to give rise to some manifestation of the right divine.

To recapitulate, the theory of the king's divine right is certainly present in Hindu thought. In some cases, as we have seen, there is even an undue emphasis on the king's divinity. However, the Hindu theory does not aim at justifying misrule. The king has no right divine to go wrong. The theory of divine right is in no way an adequate explanation of political obligation. And the Hindu thinkers have certainly not offered the divine right theory as the sole justification of the king's authority. They give us further hints of some other theories also which throw light on the problem of political obligation. These we shall consider in the next three chapters.

Chapter II

The Contractual Theory of Political Obligation in Hindu Thought

We remarked, towards the close of the last chapter, that in our ancient works we come across various hints, at different places, suggesting, though vaguely different, explanations of political allegiance. Having discussed the implications of the theory of the king's divine right, we shall now see whether and how far the contractual view of political obligation has been suggested and developed by our authors. We shall also work out the implications of the various relevant hints and compare them with the European theories of contract. And finally we shall indicate the element of value in the contractual theory of political obligation.

In the *Brāhmaṇas*, there occur a few references to the origin of sovereign authority among the gods. The subject in hand in these compositions is the sovereignty of Indra. But man makes gods after his own image. The celestial sovereignty of Indra therefore may well be taken as the reflex of the sovereignty of the earthly king.[1] The *Aitareya Brāhmaṇa*, for example, thus describes the origin of lndra's sovereignty:

> "The gods headed by Prajapati said to one another (pointing with their hands to Indra): 'This one is among the gods the most vigorous, most strong, most valiant, most perfect, who carries out best any work (to be done). Let us instal him (to the kingship over us).' They all consented to perform just this ceremony (mahabhisheka) on Indra."

---

1. Bhandarkar: *Score Aspects of Ancient Indian Polity*, p. 127.

The sovereignty of Indra is thus the result of his election by the gods, headed by Prajapati. There is, however, no contract at all as between the gods and Indra. The passage seems to be merely indicating the acceptance by the gods of the sovereignty of Indra, which was probably a foregone conclusion already. There is no indication in the passage of the terms on which Indra retained his authority. It is hardly defensible to read here any 'resemblance to the social contract theory of the western political thinkers' as Dr. Bhandarkar has done.[2] There is another passage in the *Aitareya Brāhmaṇa*[3] which Jayaswal takes to signify the contractual basis of kingly rule. It represents the 'coronation oath' to be taken by the king-elect. He is to repeat with faith (śraddhayā): "Between the night I am born and the night I die, whatever good I might have done, my heaven, my life and my progeny may I be deprived of, if I oppress you."[4] One fails to see where the 'contractual nature of the oath' comes in at all. There is no reference here to the people as the electors of the king. The oath does not represent an undertaking given by the king to the subjects to rule according to any specified principles. The nemesis of misrule is not said to be any penalty at the hands of the subjects. On the other hand, the oath only recounts the spiritual penalties for oppression; for, the penalties mentioned are loss of life, of progeny and of heaven. It involves, therefore, a gross misunderstanding to interpret the passage as implying a contract between the king and the subjects. In the *Śatapatha Brāhmaṇa* there is a passage which explains the sovereignty of Indra as being founded on an agreement between the gods.[5] A passage in the *Aitareya Brāhmaṇa,* again, speaks of the office of kingship as being created or perhaps acclaimed by common consent.[6] Passages such as these do not really postulate a contract on definite terms between the ruler and the ruled.

---

2. *Some Aspects of Ancient Indian Polity,* p. 128. Dr. Bhandarkar himself recognises, however, that "the most important feature of the theory is conspicuous by its absence, namely, the governmental pact entered into by both parties."
3. *Aitareya Br.,* VIII, 15, p. 332 (Keith's translation).
4. *Hindu Polity,* Part II, p. 28.
5. III, 4. 2 (S. B. E. Vol. XXVI, p. 93).
6. I, i, 14, p. 117 (Keith's translation).

In the *Dharmasūtra* of Baudhāyana the king is enjoined to protect his subjects, receiving as his pay a sixth part.[7] This view is certainly common in Hindu thought.[8] It emphasizes the duty of the king to protect the subjects in return for the taxes he receives from them. The king would not be justified in accepting or exacting the taxes from the people, unless he discharged his duty of 'protection.' This does not imply a contract between the king and the people. It only points out the moral responsibility of the king for the 'protection' of the subjects inasmuch as he receives taxes from them. The subjects have no means at their command to enforce the king's compliance to this injunction. It is too much, therefore, to conclude, with Dr. P.N. Banerjea, on the strength of these injunctions, that the relations between the ruler and the ruled were contractual.[9]

Let us now consider the evidence of the *Arthaśāstra* of Kauṭilya. Dr. Bhandarkar[10] emphatically asserts that "the mental restlessness" associated with the social contract theory was not confined to Europe only; it certainly "manifested itself in the political horizon of ancient India." "The theory of the social contract," the Doctor observes, "was certainly known to Kauṭilya, and is referred to by him with approval."

Kauṭilya opens his discussion on this point by visualising a state of affairs in which there is no political authority. 'The state of nature' so visualised is one where the 'logic of the fish' has full sway. It is a state of affairs in which the people know no law but their savage appetites and instincts. They only prey upon one another. Security of life or property there is none. An escape from such a state would certainly be desirable. And this is effected, says Kauṭilya, by people making Manu their first king. Kauṭilya does not discuss why they selected Manu. But Manu is said to be the son of Vaivasvata. This mythological setting of the story may, as

---

7. I, 10, 18, I.
8. cf. Artha., Bk. II; Manu: VIII, 309; Śukra: I, 255.
9. *Pub. Admn. in Ancient India*, p. 72.
10. *Carmichael Lectures*, 1918, p. 119.

we have seen already,[11] be regarded as one factor, surrounding the king with a halo of sanctity. To Manu, the people, we are told, allotted one-sixth of their grains and one-tenth of their merchandise as the sovereign's dues. Fed by this payment, the kings took upon themselves the responsibility of maintaining the safety and security of their subjects.[12]

What are the implications of these remarks? It must be noted at the outset that these remarks are immediately followed by the exposition of the king's divinity, and the king is said to be answerable for the sins of his subjects. So far, however, as the passage in question is concerned, we must point out that it is not clear whether Manu on his part makes any definite promise to the people. Kauṭilya does not tell us if Manu agreed to or accepted the conditions offered by the people. We may say that the contract between Manu and the people must be regarded as only implicit. The implications of this implicit contract would be that the people should obey the king and pay taxes and the king on his part should not fail to protect them. Kauṭilya, however, draws only the one-sided conclusion that even the hermits must pay the king's dues.

If we attempt a critical examination of the theory as stated by Kauṭilya, we vividly realize its inadequacy. The people, in the absence of the kingly office, were, we are told, in a state of nature, where they suffered all sorts of privations owing to the operation of the "matsyanyāya." In such a state, their life would evidently be, like the life of men in the Hobbesian pre-social state, "solitary, poor, nasty, brutish and short." Kauṭilya does not explain how from this lawless state emerged civil-society. He does not stop to postulate a 'social' contract. He rather goes on immediately to describe what may be called the 'governmental' compact. But the problem is: if people were merely praying upon one another like fishes, in the absence of a ruler, how can an agreement between them be postulated? If really the state of nature was a state of mutual animosity, if really there was no principle in it but the

11. See Ch. I, p. 48.

12. *Arthaśāstra*, Bk. I, Ch. 13.

rule of the strong, how can we account for this sudden change in their nature, whereby, as Vaughan[13] so picturesquely puts it, 'the same beings, who, one moment, have been flying at each other's throats, should, the next moment, with equal eagerness be flying into each other's arms?' It is difficult to understand how people subject to "matsyanyāya" could any time come together and agree to live peacefully with one another under the authority of a king.

Further, even if such a phenomenon does take place, what guarantee is there that the agreement so arrived at would be honourably kept ever afterwards? It is probably in an attempt to explain this inconsistency that Hobbes lands himself into another. Side by side with the law of nature, which was merely another name for the rule of brute force, he postulates another law, a law of right reason, that exists somehow alongside with the law of the sword. This law requires that "every man ought to endeavour peace, as far as he has hope of attaining it;" that "whatsoever you require that others should do to you, that do you to them," and that "men perform their covenants made."[14] It is difficult to comprehend how such a law could at all exist in a world, where force and fraud are stated to be cardinal virtues and where "the very notions of right and wrong, justice and injustice are unknown."[15] If, however, such a law was really recognised in the pre-social state, then we might as well speak of such a society, as Green points out,[16] as already a civil society.

Such difficulties do not confront Kauṭilya. He does not search out the sanctions behind the contract. He is silent as to how the obligation of the subjects to obey kings subsequent to Manu is to be explained. Even the terms of the so-called contract are not quite clear. They do not really indicate the sphere of the State. There are no "natural rights" which the State must consider sacrosanct. Really speaking, the contractual element in the theory

---

13. *Studies in the History of Pol. Phil.*, pp. 32 and 51.

14. *Leviathan*, pp. 66 ff.

15. *Ibid.*, pp. 63 ff.

16. *Principles of Political Obligation*, pp. 70-71.

is very weak. At most, we might say that the idea of a contract is vaguely suggested when it is said that "people made Manu their first king." The doctrine of "matsyanyāya," however, makes the idea of a contract a logical absurdity. And having selected Manu as their first king, the people seem to relapse once again into nothingness. The king is legally in a position to enforce obedience and to exact the sovereign's dues. The subjects are, on the other hand, quite helpless; for they have no constitutional means at their command to compel the king to observe the terms of the agreement. If the statement that Manu was selected by the people themselves suggests the conception of "popular sovereignty," such a conception quite disappears towards the end, when we are told that "whoever disregards kings will be visited with divine punishments too."

In fact, Kauṭilya is far from logical in the statement of his theory. We are only left to make conjectures as to its implications. Kauṭilya himself, as we have seen, concludes that the people, including the hermits, must pay the taxes and must obey the king. He does not, on the other hand, even mention the reciprocal duty of the king to his subjects.[17] If Kauṭilya really wanted to inculcate the contractual basis of political obligation, he would certainly have defined with more exactitude the sphere of the State and would also have pointed out how the subjects were to see that the king duly kept his word. The exposition in the *Arthaśāstra*, again, involves the doctrine of the king's divine right, as we have seen in the last chapter. It is quite misleading, therefore, to assert that "the theory of the social contract was known to Kauṭilya," and that it is "referred to by him with approval."[18]

When we turn from the *Dharmasūtras* and the *Arthaśāstra* to consider the political ideas embodied in the copious literature of

---

17. cf. Dr. Keith's remarks on the Kauṭiliyan State in his *History of Sanskrit Literature*, pp. 455-56.

18. cf. D. R. Bhandarkar: *Carmichael Lectures*, p. 119. On the other hand, the general trend of the whole passage points the other way about. Kauṭilya himself explicitly tells us that the object of the whole explanation is to silence 'the treacherous opponents of sovereignty.' How could he, then, ever refer to the contractual theory with approval?

the Buddhist canon, we are at once struck by the contrast between the orderly presentation of rules and maxims in one case and the merely incidental and fragmentary notices in the other.[19] The word "Khattavijja" in the Pali canon probably corresponds with the word Daṇḍanīti and Rājavidyā and it is remarkable that this "science" is looked down upon by Buddhist authors. Thus, very little of political thought is traceable in Buddhist literature. The main aim of this literature is evidently not to expatiate on things mundane but rather to describe whatever would contribute to the spiritual welfare of man. There are, however, a few passages which deserve our attention in this connexion.

The Buddhist view of the origin of kingship is expounded in the *Dīgha Nikāya* in the course of an enquiry into the claim of the Brāhmaṇas for superiority.[20] The author starts by visualising a fanciful age, when people were all perfect. In this original "state of nature," the people had nothing corporeal about them. The ethereal beings shone in splendour, enjoyed peace and affluence, danced in the air and lived long. The picture presented to us here is even more fanciful than that of the Satya Yuga occurring in other works. In this golden age, which reminds us of the stoic golden age, there could evidently be no scope for the State. The distinctions of colour and sex gradually manifested themselves. At this stage arose the need for the satisfaction of the primary appetites, food, clothing and shelter. Institutions like the family and private property were set up, we are told, by mutual agreements. But it was found impossible to pull on with this arrangement. Theft appeared and also certain other forms of unsocial conduct. Then, it is said, the people came together and said, "What if we now elect some one of us who shall get angry with him who merits anger, reprove him who merits reproof and banish him who merits banishment. And we will give him in return a share of our rice." So they selected the most beautiful, gracious and powerful individual as chief. He was called the Great Elect for

---

19. cf. Ghoshal: *Hindu Political Theories*, pp. 63-64.

20. Vide B. Prasad: *Theory of Government in Ancient India*, p. 205. Ghoshal: *Hindu Political Theories*, pp. 65 ff. Warren: *Buddhism in Translations*, pp. 315 ff.

being chosen by a great multitude of men; as he was lord of the fields, he was called Khattiya and as he delighted the others in accordance with law (*Dharmena*) he was called "Rājā." Similar are the versions of the theory occurring in other Buddhist writings.[21] What is the significance of this story? It starts with the conception of a mythical perfect age when men were not subject to the ills of the flesh and the frailties of human nature. The picture is highly imaginative and is not really connected with the rest of the theory. It is with the next stage, therefore, that we must concern ourselves. We do not know what 'original sin' led to the fall. But the point to note is that the moment people descend to the physical plane, the moment they feel the pressure of human needs, some social organisation becomes absolutely necessary. If the idea here is that the origin of the State must ultimately be traced to the fundamental needs of life, then, certainly, the theory has a sound kernel of truth in it.[22] It is also remarkable that life in society, it is recognised, is not really possible, so long as there is no institution to adjudicate between conflicting claims. The story tells us how the institution of kingship came into existence primarily in order to check unsocial forms of conduct.

The theory as stated here differs in certain respects from the exposition of the theory by Kauṭilya. The conception of the original state of perfection is not found in the *Arthaśāstra.* The conception of "matsyanyāya" as the immediate prelude to the institution of government is absent in the Buddhist story. Here, the institution of kingship is said to be necessitated by the appearance of only some forms of unsocial conduct. Human nature is not in this passage conceived of as being essentially so wicked as to be inclined merely to prey upon one another in the absence of control. Strictly speaking, the Buddhist theory does not postulate a state of nature, prior to the formation of civil society. It only

21. *Mahavastu,* ed Senart, I, 347-48; *The life of Buddha,* translated by Rockhill, referred to by Beni Prasad, *Theory of Government,* pp. 206-208; also see Ghoshal: *Hindu Political Theories,* p. 66; and N.N. Law: *Some Aspects of Ancient Indian Polity,* pp. 94-95.

22. cf. Aristotle: *Politics,* Ch. II.

gives us a glimpse into a dreamland where mankind lived a life of perfection. But it recognises that as soon as men descend to the physical plane, that is to say, as soon as men become really ordinary human beings, social institutions arise. And these social institutions, says the story, proved to be unavailing in the absence of some definite sanction behind them. Government, in short, arises because of the need for the maintenance of order in society. We do not know if the author intended to make his theory correspond to the facts of history in this respect. He wins our admiration for his sound instinctive recognition of the fact that life in society must involve definite restraints and that the origin of government must be traced to the need for the preservation of order. Here, in Hindu thought, we may say, is the theory of the origin of kingship which may well be taken as complementary to that in the *Aitareya Brāhmaṇa*, where the origin of government is ascribed to the necessity of leadership in war. This seems to us to be the real significance of the story.

A difficulty arises when we try to understand the legitimate sphere of government and the nature of the relation between the king and the subjects in the light of the account presented to us here. If we study the wording of the story itself, it does not appear that the king on his part made any definite promise to the people. We cannot, therefore, speak of a contract in the full sense of the term as between the king and the subjects. We might say, at most, that the contract is implicit here. The duty of the king would, then, be to act as judge and punish those who commit theft or such other crimes. The duty of the people would be to pay a share of their produce. The literal meaning of the terms of the implicit agreement lends colour to the view that the state is here conceived of as a necessary evil, to be tolerated because of the existence of unsocial men in society. The function of the State would then be merely to act as Police and leave the rest to the subjects themselves. It is even possible to read in the passage a recognition, even if latent, of popular sovereignty.[23] If this interpretation were justified, we shall certainly agree with

23. cf. Ghoshal: *Hindu Political Theories*, pp. 67-68.

Dr. Ghoshal in characterising the theory as marked by originality in many points. We would even go further and assert that the Buddhist theory with its fiercely individualistic implications stands in a category by itself apart from the rest of Hindu thought.

We feel, however, that such are not really the implications of the story presented to us here. The important point to bear in mind in this connexion is that the Buddha was not at all a social reformer.[24] The Buddha's doctrine did not aim at a transformation or an improvement of the social conditions. The worldly life is a matter of indifference to the virtuous Buddhist who renounces the world. Life, according to the Buddhist teaching, is all misery and Nirvana the "summum bonum." It is in Nirvana that the end of all that aggregation of pain which is life is brought about.[25] The doctrine of Karma is too strongly embedded in Buddhist thought to allow it to consider that life on earth could ever be anything else than what it actually was. "It is Karma," we are told, "that divides men into low and high."[26] Thus, the Buddhist author could hardly have thought of propounding a new theory to explain political obligation.

Further, we have it on the authority of Dr. Keith[27] that logically no such thing as political or social philosophy could be possible in Buddhist thought.

Even granting for the moment that political or social philosophy may nevertheless be traced in Buddhist thought, it is highly improbable that the author in this case was trying to forge "a weapon which might be used to justify almost any degree of popular control over the king." For, if that were so, should we not expect that his treatment of the subject would have been less fragmentary? Should we not expect that he would work out the implications of his theory so as at least to point out his distinctiveness or his departure from traditional thought?

---

24. Fick: *Social Organisation*, p. 335.
25. *Questions of Milinda*, p. 107.
26. *Ibid.*, p. 108.
27. *Buddhist Philosophy*, p. 120.

We must also take into account the setting of the story itself, which is essentially mythological. Thus even the sun and the moon are described as having come into existence in response to human need.[28] It is also significant that "the most handsome, the most pleasing of appearance, possessing of the greatest influence and wisdom" at the time happens to be no other than the Buddha himself. And lastly the story concludes by inculcating the precedence of the warrior-caste above the rest. It seems really that the whole story is an attempt to glorify the Buddha and the Kshatriyas and that the implicit contract cannot be interpreted literally.

The passage in question, thus, cannot be regarded as giving us a new basis for political obligation. We do not come across evidence elsewhere in these works suggesting that the Buddhist theory of political obligation involved a distinct departure from the traditional view. Nowhere in the Buddhist Jataḳas, in the *Jatakamala* of Aryasura or in the *Buddha-charita* of Asvaghosha do we find a reference to an attempt to delimit the functions of the State so as to reduce it to a Police State. The Edicts of Asoka, on the other hand, imply a theory of paternal despotism, recognising no limit to the scope of governmental interference. The failure to observe this fact seems to be responsible for the statements of some of our scholars to the effect that the Buddhist theory is "the individualistic theory which prevailed in the West in the seventeenth and eighteenth centuries."[29]

We may say, then, that the author of the *Dīgha Nikāya* brings in the idea of a pact not in order to inculcate by means of it a complete theory of the State but only to explain the origin of government as a necessary institution for the maintenance of order in society. The punishment of wrong-doers would thus be an important function of the king. But that is not all. The story admits that the king was the lord of the fields and also the cause of delight to the people. Evidently the lordship of the fields cannot

---

28. Refer Warren: *Buddhism in Translations*, p. 315.

29. Dikshitar: *Hindu Administrative Institutions*, p. 63.

be justified if we look to the terms of the suggested pact; nor is there any ground for his being the cause of delight to the people, if he is a mere magistrate elected by the people for the purpose of punishing wrong-doers.[30] We must note in this connection that in the passage before us, the intervention of any divine power is clearly absent and that the *Dharmaśāstra* doctrine of the necessary relation of taxation to protection is brought out here with an added emphasis. There is, however, a good deal of vagueness about the actual terms of the suggested pact, and there is no provision to secure the conformity of the two parties to its terms.

In the *Mahābhārata*, we get an elaborate account of the state of nature and the duties of the king. The supreme importance of Daṇḍanīti, the science of Government, is a favourite theme of the Epic. Daṇḍanīti is "the refuge of all creatures;" "Dharma, Artha and Kama depend on royal duties," nay, "the practices which lead to liberation equally depend on them."[31] As the discourse proceeds, Yudhishṭhira puts his famous question, which is no other than the question why men obey the State.[32] In reply, the venerable grandfather starts with the description of "how in the golden cycle sovereignty was first instituted."

There was a time, a golden age, when "there was no sovereignty, no king, no punishment and no punisher."[33] Men lived in peace and were equal to gods. They used to protect one another piously. In a word, it may be said, "the state of nature was the reign of God."[34]

However, this state of perfection was not destined to last long. As in the Buddhist theory so here the fall soon comes on. "Error possessed their hearts" and men found the task of protecting one another to be painful. Virtue began to wane. Men became

30. The fact of his delighting the people is connected really with his association with the conception of *Dharma*. (*cf. Dhammena pare ranjettiti raja.*)

31. *Śanti Parva,* LVI, 2-9.

32. *Ibid.*, LIX, 5-12.

33. *Ibid.*, LIX, 13 ff. and *Vana Parva,* CCIX, LVII, 15.

34. Pope's *Essay on Man,* Epistle iii, i, 148—quoted in Tozer's Introduction to Rousseau's *Social Contract,* p. 26.

covetous. Lust seized them. Anger overtook them. As a result, we are told, in words reminiscent of the *Bhagavad-gītā*,[35] they lost all considerations of what should be done and what should not be done. In this confusion, the Vedas disappeared and with them all righteousness. The gods were overcome with fear and they sought the help of the Brāhmaṇa.

We do not know what 'original sin' was responsible for such a fall. In fact, this notion of the inherent tendency of men and societies to decline inevitably is found to be a common characteristic of Hindu thought. The Vana Parva gives us an animated description of the successive stages of the fall through the ages.[36] Manu describes the four Ages, and lays down different duties for each. In the Krita Age, *Dharma* is four-footed and entire and (so is) truth; nor does any gain accrue to men by unrighteousness; in the other (three ages) by reason of (unjust) gains, *Dharma* is deprived of one foot, and through (the prevalence) of theft, falsehood and fraud, the merit (gained by men) is diminished by one-fourth (in each).[37] The same conception seems to underlie the oft-quoted assurance of Lord Krishna to his devotees that whenever piety (*Dharma*) languishes and impiety becomes ascendant in this world, He in His mercy and love takes birth in order to re-establish *Dharma*.[38] We may not pause at this stage to estimate the influence of such a conception on the people's outlook on life. It is enough here to say that there is no conception in Hindu thought of the gradual perfectibility of man, no conception of progress, bringing in its train freedom broadening down from precedent to precedent.[39]

So deep-rooted is this conception, that from the initial state of idyllic peace and felicity, men are said to have degenerated to

35. II, 62, 63.

36. CXLL.

37. I, 81-86.

38. *Bhagavad-gīta*, 1V, 7-8.

39. And this is not surprising, since the conception of progress is essentially modern. cf. Jowett's Introduction to Plato's *Republic*.

such an extent that they became like a herd of cattle[40] without the herdsman, like fishes in shallow water, feasting upon their kindred. In such a state might becomes right; "wives, sons, foods and other kinds of property cease to exist." Such a state is indeed intolerable and a way out must be discovered.

The *Mahābhārata* offers two accounts of how this state of affairs was remedied. According to one,[41] with the disappearance of the Vedas and of righteousness, the gods were overcome with fear. They approached Brahma and narrated to him how they were about to be reduced to the level of human beings. This became an occasion for the divine Grandfather to compose a comprehensive treatise on Dharma, Artha and Kāma. Vishṇu was then approached by the god and was requested to point out that one among men who deserved to reign supreme over the rest.[42] Pṛithū ultimately became the first king, and his divinity is expounded by the Epic in more ways than one.[43] With that part of the discussion we are not concerned here. What interests us here is the suggestion of a pact which is introduced into the description at this stage. That Pṛithu was the king-elect by the will of Vishṇu is evident. Still, the *Mahābhārata* tells us that Pṛithu was asked by the gods and Rishis present there to make a definite promise, which represents his coronation-oath. The Rishis and the gods thus describe the duties which he should perform:

> "Do you perform fearlessly all sorts of righteous works. Without caring for what is dear and what is not dear, regard all creatures with impartiality. Renounce lust, anger, covetousness and pride and always following the dictates of righteousness, do you punish the man, whoever he may be, who does not discharge his duty. Do you also swear that you would in thought, word and deed always maintain the religion (*Dharma*) laid down on earth by the Vedas. Do you also swear that you would fearlessly follow the duties laid down in the Vedas with the help of the science of punishment, and that you would never act capriciously. O powerful one, know

40. *Śānti Parva*, LXVIII, 10-31.

41. *Śānti Parva*, LIX, 23 ff.

42. *Ibid.*, LIX, 87 ff.

43. See Ch. I, Supra.

that Brāhmaṇas are exempt from punishment, and promise further that you would protect the world from an intermixture of castes."[44]

To these terms, Pṛithu agreed.

There is evidently no contract here between the people and the king. The people have no share at all in the choice of the king. Nor do they ever determine on what terms the king must exercise his power. The theory in the *Mahābhārata* emphasizes, as we have seen, the divinity of the king. But the terms on which his power is to be exercised are here laid down. It may be noted that the absence of the participation of the people in this affair is quite consistent with the supposition of 'the state of nature' as a state of chaos. The people being under the operation of the "matsyanyāya" could obviously not be in a position to come together and dictate terms to the king-elect. It is only to the gods and the Rishis, in other words, to divine or semi-divine persons that the king makes his pledge. The pledge is to the effect that he would rule according to *Dharma*. There is no mention, however, of any sanctions behind this agreement. Prithu takes the oath as suggested by the gods and Rishis and the latter are satisfied. The question "what if the terms of the oath are not kept" does not seem to arise at all.

In this passage, then, there is certainly no contractual view of political obligation. The king, however, exercises his authority on definite terms laid down in the oath, taken in the presence of the gods and Rishis—the divinely gifted wise men and well-wishers of the human race.

The second version of the account[45] starts by describing the evils of anarchy. These, in the opinion of Bhisma, are so serious that people should never live in a kingdom in which they prevail. They must rather submit to a usurper, for "the man who bends his head to a powerful person really bows his head to Indra." The text then goes on to describe the origin of the institution of kingship. It is said, that "men in days of yore were ruined in

---

44. *Śānti Parva,* LXIX, 103-108.

45. *Ibid.*, LXVII.

consequence of anarchy, devouring one another like stronger fishes devouring the weaker." Thus, in the absence of the king, the people lived a life of incessant struggle and warfare, recognising no ethical considerations. In order to avoid this, however, they assembled together and made certain agreements saying: "He who becomes harsh in speech or violent in temper, he who seduces other people's wives or robs others' wealth should be renounced by us."

We have no means to judge whether the *Mahābhārata* seeks to maintain here that men enter the civil state by means of a compact. It would seem that this is so. The difficulties that arise in that case are obvious. If the people were really devouring one another, how could they think of assembling together? How could they arrive at the norms of conduct which they thenceforth agree to maintain? The text does not tell us what authority the people set up in this case to detect and punish the crimes referred to above. Any way, the experiment, we are told, proved a failure. The people had therefore to approach Brahma and to request him to appoint some one as their king. It is a bit puzzling to note that the people, who could see how to escape from the state of anarchy with all its evils and could think of organising their life on the basis of an agreement, could not appoint a king for themselves on their own initiative. Shall we presume that they relapsed into the state of anarchy? If that be so, again, how could they themselves think of approaching Brahma and requesting him to appoint a king for them? Well, Brahma, we are told, asked Manu to be the first king. But the latter was reluctant, as he was afraid of incurring sin by having to govern men always false and deceitful. Thereupon, 'the denizens of the earth' assured him that the sins of men would affect only those who committed them. Further, they promised him a fiftieth part of their animals and precious metals and 'a tenth part of their grain.' They also promised him a large retinue of able warriors and also added: "A fourth part of the merit which men will acquire under your protection will belong to you. Strengthened by that merit do you protect us. Crush the pride of enemies and let righteousness be always victorious!" Thus assured by the people, Manu, we are told, went round the world, suppressing everywhere all acts of wickedness and compelling all men to follow their respective duties.

It will be noted that even in this version there is no contract between the King and the people; for, while the people pledge themselves to fulfil certain conditions, the king makes them no promise in return. He was selected by Brahma; and he is content with this assurance from the people. It is thus a one-sided bargain. We may grant that he accepted the obligation of protecting the people and of maintaining the integrity of *Dharma* referred to by the people. We are not entitled to say, however, that he would be responsible to the people for the due discharge of these duties. In this case, too, there is no provision to see that obligations on either side are duly fulfilled. It must also be noted that people are here described as promising a fourth part of the merit which men would acquire under the protection of the king. They also guarantee that the sins will affect those who commit them and not the king. The question is: how could the people be an authority in matters spiritual? How could they determine spiritual awards or penalties? And what would be the value of such a pledge or assurance from the people, who, as we are told, were perishing without a king to keep them in check?

Judging from the setting of the description and also the spirit of the description itself with all its inconsistencies, we come to the conclusion that here also there is strictly speaking no contract postulated in order to explain the relation of the subjects to the ruler. Certain statements are only put in the mouth of the people by the author probably to emphasize the imperativeness of their duty to obey the king and pay him taxes. Side by side with the duties of the people are also mentioned the duties of the king. The king has certain duties which he must always perform; similarly the subjects also have their own duties. These are pointed out, it seems, by means of the peculiar expedient of representing the people as agreeing to impose certain duties on themselves. But this, as we have remarked is incompatible with the doctrine of 'matsyanyāya' and the picture of the state of affairs in the absence of the king. We must, then, be content to note the general trend of such passages. They emphasize finally the fact that the institution of kingship is essential in society for the preservation of order and also for the general well-being of the people. It becomes the imperative duty of the people, therefore, to render obedience to the king and to pay him taxes. Secondly, the king on his part must 'protect' the people and uphold *Dharma.* It is evident that there is no conception here of 'natural rights' which the king must guarantee. Nor is there a hint that the subjects have in any definite sense the power to influence the conduct of the king in administering the affairs of the State from day to day. In a word, in the *Mahābhārata,* we may say, political obligation is not regarded as essentially contractual in nature, depending on the scrupulous performance of definite duties by both parties. That this is correct may be seen *inter alia* from the fact that the inhabitants of the earth became stricken with fear when they saw the power of Manu.[46] The essential implication of a contractual theory is that people have themselves realised the necessity or the advisability of having a supreme authority for the management of their affairs. The king would then be an official commissioned by the people to discharge certain functions on definite terms. It would mean, in short, that the basis of the king's authority is consent and that the obedience of the people is thus voluntary.[47] There would clearly be no reason why the people should get stricken with fear on seeing the might of the king. In fact, the various implications of the contractual view cannot be reconciled with the statement of the duties of the king and of the subjects that we come across in different contexts in our ancient Epic.

After the *Mahābhārata,* the law-books constitute one of the most important sources of Hindu political theory; and of the law-books, the *Manu-smṛiti* is probably the most important. This work is as sacerdotal in tone and as partial to the *Brāhmaṇas* as the *Mahābhārata.* The social ideas of the two works are in

46. *Śānti Parva,* LXVII, 31-32.

47. As Vaughan puts it, "The idea of contract once given, the only natural application of it is that which turns it to purposes of democracy" (*Studies in the History of Political Philosophy,* I, P. 14).

remarkable agreement. The superiority of the Brāhmaṇas is greatly emphasized in the *Manu-smṛiti.* Among men they are said to be the most exalted. A Brāhmaṇa, it is laid down, is 'an eternal incarnation of the sacred law,'[48] 'the highest on the earth' and 'the lord of the created beings.'[49] Thus, 'whatever exists in the world is the property of the Brāhmaṇas,'[50] 'other mortals subsist through the benevolence of the Brāhmaṇa.'[51] A king must be particularly careful not to enrage a Brāhmaṇa, or else he would instantly destroy him together with his army and vehicles. And lest we should entertain any doubt as to whether all this applied to an ignorant Brāhmaṇa also, the Smriti text lays down that "a Brāhmaṇa, be he ignorant or learned, is a great divinity just as the fire, whether carried forth (for the performance of a burnt oblation) or not carried forth, is a great divinity."[52]

With this social background, the *Manu-smṛiti* launches upon the discussion of royal duties. There is not the slightest suggestion of a contractual view here. On the other hand, the assertions of the divinity of the king and of the supremacy of the Brāhmaṇas are unequivocal and dogmatic. The state of nature, the kingless state, is one of fear and force.[53] The creatures, without a king, disperse in all directions, being oppressed by the sense of fear. This, however, is not a prelude to any contract with or without the intervention of the divine element. The state of sheer lawlessness moves the Lord, who immediately created a king for the protection of this whole creation out of the particles of different gods. Thus the king derives his authority from the divine will. The idea of the coronation-oath and the acceptance of the king's authority by the people does not appear here. Even as an infant, the king is a great deity in human form.[54] In the discharge of his duties

---

48. *Manu,* I, 98.
49. *Ibid.,* 99.
50. *Ibid.,* 100.
51. *Manu,* I, 101.
52. *Ibid.,* IX, 313-321.
53. *Ibid.,* VII, 3 and 20-21.
54. *Ibid.,* VII, 8.

he is to emulate the energetic action of Indra, of the Sun, of the Wind, of Yama, of Varuṇa, of the Moon, of the Fire, and of the Earth.[55]

Manu's tone is all through authoritarian. However, it would be wrong to conclude that for him the State is force and the king an irresponsible despot. For, even he is careful enough to emphasize that "a king who punishes those who do not deserve to be punished and punishes not those who deserve to be, brings great infamy on himself and sinks into hell."[56] Daṇḍa is a principle that "strikes down the king who swerves from his duty."[57] Does this not involve a recognition, however vague and implicit, of the fact that political obligation must be founded on something more rational than divine right? Divine though the king is, there is a principle to which he must acknowledge allegiance: This principle is not indeed that of the consent of the people. That the king's authority must ultimately be accepted by the people was never explicitly recognised by Manu. However, the king's life and conduct have to be regulated, so that there may be the necessary adjustment inevitable for any good system of government. That is why Manu lays down various restrictions and regulations which the king must abide by.[58] Thus, Manu insists that "the highest duty of a Kshatriya is to protect his subjects, for the king who enjoys the rewards just mentioned is bound to discharge that duty."[59] A sure suggestion of mutual obligation, indeed. It is thus that the old doctrine that taxation is a reward or remuneration for protection reasserts itself! There is certainly no contract in Manu, but is this not after all a homage, however indirect, to the principle that "living in society renders it indispensable that each should be bound to observe a certain line of conduct towards the rest?"[60]

---

55. *Ibid.*, IX, 303 ff.
56. *Manu*, VIII, 128; also VIII; 307-309.
57. *Ibid.*, VII, 28.
58. *Ibid.*, 144.
59. *Ibid.*, VII, 111-113.
60. Mill: *On Liberty*, p. 110.

The *Yājñavālkya-smṛiti* is next in importance to the *Manu-smṛiti.* It only enumerates in detail the duties of the king without explaining the principle behind them and therefore without propounding theories. Thus, we have here neither the theory of the king's divinity nor the theory suggestive of a contract. The duties of the king are multifarious. The scope of his activity coincides with the whole field of human life. He is to protect the people with justice,[61] to wield the rod of justice,[62] to set right families, castes, śrenis etc.,[63] to acquire by fair means, to protect what has been acquired, to increase what has been protected,[64] to appoint supervisors in departments of Dharma, Artha and Kāma,[65] to acquire wealth from war and to be a father to servants and subjects. It must be noted that Yājñavālkya insists on a higher standard of conduct than Manu. Punishment is to be meted out to all equitably, be the offender the father-in-law or the maternal uncle.[66] There is no injunction here such as there is in the *Manu-smṛiti* not to despise even an infant king, no injunction not to doubt the king's wisdom in treating his favourites with partiality. Brāhmaṇas have, indeed, a peculiar sanctity about them and "there is no higher virtue for kings than acquiring wealth by war, and giving that property to Brāhmaṇas."[67] The king is also enjoined to "be lenient towards Brāhmaṇas."[68] But the worship of the ignorant Brāhmaṇa is not insisted on by Yājñavālkya. "The lords of all are the Brāhmaṇas," says the text, but there is a qualifying phrase, "versed in the study of the Vedas" and "among them, those who perform observances are superior;" "even among the latter are those best who are knowers of the science of the spirit."[69] With

61. *Yāj.*, XIII, 334-337.
62. *Ibid.*, 354-359.
63. *Ibid.*, 361.
64. *Ibid.*, 317.
65. *Ibid.*, 322.
66. *Ibid.*, 358.
67. *Ibid.*, 323.
68. *Ibid.*, 334.
69. *Yāj.*, IX, 199.

reference to the subjects generally the injunction to the king to behave as a father has already been noted. Further the king is not to make illegal exactions or cause suffering to the subjects.[70] The fire arising from the heat of the sufferings of the subjects does not cease without fully burning the family, fortune and life of the king.[71] Nor is the doctrine of the relation between taxation and protection lost sight of. 'When not protected, whatever sin subjects commit, from that verily goes to the king one-half because he takes taxes from them.'[72] This statement has an importance of its own. At first sight it seems that this relation of taxation and protection makes the relation between the subjects and the king contractual. The statements on this point that we have so far noticed, if taken by themselves, might yield this interpretation. That they are not to be so judged as standing by themselves is what we have maintained all along. And here we are told definitely that the failure on the king's part to afford 'protection' does not absolve the subjects from the duty of obedience. It only means that the sins of the subjects are partly visited on the king. This is essentially a sacerdotal conception and cannot be reconciled with any contractual and therefore legal idea. All we are entitled to say is that though there is no clearly laid down theory in Yājñavālkya, the work is on the whole an attempt to balance the duties and privileges of the king; and, in this attempt fortunately the interests of the Brāhmaṇas do not come in so often as in Manu.

The *Vishnu-smṛiti* generally follows Manu, though with a few minor differences. It has a preference for the Brāhmaṇas, who are to be exempted from paying taxes[73] and are to be revered.[74] There is no idea of a contract to explain the relations between the ruler and the ruled, but the importance of keeping the subjects well-satisfied with the administration is certainly realised. As the author puts it, "That king who is pleased when his subjects are

---

70. *Ibid.*, XIII, 340.

71. *Ibid.*, 341.

72. *Ibid.*, 337.

73. Vishṇu, 26, 27.

74. *Ibid.*, 76.

joyful and grieved when they are in grief will obtain fame in this world and will be raised to a high station after death."[75] There is an identity of interests between the king and the subjects, because they are co-sharers in spiritual merit as well as sin.[76] In this respect, the *Vishnu-smṛiti* goes further than the *Mahābhārata*, where the sins committed by the subjects are to fall on them alone, while the king was to share their spiritual merit.

Thus, even the hints about the implicit contract between the king and the people gradually disappear. Only the insistence on the duty of protection in return for taxes still remains. Even Nārada, who preaches meek submission to the king's authority, characterises the king's dues as "the reward for the protection of his subjects."[77] So popular is this doctrine with Hindu writers, that Śukra even connects it up with the idea of the divine creation of the king. That the king is divine because he has been made out of the permanent elements of various gods has been made clear by the author.[78] This divinity is not, however, a title to license or capriciousness. It is pointed out that "gods ruin and cast down a king who is not a protector."[79] Nay, his divinity only makes him a servant. "The ruler," says Śukra, "has been made by Brahmā a servant of the people getting his revenue as remuneration."[80]

It is interesting to note that while the semblance of a contract that we have in Kauṭilya is made to support and exalt the authority of the king, the idea of his divinity in Śukra emphasizes only his duties as 'a servant of the people.'[81]

To recapitulate, we do not strictly speaking get a contractual view of political obligation in our ancient works. There are indeed

75. *Ibid.*, 98.

76. *Ibid.*, 28

77. *Nārada*, XVIII, 48.

78. *Śukra*, 1, 141-154.

79. *Ibid.*, 1, 239.

80. *Śukra*, I, 375.

81. We are not suggesting that Śukra's view of the king's office is radically different from that of Kauṭilya. We only draw attention to the danger of coming to a hasty generalisation.

a few hints, particularly in the *Arthaśāstra*, the *Mahābhārata* and in Buddhist works. It would, however, be misleading to generalise from these hints that the relations of the ruler and the ruled were at bottom contractual. Our analysis has shown that the elements of a contractual view are not really present in our ancient works. If, therefore, we institute a comparison between the Indian and the Western theories in this respect, we should do it with great caution and point out where exactly the similarity lies. A bare statement, for instance, to the effect that "clearly, the theory of social contract was not unknown in ancient India" is of little value, if not positively misleading.

We must first try to understand the exact significance of the contractual theories of political obligation as propounded by different Western thinkers.

The idea that governmental authority is based on a compact between the ruler and the subjects seems to be of ancient origin. It was prevalent among the Hebrews.[82] In the *Republic* of Plato, the idea is put forward by Glaucon, who maintains that laws are the result of an agreement between doing evil and suffering evil.[83] It was accepted by the Roman jurists under the Empire,[84] and the whole feudal system was saturated with ideas of contract.[85] It was, however, not till the Reformation created the strong bias towards individualism that the hour of contract can be said to have fully struck. John Althusius[86] asserted that sovereignty resides in the people and that kings are only their magistrates. Hooker, in his *Ecclesiastical Polity*, gave expression to the dictum, "Laws human of what kind soever, are available by consent."[87] Grotius pays at least a passing tribute to the theory, although the idea of a free contract as the foundation of civil society had not yet a very deep

82. Vide Willoughby: *The Nature of State*, p. 57.
83. *op. cit.*, p. 38.
84. Willoughby: *op. cit.*, p. 56.
85. H. Maine: *Ancient Law*, p. 353.
86. Vaughan: *Studies in the History of Pol. Philosophy*, Vol. I, p. 22.
87. Rousseau: *Social Contract*, ed. Tozer, Introdn., p. 13.

hold on his mind. The first formal statement of the theory is to be found in Hobbes; and the names of Locke and Rousseau are associated with the logical development of the theory.

The social contract theory envisages an original pre-social condition of men when there was no government. This 'state of nature' was sometimes conceived of as an ideal state of peace and felicity and sometimes as one of mutual war. The transition from this state to civil society was explained in terms of a compact. The governmental compact further determined the scope of governmental action. There are thus three essential elements of the theory, the state of nature and natural law, the political or social compact and the governmental compact.[88] These conceptions were made to yield different conclusions regarding the nature and basis of political obligation. Thus, to Hobbes, the contract is no less than a charter of despotism. The 'natural rights' of the people are surrendered to the sovereign and the people have by their own act lost not only the power but even the right to question or resist.[89] To the possible objection that the condition of subjects in this case is very miserable, Hobbes gives a very characteristic reply. The state of man, he says with an air of pessimism, can never be without some inconvenience or other. The inconvenience that may result in the civil state under the authority of the sovereign is thus inevitable. Nay, it ought rather to be welcomed, for the only alternative is a civil war or a state of anarchy with far greater miseries and calamities. Hobbes thus forged out a weapon to justify the absolutism of the Stuarts, without having recourse to the theory of divine right.

Spinoza does not create the impassable barrier between the state of nature and the civil state that Hobbes does. He equates 'jus' with 'potentia' both in the state and in the individual. His conclusion, therefore, is that the 'right' of the state against its members is only limited by its 'power.'[90] As in the state of nature, so in the civil state, there is a struggle for existence between

88. Gettell: *Introduction to Political Science*, pp. 82-83.

89. *Leviathan, Chs.* XVII and XVIII.

90. See Green: *Principles of Political Obligation*, pp. 49-51.

the powers of the individuals and the State. The State in this view represents nothing but superior power. The State can do no wrong, in the sense that there are no rights that it can violate. Limitations on the power of the State may all be summed up in one phrase, 'the danger of rebellion.' The sole motive power which Spinoza recognises, the only consideration binding either on the Government or the governed, is expediency. Now, what expediency means it is always difficult to say. The State may on the one hand push its claim to the farthest limits, and so on the other hand the individual may push his claims—his rights of resistance—to the farthest limits. The weakness of such a system is obvious. The chief error of Spinoza is in holding that rights can exist apart from society. And no wonder, he is soon compelled to throw consistency to the winds. He admits that while everything is "lawful" for the State, everything is not the "best;" the "best" State is that which secures a life of peace, for "no price paid for peace can ever be too great."

The contract in Spinoza is thus an absolute surrender on the part of the individuals. As Spinoza himself puts it, "henceforth all are to be controlled as it were by one mind," and "all submit their lives to the common good of all." In making the State an institution to secure the common good of all to be controlled by one mind, Spinoza's doctrine has a real affinity with Rousseau's.[91] But on the whole, for Spinoza "might is right" and "right is might" and his system leads to despotism—a despotism to which his nominal citizens are consenting parties.

The social contract theory becomes a gospel of freedom and democracy at the hands of Locke. His 'state of nature' is, unlike Hobbes' and Spinoza's, a state of "peace, good-will, mutual assistance and preservation."[92] The state of nature is governed by a "natural law." This law requires that "being all equal and independent, no one ought to harm another in his life, health,

---

91. cf. Vaughan: *Studies in the History of Political Philosophy,* Vol. I, pp. 125 ff.

92. *Civil Government,* Bk. 11, Ch. 3, p. 126.

liberty or possessions."[93] Every man must obey this law of nature and be also prepared to punish a breach of it by others. Thus in the state of nature every man has a power to kill the murderer, who has by his act renounced reason and declared war against mankind. This constitutes the inconvenience of the state of nature; men are obliged to be judges in their own case and it is likely that ill nature, passion and revenge may carry them too far in punishing others. The only remedy for this is to establish or to pass into the civil state. The civil state is the only remedy for the want of an established, settled, known law, of a known and indifferent judge and the power to enforce the claims of right."[94] "Wherever any number of men so unite into one society as to quit every one his executive power of the law of nature and to resign it to the public, there and there only is a political or civil society."[95]

The ruler is a party to this contract and it is as binding on him as on the ruled. The society, according to Locke, always retains the right of resuming the powers thus delegated to the ruler. Revolution is justified when it is an act of the whole sovereign people.

Consent is thus from beginning to end the keynote of Locke's theory. Consent is formally embodied in the "original compact;" consent is necessary for the establishment and maintenance of the civil Government; and consent is the basis of the law of nature which furnishes the sanction to the contract. Locke's theory along with Spinoza's has the credit of being the most consistent ever built upon the theory of contract.[96]

Let us pass on to Rousseau: His 'state of nature' is similar to Locke's. It has to be abandoned because "men have reached a point at which the obstacles that endanger their preservation in the state of nature overcome by their resistance the forces which

93. *Ibid.*, Bk. 11, Ch. 2, p. 120.

94. *op. cit.*, Bk. II, p. 180.

95. Ibid., p. 160.

96. Vaughan, Vol. I, p. 157.

each individual can exert with a view to maintaining himself in that state."[97] The problem according to Rousseau is: "To find a form of association which may defend and protect with the whole force of the community the person and the property of every associate, and by means of which, each coalescing with all, may nevertheless obey only himself, and remain as free as before." "Each giving himself to all gives himself to nobody." The terms of the contract are, in short, that "each of us puts in common his person and his whole power under the supreme direction of the general will, and in return we accept each member as an indivisible part of the whole."[98]

And what is the "general will"? It is distinct from the "will of all;" it regards only the common interest and is not to be looked upon as "a sum of particular wills."[99] It is the outcome and the expression of the organic, corporate life in the State. Laws are the acts of the general will. In obedience to the general will man finds his true freedom. The passage from the state of nature to the civil state thus elevates a man to the rank of a moral agent. Justice is substituted for instinct. Slavery to appetite gives place to the moral freedom which consists in obedience to the self-imposed law. It is this conception of the general will and not the idea of the contract, which forms the kernel of Rousseau's theory. Rousseau, in fact, recognises that the State is not a mere aggregate but a moral organism. And from this point of view it may well be said that the social contract theory received its death-blow partly from the Utilitarians and partly from the hand of Rousseau, though he himself was but half aware of what he was doing.[100]

A detailed criticism of the social contract theory need not be attempted here. Various criticisms have been levelled against

97. Rousseau: *Social Contract*, Ch. VI, p. 109.

98. *op. cit.*, Ch. VI, p.109 ff.

99. *Ibid.*, Bk. II, Ch. III.

cf. 'The General Will aims at a common interest; and it is this community of interest, and not the number of votes in which it may find expression which in truth generalises the will'.—Bosanquet: *The Phil. Theory of the State*, pp. 104 ff.

100. Vaughan: *op. cit.*, Vol. II, Introduction, p. I.

it. It has been called bad history, bad logic and bad ethics.[101] Maine has attempted to demonstrate the error of the theory on historical grounds. He tells us that history shows society beginning not with individual rights but with group status, and not with free contract but with paternal power.[102] Bluntschli also notes that "the evidence of history is thus absolutely opposed to this theory."[103] This criticism must be pronounced as being beside the mark. For, the apostles of natural right and social contract were not concerned so much with historical origins, not with chronological antecedents, as with the logical presuppositions of political society.[104] Hobbes and Locke and to some extent even Rousseau assume the state of nature and the contract to have been a historical reality. So far, indeed, the criticism is justified. But if this belief has no effect on the subsequent development of the argument, the error is of no practical significance.[105]

There is more force in Spencer's statement that society is a growth and not a manufacture.[106] The sins of the legislators he attributes to the fact that society is looked upon as a manufacture, to be tampered with at will. Burke's attack on the theory of the French Revolution is also based on similar grounds.[107] The social contract theory errs in regarding a slow, unpremeditated development as a conscious act.

There are other objections to the theory. As the juristic school would put it, "On what authority can authority itself be set up and if on no authority, what sanction has the social contract to induce men to obedience to authority?"[108] To put it differently,

---

101. Catlin: *Principles of Politics*, p. 166.
102. *Ancient Law*, p. 141.
103. *Theory of the State*, p. 295.
104. cf. Barker: *Political Thought in England*, 1848-1914, p. 166.
105. cf. Vaughan: *op. cit.*, Vol. I, p. 28. Also *Social Purpose*, p. 37.
106. *Man versus the State*, p. 63. It is curious that Spencer himself has postulated a hypothetical contract. See Barker: *op. cit.*, p. 125.
107. cf. Vaughan: *op. cit.*, Vol. II, pp. 24 ff.
108. Catlin: *Principles of Politics*, pp. 171 ff.

the theory starts with assuming the very conditions which it seeks to prove.

The conception of natural rights and the idea of a contract involving an exchange of obedience for protection are also fallacious. Rights cannot be conceived of apart from society. They involve a recognition by members of society of a correlative claim upon and duty to each other as all interested in one and the same good.[109] And the State is much more than an association for mutual protection. It comes into existence to make life possible, but as Aristotle put it, it continues to exist to make good life possible. However, the theory has a valuable element of truth in it. It points out that the government rests ultimately on the consent of the governed. Thus, if Hobbes is out to justify despotism, he has to justify it ultimately on the ground that people have themselves entered into the compact. They are thus themselves the source of their proper woe. If we look upon the contract as an ideal contract, the terms of which have not been finally laid down, but which we are trying to reach up to, then, indeed, it emphasizes an important point. The contract is, as Kant put it, an idea of reason. If society is a contract, it is a contract that binds the past, the present and the future generations. The State is much more than a partnership in things subservient only to the gross animal existence and therefore of a temporary, perishable nature. "It is a partnership in all science; a partnership in all art; a partnership in every virtue, and in all perfection."[110] This brief survey of the theory in the West must enable us to say how far there is an affinity between the Hindu and the European theories.

---

109. Green: *Political Obligation*, p. 56.

110. Burke: *Reflections*, i, p. 417, quoted by Vaughan *op. cit.* cf. also McKechnie: *The State and the Individual*, p. 67.

"That all men ought to have a share in moulding the form of constitution of a State is a logical and intelligible position, but to hold that the individual atoms vote the State itself into existence as a result of a unanimous plebiscite is absurd. It is to ignore the great truth established for all time by Aristotle that man is by nature a social and political animal and therefore necessarily the member of some state, however crude."

It becomes evident even at first sight that there is a fundamental difference in the methods of treatment. For the Hindu authors, the exposition of political theory is merely incidental to their main purpose, which is to discuss the social and religious duties of man comprehensively. The Western thinkers on the other hand make political problems the main object of their study. Their views are set forth in great detail. Their consequences are worked out. Objections are anticipated and answered. There is hardly the authoritarian tone about them, which is characteristic of Hindu thought. The closely-reasoned method of the Western theory presents a striking contrast to the popular, almost story-telling tone of the Hindu theory.[111] If there is any remarkable similarity, it is in the conception of the pre-social state. Thus most Hindu writers speak of a 'state of nature', where the strong devour the weak, where the castes get intermixed and righteousness is absent. This view of the pre-social state corresponds with Spinoza's and Hobbes' noted above. The state of perfect freedom and equality and peace which Locke and Rousseau speak of has a counterpart in the picture of the golden age in the *Mahābhārata* and the Buddhist works.

But there the similarity ends. The conception of the state of nature is important in Western political thought in so far as it is governed by the law of nature. That the theorists in question have confounded the various meanings of 'the law of nature' and have employed the concept to suit their own immediate purpose may at once be admitted. Hobbes has used it at will in the sense of the sway of brute instinct and also in the sense of a moral ideal. To Locke, the law of nature is, at one time, operative in the pre-social state and at another time, it is that which the state comes into existence to bring out and maintain. To go farther back, the law of nature suggested to Plato the famous allegory of the metals and it became an instrument to justify slavery in the hands of Aristotle. To-day, we know that "there is a system of rights and obligations which *should* be maintained by law, whether it is so or not, and which may properly be called 'natural;' ......

111. Ghoshal: *History of Hindu Political Theories*, p. 247.

'natural' because necessary to the end which it is the vocation of human society to realise."[112]

In spite of this confusion, however, the conception of the state of nature with its law of nature is made to throw light on the nature of the ensuing contract and the nature and extent of obligations resulting therefrom. Such conclusions are not drawn by our ancient writers. The contract itself, as we have seen, is at best implicit. Its terms are uncertain. Only the duty of obeying the king is emphasized, or the king's duties are indicated by the way. In other words, the state of anarchy with all its evils is presented as the only alternative to the king's rule. The state of nature is thus a foil to show clearly the necessity and importance of government and no more.

The terms of the implied or suggested contract, as we just noted, are left vague by Hindu authors. The questions such as the proper sphere of the State, the limits of governmental action and the right—or rather the duty—of rebellion, are left as problematic as ever. The implications of the statements suggestive of a contract as found in different writers have been already worked out.

They differ *inter se* and are very unsystematic. We are tempted to doubt if the authors were themselves perfectly clear about the various implications of such statements.

In the light of all these considerations, it is impossible to accept the statements characterising the relations of the ruler and the ruled as 'at bottom contractual.' Jayaswal's view that the Hindu kingship was a contractual agreement must therefore be pronounced to be unwarranted and misleading.

Dr. Bhandarkar[113] has instituted a comparison between the social contract theory as found in Hindu works and the Western theory. The *Arthaśāstra* theory is pronounced to be superior to Hobbes'. The reason is, the latter involves an irrevocable surrender on the part of the people to the sovereign, while the former looks

112. Green: *op. cit.*, pp. 33-34.

113. *Carmichael Lectures*, 1918, pp. 119 ff. cf. also *Some Aspects of Ancient Indian Polity*, pp. 154-155.

upon the king as the servant of the people. Two objections may be pointed out to this conclusion. Firstly, Hobbes does recognise occasions when a man is not bound to obey the sovereign;[114] and, secondly, the statement of the contract theory such as it is in Kauṭilya is used to justify the authority of the king. The view that the king is the servant of the people paid by them for his services is certainly a common feature in Hindu political thought. But the contractual idea itself is not worked out so as to suggest this conclusion. The superiority of the Hindu theory cannot be accepted—nay, the very comparison as made by Dr. Bhandarkar is not justified, because the conception of the king as a servant of the people is not the result of a contract. In fact, the idea was popular with the authors of the *Dharmasūtras.* The *Mahābhārata* also has this view (see LXIX, 25). To us it seems that the king is called a servant of the people only to emphasize his duty to fulfil his *Svadharma.* As such, it is but one more illustration of the tendency of Hindu thinkers to put their statements in exaggerated forms.

It would be an error to interpret such statements too literally. They cannot mean that the king was in any constitutional sense responsible to the people. The people have no right to call in question any of the acts of the king because a contractual view of political obligation with all its implications is not really propounded by Hindu thinkers. Their view of the relation between taxation and protection is often so expressed as to suggest a contractual basis. In truth, the obligation that is so inculcated is an obligation in the light of the conception of *Dharma.*

---

114. *Leviathan,* Ch. VI, p. 114. cf. Ghoshal, *op. cit.,* p. 248, footnote.

Chapter III

The Theory of Force in Hindu Political Thought

We have now to find out how far our ancient thinkers regarded force as the basis of political obligation.

Man is a centre of diverse social relationships. He realises—or at least attempts to realise—his purposes through membership of various associations and institutions. Every such institution then objectifies a social purpose. For expressing and fostering its purpose certain rules of conduct have to be observed by all members and a penalty is attached to a breach of these rules. Thus coercion, however slight, is potentially at least at the back of such institutions. It is remarkable, however, that this element of coercion is never regarded as the ultimate sanction behind the rules of these institutions. Coercion might be a method of enforcing obedience; it is not in itself the basis of the institutions. We do not say that the members abide by these rules because of the fear of coercion behind them. In other words, coercion, though a valuable element in the background, is not of the essence of these institutions.[1]

The problem is: does the State stand in a category apart from other social institutions? Is it, we ask, correct to regard it as an organisation of force par excellence? It seems at first sight that the State is essentially force. It seems to stand in a category by itself, because it is a compulsory form of association. You cannot resign membership of it in case of differences of opinion. The

1. J.S. MacKenzie: *Outlines of Social Philosophy*, p. 133.

State, again, is the only institution able to take the life of the individual in the last resort. The consequences of disregarding a law of the State are generally far more serious than those of breaking a rule of an ordinary association. The force exercised by and at the command of the State is so great that the obedience of the people seems to be founded on it alone. The individual seems to obey the State because he is compelled to do so. Law appears to be nothing but command backed by force. The individual is helpless before the superior might of the State. In such a view, might is indeed right and capacity to coerce the sole justification of State authority.

A little reflection, however, shows that the State does not really stand in a separate category apart from other institutions. The difference between its coercive power and that of other institutions is one of degree. It is true to say that force has played an important part in the formation of some states. Herbert Spencer even declared that the State is begotten of aggression and by aggression and hears about it the marks of its parentage.[2] The sovereignty of the State suggests that the State is essentially a force recognising no moral obligation. But the plausibility of these considerations need not blind us to the truth that it is not force as such, but force exercised in a particular way and for certain ends, that makes a State.[3] The sovereignty of the State is not immunity from moral obligation. It is only the necessary imperative of a true collective will.[4]

---

2. *Man vs. the State,* p. 40.

3. Green: *Political Obligation,* p. 136.

4. Follett: *The New State,* p. 271. Much of the distrust of the conception of sovereignty is, we feel, due to the view that the State is nothing but government. A hiatus is assumed between the government and the governed and the will of the former is regarded as being presented to the latter for acceptance. The sovereignty of the State is thus taken to imply the irresponsibility of the government. It is this attitude that explains Spencer's tirades against the "Divine Right" of the State to control individuals and we cannot help feeling that it is this attitude that lies at the back of Hobhouse's distinction between what he calls the metaphysical State and the democratic State. cf. D.G. Ritchie: *Principles of State Interference,* p. 65.

Force by itself is disruptive. It may be a useful ally of right but it cannot create any right. Thus, though force or the fear of force may be a pervasive element in the State, its proper place is only in the background. The State, therefore, is not mere force. The force that it exercises rests on a union of wills.[5] Like other social institutions the State has a definite end. For the realisation of this end, obedience to laws is necessary. It is on such recognition, then, that political obligation rests. All the same, there have been thinkers who regarded obedience to the State as founded on force. Let us, therefore, see what the Hindu authors have got to say about this problem. What, in other words, is the proper function of force in the State, according to them?

That the Hindu authors attached great importance to force as an element in the administration of the State is seen from the very title they gave to the science of Politics. Daṇḍa-nīti is the word used to signify Politics or rather the art of government. The end of the Hindu State is declared to be the maintenance of *Dharma.* In order to achieve this, the king has to discharge manifold functions. This is sometimes summed up by saying that the most important duty of the king is to protect the people by administering Daṇḍa. Without the proper administration of Daṇḍa, the maintenance of *Dharma* would be impossible.

On Daṇḍa, says Kauṭilya, depends the well-being and progress of the science of Ānvīkshakī, Trayī and Vārtā. Daṇḍa, therefore, must be constantly administered. This does not however mean that the king is to punish the subjects indiscriminately. Daṇḍa is not mere punishment. "Whoever imposes severe punishment becomes repulsive to the people." It must, therefore, be awarded with due consideration. So awarded, it makes people devoted to duty. Daṇḍa is thus 'the grand engine of social order.' If Daṇḍa were to be held in abeyance, the stronger would devour the weaker.[6] In other words, on the proper administration of the coercive authority of the State depend the security and well-being of the people. Force

5. Hobhouse: *Social Development,* p. 57. cf. Mac Iver: "Force always disrupts unless it is made subservient to the common will", *The Modern State,* p. 212.

6. *Arthaśāstra,* Bk. I, Ch. IV.

or coercion is not an end in itself. Its function is to ward off "the law of fishes." It is to be the champion of right as against might.

The *Mahābhārata* attaches great importance to Daṇḍanīti. It is the refuge "of the whole world of life." As the reins check the steed, or as an iron hook controls the elephant, so Daṇḍa-nīti keeps the world under restraint. It destroys every evil as the sun destroys darkness.[7] Daṇḍa alone enables the king to enjoy the earth and the subjects to enjoy happiness.[8] The three-fold objects of life, Dharma, Artha and Kāma cannot he attained without Daṇḍa.[9] So important is the function of Daṇḍa as a guarantee of Righteousness that it is identified with Righteousness itself.[10] Daṇḍa, again, is not an instrument merely to punish the wicked. Force, in other words, is not confined merely to the restraint of disorderly persons and the punishment of intentional law-breakers.[11] There is a class of people, says the Epic, who refrain from wickedness only because of the fear of chastisement. Nay, in the absence of this fear, the Brahmachārin, the Householder, the hermit and the religious mendicant would not follow their respective duties.[12] In short, to use the same phrase as Kauṭilya's, the stronger would devour the weaker like fishes in water.[13] To emphasize the importance of Daṇḍa, it is even personified and declared to have been created by the Creator himself.[14] Nay, Daṇḍa is the holy Vishṇu, the powerful Nārāyaṇa, the dreadful Mahāpurusha.[15] All this glorification and deification of Daṇḍa is called forth by the peculiar Hindu view that man by nature is prone to evil. But for the fear of force the

---

7. *Śānti Parva,* LVI, 3-7.
8. *Ibid.,* XIV, 13.
9. *Ibid.,* XV, 3.
10. *Ibid.,* XV, 2.
11. cf. Bosanquet: *Phil. Theory of the State,* p. 141.
12. *Śānti Parva,* XV, 12. It is quite likely that these hyperbolic descriptions of the state of anarchy were suggested to the author by the actual conditions in India in the absence of a ruler to maintain the Aryan tradition; see Havell: *Aryan Ride in India,* p. 35.
13. *Śānti Parva,* XV, 30.
14. *Ibid.,* XV, 35; CXXII, 24.
15. *Ibid.,* Ch. CXXI.

world, it is believed, would sink into darkness, chaos and confusion. The evils of anarchy is a favourite theme of Hindu authors. In order to avoid anarchy the *Mahābhārata* justifies submission even to a usurper. "If a powerful king," it is said, "approaches a kingdom weakened by anarchy with a view to annex it to his dominions, the people should go forward and receive the invader with honour." In this connexion it seems as if the Epic justifies political allegiance on the basis of the superior force of the king. "Men," we are told,[16] "should bow before those that are powerful. The man who bends his head to a powerful person really bows his head to Indra." Passages like this taken by themselves would suggest that the State is mere force and political obligation an act of sheer necessity. What we have here, however, is not really the glorification of force as such. All this is to he understood as an emphasis on the absolute necessity of preserving *Dharma.*

Thus we find that the author warns the king that Daṇḍa is not to be divorced from *Dharma.* It is to be a servant of *Dharma* and is to further its purposes. That is why "punishment should be meted out with discrimination, guided by righteousness and not by caprice."[17] Daṇḍa is explicitly defined as that by which Dharma is maintained;[18] and the king, who wields the rod of punishment impartially and protects all creatures, the loved and the hated equally, is said to be *Dharma* incarnate.[19]

The *Manu-smṛiti*[20] finds itself in agreement with the *Mahābhārata* so far as the duty of the king to protect the people is concerned. The king is said to have been created by the Lord, out of the particles of various gods, for the protection of the people. Being thus a great deity in human form, he exacts the obedience of all. To help him in his work the Lord created Daṇḍa, the protector of all creatures. If the king did not without tiring inflict punishment

16. *Ibid.*, LXVII, 6-11.
17. *Śānti Parva,* CXXII, 40.
18. *Ibid.*, CXXI, 9.
19. *Ibid.*, CXXI, 10-11.
20. *Vide* Ch. VII.

on those worthy to be punished, the stronger would roast the weaker; all castes would be corrupted, all barriers would be broken through and all men would rage against each other. It is thus that Daṇḍa governs all created beings and watches over them. The *Manu-smṛiti*, like the *Mahābhārata*, personifies Daṇḍa. It is through fear of him that all created beings allow themselves to be enjoyed and swerve not from their duties. Behind these eulogies of the function of Daṇḍa lies the same conception of human nature as was noted in the *Mahābhārata*. "A guiltless man," the text runs, "is hard to find." But the king must possess the necessary qualifications to be able to wield Daṇḍa properly. Manu enjoins the subjects not to transgress the law of the king with respect to his favourites and never to despise him even as an infant. At the same time he insists that the king on his part is to inflict punishment for the good of his subjects. Daṇḍa is a double-edged weapon. "It strikes down the king who swerves from his duty, together with his relatives." The sovereignty of the king is itself subject to a higher law. If he breaks this higher law, he would be ruined, himself and his family. Thus, in the *Manu-smṛiti*, as in the *Arthaśāstra* and the *Mahābhārata*, there is no deification of brute force.

Yājñavālkya[21] re-echoes Manu. "*Dharma* was created of yore by Brāhmā himself in the shape of Daṇḍa." It is the duty of the king to hurl it on the evil-doers. It will be possible for him to do this properly only if he is "true to his promise, pure, well-assisted and wise." Yājñavālkya, it may be noted, does not dwell on the depravity of human nature. He is content to say that Daṇḍa must be applied equitably to those who fall away from their duty. It is no respector of persons. Even a brother or a son, if guilty, must be punished. Thus wielding Daṇḍa equitably, the king earns for himself victory, glory and heaven. But if he misused his power, he would be ruined. Thus, the king is under an obligation to punish the guilty; and in doing so, he is carrying out the divine purpose; for, Daṇḍa is God's creation.

21. *Vide* XIII, 354-359.

Vishṇu's treatment[22] of the functions of Daṇḍa is similar. The king is to inflict punishments upon evil-doers corresponding to the nature of their offences. Punishments must be based on justice. The king who does inflict punishment with justice wins fame and makes his people prosper. The function of force or coercion as something more positive than the punishment of wrong-doers is not clearly brought out here. What interests us, however, is the fact that Vishṇu also does not think that force is of the essence of the State.

Nārada expounds the function of Daṇḍa at considerable length. "The king has authority to punish,"[23] because he has been appointed for the purpose. "The king is the fountain-head of justice."[24] As such, he is exempt from censure and corporeal punishment in this world.[25] He is, therefore, to be implicitly obeyed. If a man censures a king devoted to his duties, he shall have his tongue cut out.[26] Nārada seems even to regard law as the king's command. "That wicked man who does not act up to the laws proclaimed by the king, shall be fined and corporeally punished, as offending against the king's commandments.[27] It would seem from Nārada's authoritarian tone and his extreme statements that the function of Daṇḍa, according to him, is to exact obedience to the king's commands, whether right or wrong. He even says, "Whatever a king does is right."[28] It is hardly likely, however, that Nārada intends to depart from the traditional theory. All that he probably means to assert is that in a sense, the actions of the king are always right from the point of view of the subjects, whose duty is merely to obey the king's commands. The king, however, on his part, is enjoined to "be equitable towards all

22. Vide III, 35-36, 190-96.

23. Narada, I, 2.

24. *Ibid.*, III, 6.

25. *Ibid.*, XV, XVI, 20.

26. *Ibid.*, 3o.

27. *Ibid.*, XVIII, 13.

28. *Ibid.*, 21.

beings, to disregard selfish interests and act the part of Vaivasvata.[29] On the adequate discharge of his duties in respect of Daṇḍa depends the welfare of the world, the observance of their duties by the castes and the success of right as against might.[30] Here, as in the *Kauṭilya*, the *Mahābhārata* and the *Manu-smṛiti*, Daṇḍa is declared to be the preserver of the social order. If the king fails to administer Daṇḍa, the sin committed by the wrong-doer falls on him. Thus, although Nārada insists on the duty of the subjects to obey the king implicitly and to worship him even if he is worthless, on the whole, his view of Daṇḍa is not different from that of his predecessors. It is correlated to *Dharma*.

Among the Purāṇas, the *Bṛihaddharma* and the *Bhāgavata Purāṇas* support the traditional views of the function of Daṇḍa.[31] They hold that the State must maintain the social order as the concretised embodiment of eternal *Dharma*. If the rod were laid aside, there would be utter confusion and chaos. The king's duty of protection thus involves the punishment of the wicked and the suppression of sin. Only a wise and learned king can do this properly.

The *Nītivākyāmṛita*, though a Jaina work, repeats the traditional conceptions in the field of Politics. It dwells on the enormous importance of punishment; but adds at the same time that it is not to be prostituted for monetary or selfish ends. Its function is to maintain order in society and in this respect it is similar to medicine. Unjust punishment ruins the king himself.[32]

Kāmaṇḍaka, with his usual fidelity to his master points out the evil of severity as well as of leniency[33] and recommends the infliction of just punishment. The universal wickedness of men would lead to anarchy in the absence of Daṇḍa. It is the duty of the king to save the world from such ruin by means of Daṇḍa.[34]

29. *Ibid.*, 1, 34.

30. *Nārada*, XVIII, 14-16.

31. Refer Beni Prasad: *Theory of Government in Ancient India*, pp. 194-200.

32. *Ibid.*, p. 233.

33. *Nītisāra*, V, 37.

34. *op. cit.*, V, 40-41

The *Śukra-nīti* mentions constant punishment of offenders as a distinct function of the State along with protection.[35] The king is enjoined to make the subjects acquire the habits of performing their duties by the use of his terrible sceptre.[36] It is only through the fear of punishment that each man does his duty.[37] Without the governor the subjects do not keep to their own spheres.[38] In his capacity as the wielder of Daṇḍa, the king resembles Yama. If, then, the function of punishment is so important, the qualities needed in the holder of the office are equally numerous. In particular he must discipline himself, before he thinks of governing his subjects.[39]

To recapitulate, there is a remarkable unanimity amongst Hindu thinkers as to the function of Daṇḍa or the place of force in the State. Force, it is recognised, is not an end in itself. It must not be applied in order to extort money or for like purposes. Force is not of the essence of the State but it is certainly a powerful instrument at the command of the State. No force, no *Dharma*; and *Dharma* must be maintained by the State. It cannot be maintained without the actual use of force in some cases and the fear of force in others. It is important to note that all along human nature is conceived of as essentially wicked. There is no will to good in man. Potentially every man is a sinner. The Hindu authors fail to grasp the correct nature of morality. Outward conformity to certain codes is not morality. The morality of an action depends upon the state of the will of the agent. With the help of force, all that the State can do is to secure outward conformity but such outward conformity often destroys the moral character of the act which really depends on a certain motive and disposition.[40] Life in society is impossible unless men are capable of being

35. *Śukra*, V, 27-28.

36. *Ibid.*, I, 50-51.

37. *Ibid.*, I, 45-47.

38. *Ibid.*, I, 131-32.

39. *Ibid.*, I, 183-85.

40. cf. Green: *Political Obligation*, p. 34.

determined by the conception of a common good, unless they have, what Miss Follett calls, "the will to will the common will." But the Hindu view underlying the function of Daṇḍa with its low estimate of human nature, regards society as an aggregate of mutually repelling atoms, which can be held together only by great external pressure. That is why Daṇḍa does not aim at the reformation of the criminal's will. It is "a reaction of the social order against an unsocial tendency."[41] The social order, in turn, is not even ideally willed by the men concerned; it is, as it were, imposed upon them from without; at least, it is so sacrosanct that they cannot but conform to it. The force at the command of the State, thus viewed, does not rest on a union of wills. Its source is divine. It is wielded by a divine person, who is himself presumed to be immune from the inherent wickedness of human nature, which results in the universal prevalence of violence and the triumph of "matsyanyāya." We need not pause here to raise the difficulties which the acceptance of this view involves. The fallacy of placing the king as a constant terror hanging over the heads of the subjects as the Democles' sword is obvious. Such a conception takes a false view of the nature of the relation between the ruler and the ruled. We have got to recognize that the purpose of the ruler and the ruled is at bottom identical though their functions may differ. It is only by relating the authority of the government with the will of the people that the true solution can be arrived at.

Let us, however, turn to the European theory of the place of force in the ordering of the State and see how far there is a similarity between the Hindu conception and the Western conception.

The view that the State is force is evidently a superficial generalisation that does not need great insight to arrive at. It is noteworthy, however, that the theory that the State is essentially power or force came into prominence in Europe in the birth process of the modern State. It was alien to the thought of Aquinas or Dante. It was inapplicable to the centrifugal tendencies of

41. Beni Prasad: *Theory of Govt. in Ancient India*, p. 344.

feudalism. Its first characteristic expression is found in Machiavelli. "Men," says this Italian diplomat,[42] "must either be caressed or else annihilated; they will revenge themselves for small injuries, but cannot do so for great ones." "The injury that we do to a man must be such that we need not fear his vengeance." The duty of the prince, therefore, who wishes to maintain himself in power is "to learn how not to be good, and to use it and not use it according to the necessity of the case."[43] Machiavelli seems to have had a very low opinion of human nature. Men in general, he thinks, are 'ungrateful, voluble dissemblers, anxious to avoid danger and covetous of gain.' The prince who relies on their word is ruined. It is better among such people to be feared than to be loved.[44]

It seems, then, that Machiavelli expounds here his creed of employing force or fear to gain one's end. The view that the State is power is thus associated with his name. We should, however, be doing injustice to him if we attribute to him the opinion that political obligation rests on force. Machiavelli's aim in writing his work was evidently not to expound a principle of political philosophy. It was rather written to exhort the prince to "liberate Italy from the Barbarians." From this point of view he explains the policy that the Prince should follow. It is true indeed that there is unscrupulousness about his maxims, particularly in respect of inter-state morality. He admits, however, that "it is necessary for a prince to possess the friendship of the people." This can be achieved in a number of ways which vary according to circumstances. It is characteristic of the intense realism of Machiavellian thought that the author assures the Prince that "people ask nothing but not to be oppressed."[45] In other words, the Prince may well count upon the inertia of the people, which makes them slow to resist injustice or oppression. The only limit to the exercise of arbitrariness must

42. *The Prince*, p. 8.

43. *Ibid.*, p. 60.

44. *Ibid.*, p. 66.

45. *op. cit.*, p. 39.

be determined by the possibility or the danger of provoking a rebellion. It is this exposition of the theory that is responsible for the contumely that is often poured on Machiavelli. It is not safe to be dogmatic about this practical statesman's view of political obligation, since he did not concern himself with the theory as such. It is clear, however, that the State as he sees it becomes a powerful agent wielding force and making opponents bend to its wishes.

Another exposition of the theory of force may be found in Spinoza.[46] He identifies 'jus naturae' with 'potentia.'[47] According to his view, the right of the State against its members is limited only by its power. The only limitation on its power is the potential danger of revolt. And yet it must be admitted that there are traces of a sounder theory in some of his statements. He says, for instance, that 'the right of the State is coextensive with the power of the plurality which is guided as if by one mind.' "But this oneness of minds is inconceivable, unless the State has for its main intention what sound reason shows to be for the interests of all men."[48] But Spinoza's theory, it has been said, "stands or falls by his identification of rights with powers—in other words, by his refusal to admit the idea of Right into the life of the State."[49]

To come to recent writers, a frank exposition of the Force Theory is found in the works of Treitschke. He breathes all through the spirit of militarism. "The State," he declares,[50] "is no Academy of Arts, still less is it a Stock Exchange; it is Power." There is a moral majesty about war. It lies "in just what at first sight seems to be its horror—that for the sake of their country, men will overcome the natural feelings of humanity, that they

46. See Article on "Spinoza" by Abraham Wolf in the *Ency. Brit.*; also McKechnie: *The State and the Individual,* p. 67.

47. Green: *Principles of Political Obligation,* pp. 49 ff.

48. Quoted by Green: *Political Obligation,* pp. 51 and 249; cf. also Bosanquet: *Philosophical Theory of the State,* p. xiii.

49. Vaughan: *History of Political Philosophy,* Vol. I, p. 116.

50. *Politics,* Vol. II, p. 391.

will slaughter their fellowmen who have done them no injury."[51] "Punishment," according to this authority, "is an end in itself. It is the expiation of the insult offered to the law."[52] The State, in this view, "does not ask how the people is disposed." It merely "demands obedience."

It is hardly necessary to criticise this view. As Bluntschli points out, it is favourable to despotism and it justifies every act of violence. It is a most flagrant contradiction of the conception of personal freedom as it recognises only masters and slaves. To speak of the 'right' of the strongest is misleading. Force cannot create right. If force were the basis of political allegiance, disobedience would be legitimate, if it was possible with impunity. The strongest is never strong enough to rule unless he transforms might into right. As Rousseau aptly puts it: "As long as a people is compelled to obey, and does obey, it does well; as soon as it can shake off the yoke, and it shakes it off, it does better; for regaining its liberty by the same right as took it away, either it is justified in resuming it, or there was no justification for those who took it away."[53] To speak of force as the basis of political obligation involves in fact a contradiction; for, to yield to force is an act of necessity and does not involve the action of the will at all.

The Hindu thinkers have certainly never exalted the conception of the State as Power, in the way of Treitschke. The king's duty to wield the Rod of Punishment is to be understood as necessary for the maintenance of *Dharma.* Even Kauṭilya, who has sometimes been called the Indian Machiavelli, warns the king of the danger of meting out severe punishments. It is only one "who imposes punishment as deserved" that becomes respectable.[54] It is the duty of the king rather to identify himself with the welfare of his subjects; whatever pleases himself he shall not consider as good,

---

51. *Ibid.*, p. 462.

52. *The Theory of the State*, pp. 292-293.

53. *Social Contract*, Bk. I, Chapters I and 3.

54. *Artha,* Bk. I, Ch. 4.

but whatever pleases his subjects he shall consider as good.[55] The *Manu-smṛiti* warns the king that "the intoxication of power is worse than the intoxication of drink."[56] The ethics of the battlefield and the policy to be followed in respect of a conquered prince are conceived by Hindu thinkers in a spirit which nowhere breathes the insolence of power. Daṇḍa is the means by which *Dharma* is to be maintained. No Daṇḍa, no *Dharma.* Daṇḍa and *Dharma* are thus closely related. If Daṇḍa is the authority of the State, *Dharma* is its ideal. Daṇḍa and *Dharma* may be said to be the two poles of the State, "the two faces of the political Janus, one looking to the failures, the other to the triumphs."[57] Because of this relation of Daṇḍa and *Dharma,* the State ceases to appear as mere power. It becomes an institution for the advancement of culture—a *Dharma*-producing machinery or institution securing even the ultimate salvation of all."[58]

The Hindu view of the function of force is, however, in some respects objectionable. There is a remarkable resemblance between their views of human nature and the exposition of the same by Hobbes. To Hobbes, it seemed, men were by nature enemies. He speaks accordingly of the state of nature as a state of war, a war of each against all. In this state, life is "solitary, poor, nasty, brutish and short." It is the fear of this wretched state that leads men to enter into the contract. The people submit to the rule of the Leviathan in order to escape this miserable state. And they continue to be the members of the civil society because of the fear of sinking back into the original state.[59] The fear of force is the motive that determines the conduct of men from the beginning to the end. The State is the product of fear and is sustained by fear. Now, fear in the background may be a very pervasive element in human conduct. It may be true also that "fear, partly sublimated

---

55. *Ibid.*, Ch. 19.
56. *Manu,* VII, 45.
57. B.K. Sarkar: *Pol. Instns. and Theories,* pp. 211-212.
58. J.N.C. Ganguly's Article on "Philosophy of Dharma," in the Indian Historical Quarterly, Vol. II.
59. *Leviathan,* Ch. XVIII.

into awe," supplies in communities based on conquest, a certain permanence and security to the authority of the conqueror. This is not, however, to admit that fear is the basis of community-life, as Hobbes would have us believe.[60]

But the Hindu view is in agreement with Hobbes' on this point. Our ancient authors are never tired of repeating that "chastisement is the root of the social order." Human beings are by nature supposed to be wicked and prone to negligence of duties. It is only through the fear of Daṇḍa that men perform their duties. Such a view has very dangerous consequences. It denies the moral nature of man. If we accept this view of human nature, it is evident that there is for us no problem of the ethical basis of authority. Men, in fact, are on a level of brutes. They cannot, therefore, have the faculty to correlate means and ends and so rationally determine their line of conduct. If we press the idea a little further, the State becomes a mere cattle-pan and men no more than "dumb, driven cattle," compelled to preserve order by external compulsion.

It is not necessary further to dilate on the dangers of making force or the fear of force the basis of the State. It is a conception that cuts at the very root of all morality.

The Hindu authors thus attach undue importance to the function of Daṇḍa. "The State," as Dr. Bosanquet rightly observes,[61] "as the Operative criticism of all institutions, is necessarily force." Force is the instrument at the command of the State, whereby it secures the conformity of men to the recognised modes of conduct. The State, backed by force, not only punishes the actual law-breakers but even reminds others of their duties by means of "authoritative suggestion." And yet coercive power is a criterion of

---

60. See Hobhouse: *Social Development*, p. 58.

cf. G. Wallas: "The clumsiness and uncertainty of fear, its imperfect adaptation even to the environment of aboriginal life, and its constant irrelevance to the environment of civilisation, make it of all human dispositions the least suitable as a general basis for modern government and education"—*The Great Society*, pp. 89-90.

61. *Philosophical Theory of the State*, p. 142.

the State, but not its essence.[62] It is because force is the "modus operandi" of the State, that its power is limited merely to the performance of external actions. The State can only enforce as much intention as is necessary to ensure the performance of these external actions. The inner springs of human conduct the State cannot directly touch. This distinction, too, has been ignored by Hindu authors and the individual is regarded as conforming to Svadharma because of the fear of Daṇḍa.

This explains how the Hindu conception of individuality is defective at its very root. The conception of human nature that lies at the back of the doctrine of "matsyanyāya" deserves to be abandoned. The will to good, we hold, is fundamental in man. The logic of his nature demands his membership of society and of the State. This is the truth emphasized by Plato and Aristotle. The individual, as Green points out, is capable of being determined by the conception of a common good.[63] While, therefore, we need to guard against the conception of the atomic individual and all the fallacies of the 'natural rights' theories of the nineteenth century, it is imperative that we do not reduce him to the level of an automaton. The true universalism does not exclude but includes and is the expression of the true individualism.

Moral progress, as has well been said,[64] consists in the discovery of the true individual. The State has a tremendous claim upon the citizen but that claim is only the reflection of the individual's claim upon the State. In the ultimate there is no antithesis between the claim of the individual and of the State. The perfect State encourages and develops to the full the individuality of all its citizens. It is not enough, therefore, that Daṇḍa should be correlated to *Dharma.* It should be ultimately connected with the Real Will of the individual and so turned into an instrument to help him to realise his best self rather than to curb him, to control him and to compel him to a mechanical performance of

---

62. Mac Iver: *The Modern State,* p. 223.

63. *Principles of Political Obligation,* p. 143.

64. James Seth: *Ethical Principles,* pp. 355-357.

actions, which are alien to his will. All the personification and deification of Daṇḍa that we come across in our ancient works, calculated to create terror and awe in the minds of subjects, must, thus, give way to a truer conception of the relation of the State to the individual. The realisation of the end of the State—as also of the individual—does certainly necessitate the operation of Daṇḍa according to definite principles. If the ultimate loyalty of the individual is clue to the comprehensive and fundamental principle of *Dharma* which governs the entire universe and if this loyalty is to be expressed by a constant approximation to the conception of the ideal society expressing *Dharma*, then, certainly, Daṇḍa will have an important function in the imposition of restraint on the actual and recalcitrant will of men. But Daṇḍa so administered would have the sanction of what may be called the real will of man which seeks its fulfilment in the search after Svadharma—Svadharma which is the realisation of the best that is in him, which is the expression of the true law of his being. Then will Daṇḍa appear in its true light as the necessary guarantee of freedom; then will law and liberty cease to appear as antithetic; then will the "paradox" of political obligation be resolved.

CHAPTER IV

THE ORGANIC THEORY IN HINDU POLITICAL THOUGHT

We have discussed in the foregoing chapters the divine right theory, the contract theory and the force theory, with their implications regarding the problem of political obligation. It is interesting to note that it is possible to discover various strands in Hindu political thought, having a bearing on this problem. We have got to work out the implications of these strands of thought and so arrive at the Hindu view of political obligation. We shall see in this chapter whether and to what extent there is implied or worked out the organic theory of the State in Hindu thought.

We may note at the outset that some of our Indian scholars maintain that the organic theory of the State can certainly be traced in Hindu thought. Dr. Jayaswal thinks that "the idea of the State as an organism was realised as early as the Vedic kingship."[1] Prof. B.K. Sarkar also maintains that the idea of the State "as a political organism" was known to Hindu thinkers.[2] "The organismic metaphor in Nīti-philosophy," he says, "is not merely structural or anatomical; it is partly functional, i.e. physiological as well."[3] And this view is endorsed, evidently without questioning, by Mr. Dikshitar also.[4]

---

1. *Hindu Polity*, Part II, p. 9.
2. Vide *Śukra-nīti-sāra*, p. II, foot-note.
3. *Positive Background of Hindu Sociology*, Bk. II, pp. 34-39.
4. *Hindu Administrative Institutions*, p. 5.

All these scholars have come to this conclusion on a study of the significance of the doctrine of "the seven limbs of sovereignty." We shall, therefore, first see what this doctrine is and what its implications are.

The doctrine of the "seven limbs of the State" was familiar to thinkers from early times. Kauṭilya mentions the various schools of the earliest *Arthaśāstra* literature and discusses their views on various topics. The conception of the seven limbs of the State (Rājya) seems to have been accepted by them as also certain other common concepts like the four sciences, the three Śaktis of the king, the seven royal Vyasanas divided into sub-groups, the six expedients of foreign policy (gunas) and the four means of conquering an enemy.

The seven elements of a Rājya, according to Kauṭilya,[5] are: The king (Svāmin), the minister (Amātya), the country (Janapada), the fort (Durga), the treasury (Kośa), the army (Bala) and the friend (Mitra). And what are the characteristics of each of these? The king, we are told, is to be an embodiment of various virtues. He must have qualities of an inviting nature. Born of a high family, possessed of valour, seeing through the medium of aged persons, virtuous, truthful, highly enthusiastic, not addicted to procrastination, powerful enough to control his neighbouring kings,—these are some of the qualities of an inviting nature that he must possess. Besides these he must have certain qualities of the intellect. He must also have valour, determination of purpose, quickness and probity. Self-possessed and self-disciplined he must necessarily be; and that means he must have a sharp intellect, strong memory, keen mind, and he must be free from vice, capable of paying in the same coin by way of awarding punishment and rewards, capable of taking remedial measures against dangers, possessed of foresight and clever enough to discern the causes necessitating the cessation of war or treaty with an enemy. Such are said to be the attributes of the first element of sovereignty—the king.

5. *Artha.*, Bk. VI, Ch. I.

The ministers form the second element of the State. The opinions of different thinkers have been cited and discussed by Kauṭilya, with regard to the question who should be appointed as ministers. After a discussion of these, Kauṭilya finally accepts the view of the son of Bāhudantī.[6] He goes on further to explain that the ministers should be not merely men of theoretical knowledge; they must also have had an experience of practical affairs. Further, they must be of noble birth, well-trained in arts, possessed of foresight, wise, of strong memory, bold, eloquent, possessed of enthusiasm, dignity and endurance, pure in character, affable and firm in loyal devotion. Their duty is to carry on the 'invisible' works of the king.[7] They are an important part of the governmental organisation. A single wheel, says Kauṭilya, cannot move; so, too, the king cannot carry on the work of administration without the assistance of ministers. The king, therefore, must have ministers whose opinion he must fear.[8] It is said to be the duty of the ministers to avert the calamities to the king and to play the role of king-makers on occasions.[9]

The third element of the State is the Janapada. This term includes the territory as well as the people. The qualities of the Janapada, according to Kauṭilya, are that it must be possessed of capital cities both in the centre and in the extremities of the kingdom; it must be productive of subsistence not only for its own people, but also for outsiders on occasions of calamities; it must be capable of bearing the burden of a large army and of heavy taxation, and above all, it must be inhabited by agriculturists of good and active character; it must be full of intelligent masters and servants and its population must be noted for its loyalty and good character.[10] In short, the third limb of the kingdom is good territory with energetic and loyal subjects as inhabitants.

---

6. *Artha.*, Bk. I, Ch. 8.
7. *Ibid.*, Ch. II.
8. *Ibid.*, Ch. 7, p. 12.
9. *Ibid.*, Bk. V, Ch. 6.
10. *Artha.*, Bk. VII, Ch. I.

Kauṭilya similarly lays down the characteristics of the remaining elements of the State. Into these details we need not go. The account we have reproduced above shows that the *Arthśāstra* gives us here a description of the mechanism of government and indicates the characteristics of the various elements that go to make a prosperous kingdom. The doctrine of Saptānga thus means that the State must have the king at the head. The king, in turn, must have duly qualified Ministers by his side. The territorial basis of the State must be sound. A prosperous State cannot exist apart from an adequate arrangement of forts, finances and the army. Further, the ally is also an element of the State because of his importance in view of inter-state relations.

These elements of the State are described as 'limb-like.' Kauṭilya does not, however, take this epithet to imply the supreme importance of each limb in its own place and for its peculiar functions. Nor does there seem to be any clear indication that the injury to any one limb means injury to the whole organism. So long as such recognition is not there, the real significance of the term 'limb-like' cannot be said to have been realised. This may be seen clearly from the discussion as to the relative seriousness of the calamity to any of these. On this point, again, earlier authors are cited and their views discussed. Kauṭilya's own view appears to be identical with what he calls his master's view. Of all calamities to a kingdom, those affecting the king are verily the most serious. The king is the most important of all the elements. These other elements really depend on the king. It is he who appoints ministers; the troubles of the people are remedied by him. For their progress or downfall, the people depend upon the king. Briefly, the king is the aggregate of the people.[11] That explains why the calamities to the king are the most serious of all. Then, in order of seriousness are the calamities to the ministers, to the people, to the fortifications, to finance, to the army and to the ally.[12] This arrangement in order of importance shows that the organic unity of the factors of government was not clearly

---

11. *Artha.*, Bk. VIII, Ch. I, p. 350.
12. *Ibid.*, Ch. I.

perceived by Kauṭilya. The doctrine implies merely that an efficient government means a king assisted by his ministers and foreign ally, equipped with all the necessary material appliances.[13] As Prof. Sarkar puts it, the theory of the constitution is epitomised in this doctrine.[14] Kauṭilya reveals himself here as an astute practical statesman whose obvious concern is with the relative importance of these 'limbs.' Naturally, he gives the first place to the king and not to the subjects. There is no suggestion here that the State is an organism, such that the interests and purposes of the citizens are its interests and purposes. In other words, the relations of the subjects to the king are not made to rest on the basis of an organic view of the State.

In the *Mahābhārata*,[15] the king is enjoined to take care of seven things. They are: his own self, his ministers, his treasury, his servants for inflicting punishments, his friends, his provinces, and his capital. And these are called, as by Kauṭilya, the seven limbs of the kingdom. There is no further discussion about the relative importance of these; nor are we told what exactly is the significance of calling them 'limbs.' The only thing we are informed about is that the king is the most important of these, for he is their preserver.

The *Manu-smṛiti*[16] develops the doctrine further. "The king and his minister, his capital, his realm, his treasury, his army, and his ally are the seven constituent parts of a kingdom; hence a kingdom is said to have seven limbs." As regards the relative importance of these, "each earlier-named is more important and its destruction the greater calamity." So far Manu agrees with Kauṭilya. But he does not stop here. He immediately corrects himself. The order of importance given above is not final. For, really speaking, each part is particularly qualified for the accomplishment of a certain purpose, and for this purpose, clearly, it is the most important. For

13. Ghoshal: *Hindu Political Theories*, p. 52.

14. *Political Theories and Institutions of the Hindus*, p. 167.

15. *Śānti Parva*, Ch. LXIX, 64-66.

16. IX, 294-297.

the kingdom, as a whole, there is no single part more important than the rest, by reason of the importance of the qualities of each for the others. Here, for the first time, we are introduced to what may be called the principles of "integration" and "differentiation." Manu thus presents a clearer conception of the organic unity of government than the *Arthaśāstra* or the *Mahābhārata.*[17]

The seven Prakṛitis or constituents of the kingdom are mentioned by Yājñavālkya as well.[18] He speaks also of the State as having seven 'limbs.' The *Vishnu-smṛiti* is another of the *Dharmaśāstras* enumerating the seven constituents of the kingdom. It may be noted, however, that Vishṇu does not speak of these as limbs. On the whole, with the exception of the *Manu-smṛiti,* the *Dharmaśāstras* merely mention the doctrine of the seven Prakṛitis of a Rājya and do not develop it any further.

It is in the *Kāmaṇḍakīya Nītisāra* that once again the doctrine is discussed at considerable length. Not that Kāmaṇḍaka is original in this respect. He bases his work avowedly on Kauṭilya's.[19] The elements of the State are declared to be seven.[20] As regards their relative importance also, the Kāmaṇḍakīya merely reproduces Kauṭilya's view. And yet, credit must be given to Kāmaṇḍaka, for he does not stop here. He speaks of the organic relation of these factors of sovereignty. In the same strain as Manu, he tells us[21] that these seven limbs contribute to one another's weal. Each factor has its own specific function. This it alone can adequately discharge. On this account, then, the loss even of one of them renders the whole imperfect.

The *Śukra-nīti* also treats of the seven elements of the State. It adopts the standard list of these. The relative importance of these it does not discuss. But it institutes an interesting comparison of these limbs of the State with the limbs of a physical organism.

17. cf. Ghoshal, *op. cit.*, p. 120.

18. XIII, 353.

19. I, 2-7.

20. I, 16-17.

21. IV, 1-2.

The king is declared to be the head; the ministers are the eye; the ally represents the ear; the treasury stands for the mouth, the army is the mind, while the fort and the territory are the two arms and legs.[22] The comparison is indeed novel, but its significance is not explained by the author. The idea of differentiation and integration, found in Manu and Kāmaṇḍaka, has not been clearly brought out here. It is, therefore, impossible to look upon the *Śukra-nīti* as giving us anything like a complete theory of the organic nature of government.

It becomes clear from the above survey that the doctrine of Saptānga represents only an attempt to analyse the government into what seem to our authors to be its constituent parts. These are said to be limb-like. But the organic relation of these elements of the Rājya is not brought out clearly except in Manu and Kāmaṇḍaka. The people form one of the seven elements. Beyond that, the doctrine of Saptānga throws no light on the nature of the mutual obligation of the subjects and the king. The king is the head of these factors of government. But the king by himself does not make a Rājya. He is, as it were, the key-stone of the constitutional arch. He is to preserve the welfare of the other elements. To the extent that the people form an integral part of the kingdom, we might say, he has to look after their welfare. That is all that we might infer from this doctrine as regards the relations of the rulers and the ruled. The proper functioning of a Rājya, in other words, demands a certain type of citizens, as also adequate provisions for war, sound ministerial advice, etc. Thus, the theory is not an attempt to explain the ethical basis of sovereignty. Even in its most developed form, it implies that these seven elements, having definite characteristics about them, are the necessary condition of a healthy State. Nowhere does it speak of the organic nature of the relation of the State to its subjects.

---

22. *Śukra*, I, 122-124; Elsewhere, the author gives us another comparison. "The king is the root of the State, the councillors are the trunks, the commanders are the branches. The troops are the leaves and flowers, the subjects are the fruits, and the lands are the seeds." Ch. V, 24-26. It is difficult to read any significance into this comparison. We do not know, for example, whether Śukra wants us to understand that the relation between the king and the subjects is the relation between the root of the tree and its fruits.

The significance of this doctrine is discussed in detail by Dr. Bhandarkar.[23] The seven limbs of the State enumerated by our authors represent, according to him, all the four essential factors of the State, as defined by modern writers, like Gettell and Leacock. Nay, the Hindu characterisation of the State is said to be more exact and comprehensive than that given by these authors. The State ought not to be looked upon as a static, self-sufficing unit. It is not merely an entity in itself. It stands related to other States. It is in relation to these also that the State should be really defined. And the Hindu definition, we are told, does this by including the ally among the essential elements of the State. This aspect of the State does not come out in the definition of it by Gettell and Leacock and from this point of view, the Hindu definition is said to be really superior to that given by the modern western scholars. How the mere mention of the ally could be enough to indicate the complex inter-state relations, is a problem that has not been discussed by the author. What interests us here more particularly is his attempt to interpret the doctrine of Saptānga so as to satisfy the definition of the State as given by Bluntschli also. Bluntschli speaks of the State as an organism. The State, he maintains, is not a lifeless instrument; it is a living and therefore organised being. The State has spirit as well as body; it has members with various special functions, it develops and grows; it is a moral and spiritual organism. The same meaning can be made out, says Dr. Bhandarkar, from the Hindu definition of the State. "It is quite clear," he writes,"that the State is looked upon by the authors of the Hindu polity as a living spiritual organism, where the Svāmin was the soul and the other six Prakṛtis or natural constituents the body of the State." On the whole, the author concludes, all the essentials of an organic theory of the State as laid down by Bluntschli can be found in the conception of the Rājya as having seven limbs.

Here, we have a typical instance of how some of us cannot help reading far-fetched meanings into old ideas, in order to make them correspond to modern concepts. We fail to understand the

23. *Some Aspects of Ancient Indian Polity*, pp. 65 ff.

significance of saying that "the Svāmin was the soul and the other six Prakṛitis the body of the State." Again, what exactly is the significance of saying that the State was a living and also spiritual organism? Before we attempt such comparisons it is necessary, then, to be definite about the significance of the characterisation of the State as organic. The organic theory of the State has been propounded by Western thinkers, far removed from one another in time, and it is evidently necessary to distinguish between the different versions of the theory in the works of different authors. It is only after such a study is made that any comparison would be justified.

The organic theory is, according to Jellinek,[24] one of the oldest and most popular theories concerning the nature of the State. Plato's discussion of the nature of justice is based on a parallelism between the nature and functions of the State and the individual. The best ordered State, according to him, is one whose structural organisation resembles most nearly that of the individual. The nature of the individual is said to be threefold; in other words, the individual is moved by three principles in his nature, the rational principle, the principle called desire, and the principle which may be called passion or spirit.[25] Corresponding to these are the three classes of society, the guardians, the farmers and the soldiers. Specific functions are assigned to each of these classes. The principle of Justice involves the necessity of each class performing functions to which it is particularly fitted. Thus a perfect harmony and unity will characterise the State and every person in it.[26] To Plato, the greatest good of states is unity; the greatest evil is discord.[27] The feeling of unity is to be secured by destroying the sense of "meum and teum" among the citizens. To this end, Plato is prepared to sacrifice institutions like private property and the family. In the ideal State, all must speak the language of harmony and concord. The communism of wives and

---

24. Quoted by J.W. Garner: *Introduction to Political Science,* p. 57.
25. *Republic,* IV, pp. 131-133.
26. *Ibid.*, p. 112; cf. Barker: *Greek Political Theory,* pp. 177-78.
27. *Ibid.*, V, pp. 156-157.

of property will put an end to private interests. The spectacle of some citizens in the State triumphing and the others plunged in grief will never be seen. The State will be like a living being which feels pain as a whole; when any of the parts is hurt.

Thus, Plato suggests an analogy between the individual and the State. But the analogy is not physical. He does not compare the different classes in the State to the limbs of a living being. Plato's chief concern is to discover the indwelling spirit of justice. The parallel, which he draws, may, therefore, be regarded as a spiritual parallel.[28] The analogy between the individual and the State, in respect of physical and material aspects, is but superficial. To Plato, the organic nature of the State is much more than an outward similarity to a living organism. It explains the relation of the State to the individual. The individual is organically related to the State. He cannot be spoken of apart from the State. It is in the State that he finds scope for the realisation of his potentialities. If that is so, the essence of individuality lies in the fulfilment of "my station and its duties." Briefly, with the help of the organic theory, Plato reconciles the individual and the State. A criticism of the theory would be out of place here. Suffice it to say, that Plato goes much farther than merely drawing an analogy between the State and the individual.

Such analogies have by no means been rare. Cicero compared the State to the individual and the head of the State to the spirit which rules the human body. The State was personified by medieval writers like John of Salisbury and Marsiglio of Padua. Some of the medieval comparisons were no more than "anthropomorphic conceits and fallacies which do not rise above the level of pictorial presentment,"[29] but there were some more fruitful too. From the fundamental idea of the social organism, a series of other ideas was deduced, regarding membership, differentiation, function and the like.[30] However, as in antiquity, so also in the Middle Age,

---

28. E. Barker: *op. cit.*, p. 162.

29. Gierke: *Political Theories of the Middle Age*, p. 22.

30. *Ibid.*, pp. 27-28.

the idea of organic society failed to issue in the legal idea of Personality—the only sense in which the conception becomes of service in legal science.[31]

The Leviathan of Hobbes is "an artificial man, though of greater stature and strength than the natural."[32] The public ministers are compared to "the nerves and tendons that move the several limbs of a body natural."[33] Likewise, he speaks of "the nutrition and procreation of a commonwealth," and points out how money serves the same function in the body politic as blood in the natural body.[34] But these are no more than comparisons. They do not throw light on the nature of political obligation.

It is under the influence of the biological conceptions of the nineteenth century that the organic nature of the State comes to be more fully understood.[35] Henceforward the organic theory of the State is invoked to counteract the mechanical theory of society, underlying the contract and utilitarian theories.

One of the most extreme advocates of the theory that the State is a biological organism was Bluntschli. The State, he says, is the very image of the human organism.[36] He speaks of it as a "living spiritual organic being;" he seems to recognise that the State is a moral organism. But he is so much obsessed by the biological analogy that he even imputes sexual attributes to the State and regards it as masculine. All the same, it must be admitted, he points out that the State is much more than an aggregate, even as a statue is much more than a combination of marble particles. In other words, the State is an organic whole and the individual acquires significance only as a member of it. He is not a self-sufficing entity with certain inalienable, indefeasible rights, as the contractualists would have us believe. Though the view that

---

31. *Ibid.*, p. 30.
32. cf. *Leviathan,* Ch. XVII.
33. *Ibid.*, Ch. XXIII.
34. *Ibid.*, Ch. XXIV.
35. Hetherington and Muirhead: *Social Purpose,* p. 38.
36. cf. Garner: *Introduction to Political Science,* p. 58.

the State is an organic whole has thus an important element of value in it, the conception of the State as a biological organism is defective in many respects. To this we shall turn our attention a little later.

In Herbert Spencer, we have another exponent of the biological analogy. He maintains that there is a similarity between the growth, functions and structures of animals on the one hand, and of societies on the other.[37] As in the one, so in the other, there is a sustaining system, a distributing system and a regulating system. Only in one respect there is an unlikeness. While the animal organism is concrete, its units being bound together in close contact, the social organism is discrete, its units being free and more or less widely dispersed. In spite of this distinction, however, the comparison on the whole is valid, for "the social aggregate, though discrete, is still a living whole."[38] Society is "a growth," and not a "manufacture," and "the sins of legislators" are due to their ignorance of this fact.[39] This is the only practical conclusion of the organic theory the author is prepared to accept. But, if the view that society is an organism implies that the whole is prior to the parts and that the good of the whole is something more imporant than the good of the parts, or that the good of the parts must be determined with reference to the good of the whole, then Spencer would, perhaps, not hesitate to abandon the conception. To reconcile his view of "natural rights" and of "an agreement tacitly entered into between the State and its members" with the conception of a social organism is no easy task; for "natural rights in a social organism are as much in place as a vacuum in a solid."[40] The difficulty has got to be surmounted. Spencer seems to have started with a conception of organic growth intended to justify individualism. But the conception of organic unity he arrived at, would justify even collectivism. The escape is

37. *Principles of Sociology*, Vol. I, Part II, Chs. ii to xi.

38. *Ibid.*, 221.

39. *Man vs. the State*, p. 63.

40. Barker: *Political Thought in England*, p. 129.

sought in the distinction he makes between the natural organism and the social organism. The one is 'concrete' and the other is 'discrete;' and there is nothing like a social sensorium. So, Spencer concludes that "the welfare of the aggregate, considered apart from that of the units, is not an end to be sought. The society exists for the benefit of its members, not its members for the benefit of society."[41] Once again, the welfare of the whole is set up in opposition to the welfare of the parts and we are, after all, not rid of the mathematical and mechanical view of society.[42] Thus, the distinction between the discreteness of the social organism and the concreteness of the natural organism leads to the abandonment of the social organism altogether.

Among other writers who work out the biological analogy are Schaffle, Lilienfield and Worms.[43] They look upon the State as the brain or the controlling and directing apparatus of the social organism with no limitations upon its powers except the function of promoting the welfare of society.

These comparisons of the State to an organism have indeed thrown some light on the nature of the State. They have led to the abandonment of the conception of the State as a piece of mechanism, which works in obedience to a purpose that is external to it and whose functions are thus strictly limited. The biological conception of evolution as applied to political theory has led to the perception that the State is not a manufacture but a growth. There are certain elements of resemblance between the structure and functions of the State on the one hand and those of the living beings on the other. But, in many respects, the analogy fails.

---

41. *Principles of Sociology*, p. 479.

42. Ritchie: *Principles of State Interference*, pp. 24-25.

    cf. also Barker, *op. cit.*, "The social organism will, as it were, constantly insist on coming to life and on being a living substance; and Spencer has to resort to far-fetched devices to kill it again, in order to assert a mechanical conception of the State as a compound of physical units," p. 93.

43. See Garner: *op. cit.*, pp. 62-63. Barnes: *Sociology and Political Theory*, pp. 28-29.

It fails, firstly, to express adequately the nature of the relation of the State to the individual. In an organism, the cells and the limbs have no independent life of their own. They are instruments of a central purpose. The whole, in other words, completely absorbs the parts, which have no purpose of their own. The members of the State, on the other hand, are purposive human beings. If the individual has no significance apart from the State, the State has no existence apart from the individuals. The individual has a distinct moral end in view and he contributes to the well-being of the State out of the richness of his unique experience. Further, a limb of the natural organism serves one set purpose. The individual, on the other hand, enters into complex social relationships and fulfils different duties. Moreover, every individual may be a complete expression of the whole in a way impossible for the parts of a physical organism.[44]

Further, an over-emphasis on the idea that society is a natural growth rather than the artificial product of a contract is apt to lead us to ignore the element of choice involved in human society. Whereas the natural organism changes and develops in accordance with the operation of the blind mechanical forces of nature, the growth of human society is largely the result of conscious action on the part of individuals. If, therefore, society is an organism, it is an organism of organisms, each one of which has a life of its own.[45] Or, we may rather say, society is not an organism but is like an organism in certain respects. The term organism is useful as a metaphor, but is not strictly applicable, for the social bond is a psychic relation and it cannot be expressed in biological terms.[46] Society is a union, not of bodies, but of minds.[47]

While, thus, the State is not a biological organism the conception of it as a moral organism, properly understood, is

44. Follett: *The New State*, pp. 75-78; cf. also Unwick's detailed criticism of the view that society is an organism, *Philosophy of Social Progress*, Ch. III.

45. J.S. MacKenzie: *Outlines of Social Philosophy*, pp. 49-50.

46. Follett: *op. cit.*, pp. 75-78.

47. Barker: *op. cit.*, pp. 106-107.

by no means objectionable. It goes as far back as Plato; it has profoundly influenced the thought of political philosophers since Rousseau[48] and it finds its complete expression in Hegel.[49]

The idea that the State is a moral organism underlies the conception of Justice in the *Republic.* The State has, according to this view, a definitely moral end. This moral end is adequate to the realisation of the moral end of the individual. It is only as a member of the State, discharging his specific duties as an integral part of it, that he can realise his best self. The State and the individual are thus organically connected. In such an organism, the parts are conscious and purposive. They are moral agents and know their relation to the whole. That this conception leads to the absorption of the individual in the State has often been pointed out. By attempting to make unity the greatest good of states, we may really destroy the essence of the State, which is to realise the unity in diversity. Even Plato is said to have succumbed to the temptation. He seems to insist on a bare unity in the State by destroying the institutions like private property and family. Nevertheless, he indicated the right line of thinking and the organic conception he introduced into moral thought has been, in the words of Dr. Bosanquet, the most fruitful of moral ideas.[50]

The famous opening sentence of Rousseau's *Contrat Social* which speaks of man as born free but finding himself in chains everywhere, is really no more than an unfortunate epigram that fails to do justice to the contents of the work. Rousseau only retains all along the terminology of the contract. This has misled those whom Bosanquet calls "the theorists of the first look" as to the real nature of his teaching. For, after all, Rousseau does imply the conception of the State as a moral organism.[51] The

---

48. Barker: *Greek Political Theory,* pp. 388-389.

49. Ritchie: *op. cit.,* p. 156.

50. *Essays and Addresses,* p. 151; cf. *Social Purpose,* p. 38.

51. Refer C. E. Vaughan's *Introduction to the Political Writings of Rousseau.* Also see Muirhead's Article, "Recent Criticism of the Idealist Theory of the General Will" in *Mind* Vol. XXXIII.

essence of the social contract, he tells us, is reducible to the following terms: "Each of us puts in common his person and his whole power under the supreme direction of the general will; and in return we receive every member as an indivisible part of the whole."[52] Further, we are told, as a result of this pact, "instead of the individual personalities of all the contracting parties," we have "a moral and collective body, which is composed of as many members as the assembly has voices and which receives from this same act its unity, its common self, its life, and its will."[53] In this way, Rousseau is trying to evolve out an organic whole by means of a contract, forgetting that the contracting parties, as unrelated atoms, could not at all be individual personalities, if by the phrase we mean the subjects of rights and duties. This confusion is probably due to his defective terminology. Putting that aside, we find that "the essence of human society consists in a common sense, a life and a will, which belong to and are exercised by the society as such, or by the individuals in society as such."[54] And, in words reminiscent of Plato's, Rousseau tells us how "so soon as the multitude is thus united in one body, it is impossible to injure one of the members without attacking the body, still less to injure the body, without the members feeling the effects."[55] As to the nature of the relation of the individual to the State, there is no antithesis between the two. The individual is an integral part of the whole and the whole determines the limbs or the parts. "As nature gives every man an absolute power over all his limbs, the social pact gives the body politic an absolute power over all its members, and it is this same power which, when directed by the general will, bears, as I said, the name of sovereignty."[56] It would seem that the individual whom Rousseau starts with and whose being in chains he deplores has at last slipped through his fingers to be merged into the whole represented by the State. But

52. *op. cit.*, Bk. I, Ch. VI.

53. *Ibid.*

54. Bosanquet: *Philosophical Theory of the State*, p. 87.

55. *op. cit.*, Bk. I, Ch. VII.

56. *Ibid.*, Bk. II, Ch. IV.

immediately Rousseau corrects himself and speaks of "the private persons" and of "the respective rights of the citizens and of the sovereign." In other words, he recognises that while the State is like an organism in some respects, it is not completely like it; for, the individuals are not dead material but purposive moral beings, who are not merely means to an end, like the limbs of a body.

Fichte, like Rousseau, represents the transition from the idea of contract to that of an organic whole. Citizenship rests on contract, but the conract is general and this fact forges an indiscernible unity in the shape of the social whole. To elucidate this notion, he compares the State to "an organised natural product." In the organic body every part continually maintains the whole, and while it maintains it, is itself maintained thereby; just such is the citizen's relation to the State.[57] In spite of this recognition, however, Fichte does not get rid of the idea that the basis of the State is the ego conceived as the individual self. He fails to apprehend the State "as the realisation of freedom." His freedom becomes "the freedom of the particular individuals;" "the individuals remain always hard and negative against one another;" and "the prison-house, the bonds, become ever more oppressive, instead of the State being apprehended as the realisation of freedom."[58]

It is in the writings of Hegel, Green, Bradley and Bosanquet that the antithesis of the individual and the State finally disappears. The individual, in the words of Hegel, "must in the fulfilment of his duties, in some way or other at the same time find his own interest, his satisfaction, and from his relations in the State a right must accrue to him whereby the universal interest should not actually be set aside or altogether suppressed, but put into agreement with the universal, whereby both it and the universal are sustained."[59] The State is, as it were, the Absolute, in which all differences are reconciled. The fullest development of individuality is not only not incompatible with but is possible only with the

57. cf. Bosanquet: *op. cit.*, pp. 227-228.

58. *Ibid.*, pp. 228-229.

59. Quoted by L.T. Hobhouse: *Metaphysical Theory of the State*, p. 96.

obedience to the law of the State. The law of the State is the expression of the general will and it is to the general will that the real will of the individual corresponds. In obeying the law, therefore, the individual is obeying his best self. There is thus a genuine sense in which a man is forced to be free. The State maintains the individual as a person, and not only maintains him, but promotes his welfare and protects the minor groups of family and social life in which he partially seeks his welfare. Further, "it carries back......the individual—whose tendency is to become a centre of his own—into the life of the universal substance."[60]

How far Hegel's reconciliation of the individual to the State is valid, this is not the place to discuss. It may be noted that he has been very severely criticised for it. He has been accused of missing the essence of the organic theory which really teaches that the value of the State lies in its service to the harmonious development of all its component members. From this point of view, Hegel's system is said to be a negation of the organic conception.[61] It may be admitted that sometimes Hegel is too enthusiastic about the State, and he talks of it almost in terms of rhapsody.[62] "The State is the divine idea as it exists on earth." It is "the absolute power on earth." If it goes to war, it is only an illustration "of the competence of the State in its individuality." We should bear in mind, however, that he refers to the *ideal* State as the perfect realization of freedom.

A moderate version of the Hegelian theory stripped of its exaggerations is given to us by Green. Accepting as he does the organic relation of the individual and the State, he does not forget that "to an Athenian slave, who might be used to gratify a master's lust, it would have been a mockery to speak of the State as a realisation of freedom; and perhaps it would not be much less so to speak of it as much to an untaught and underfed denizen of a

---

60. Barker: *op. cit.*, p. 28.

61. Hobhouse: *op. cit.*, pp. 96-97.

62. cf. Bosanquet: *op. cit.*, pp. 232-233, and Laski: *Authority in the Modern State*, p. 21.

London yard with gin-shops on the right hand and on the left."[63] In Green's exposition the "State does not absorb the individual."[64] If society has a claim upon him for the performance of his duty, he likewise has a claim upon society for the power to fulfil it. And yet the rights of the individual do not exist independently of society.

Just as Aristotle maintained that man is essentially a political animal, so also Green maintains that "the true conception of 'right' depends on the conception of the individual as being what he really is in virtue of a function which he has to fulfil relatively to a certain end, that end being the common well-being of society."[65] The individual, therefore, cannot be conceived of apart from his vocation as a member of society. Green explicitly makes reference to the practice of comparing the State to a living body and points out his objections to it. Such a view, he says, represents the State as a purely natural, not at all, as a moral, organism.[66] It ignores the consciousness on the part of the individuals of ends, which are "the same in principle" with that served by the State itself.

The same conception of the State as a moral organism Bradley developed in his *Ethical Studies*. "In fact, what we call an individual man is what he is because of and by virtue of community."[67] The State is looked upon as a systematic whole, informed by a common purpose or function; and its parts are themselves conscious moral agents.[68]

Bosanquet's theory of the State closely approaches Hegel's. The objections to the Hegelian conception of the State which Green pointed out are declared to be, after all, not very important.[69] The conception of the common self is emphasized. Law is conceived of

---

63. Green: *Principles of Political Obligation*, p. 8.
64. *op. cit.*, p. 56.
65. Hobhouse: *op. cit.*, p. 119.
66. *op. cit.*, pp. 132-133.
67. Vide Chapter on "My Station and its Duties".
68. Barker: *Political Thought in England*, pp. 64-65.
69. *op. cit.*, pp. 269-270.

as the expression of the general will and "the negative relation of the self to law and government" disappears.[70] Liberty is certainly the condition of our being ourselves. But in order to be ourselves, we have to be always becoming something which we are not. We have continually to be rising, as it were, on the stepping stones of our dead selves. The social order is the condition and guarantee of our becoming our true selves. Thus, there is no contradiction involved in saying that a man may be forced to be free.[71] The conception of the State as an organism is implied here, though it is a moral organism, not a natural organism. The social whole "differs from a machine, or what is called an organism, pure and simple, by the presence of the whole in every part, not merely for the inference of the observer, but, in some degree, for the part itself, through the action of consciousness."[72]

With some writers, like Cicero and various medieval authors, the organic theory, if we may call it so, is no more than just a comparison, fanciful if not fantastic, between some departments of the State and certain limbs of the body. Such comparisons do not throw light on the nature of political obligation. They do not attempt to elucidate the relation between the State and the individual. As to the appropriateness of such comparisons also we may be sceptical. They are often far-fetched and they fail to convey any sense at all.

Far more valuable is the analogy between the State and a natural organism in respect of their growth, functions and structures, worked out by Bluntschli, Spencer and others. The conclusions of these writers cannot, of course, be accepted *in toto!* The State is not an organism in the literal sense. It differs from one in certain important respects, as we have seen. All the same, it is in some respects like an organism. The distinctive value of this analogy lies in emphasizing the unity and the evolutionary character of the State.

---

70. *Ibid.*, p. 95.
71. *Ibid.*, pp. 118-119.
72. *op. cit.*, pp. 163-164.

Finally, there is the conception of the State as a moral or spiritual organism; and this view while taking over the valuable element in the biological analogy, avoids its errors.

These are what may be called the three phases of the organic theory in the West. Of the three, the last alone is an adequate explanation of the nature of political obligation, when taken along with the Will Theory of the State.

The question that now arises is: to which of these three phases of the organic theory can we trace a parallel in Hindu political thought? The significance of the doctrine of Saptānga has been already noted. It may be regarded as an attempt to sum up "the theory of the constitution." The epithet "limb-like" applied to the seven elements of 'sovereignty' suggests the idea that the authors had in view the similarity between these and the parts of a living body. This by itself is a vague analogy. It does not say which element of the State corresponds to which limb of the body. Nor does it involve the subordination of parts to the whole and their interdependence. It is only in Manu and Kāmaṇḍaka that these are comprehended. Śukra elaborates the analogy and points out that the Sovereign is the head, the Minister is the eye, the Friend is the ear, the Treasure is the mouth, the Army is the mind, the Fort is the arms and the Territory is the legs.[73] One fails to see the propriety of this comparison. Does the army perform the same function in the State as the mind does in the body? Nor is it easy to see how the fort and the territory of the State could be regarded as its arms and legs. All that we can say is we have here no more than fanciful comparisons. They remind us of similar comparisons instituted by medieval writers. Like these latter, the Hindu writers give us nothing more than what Maitland calls "anthropomorphic conceits and fallacies, which do not rise above the level of pictorial presentment." The Hindu conception of the limb-like elements of 'sovereignty' is thus comparable to the first phase of the organic theory noted above. There is nothing in Hindu political thought to compare with the second

73. I, 122-24.

phase, which is an attempt at working out an elaborate analogy between the State and a living body.

Nor does Hindu thought give us the conception of the State as a moral organism. In the *Rig-veda*[74] an organismic metaphor is employed to explain the origin of classes in society. The Purusha-sūkta describes how out of the Purusha's mouth came the Brāhmaṇas, how the Kshatriyas were born of his arms, how his thighs became the Vaiśyas and how from his feet sprang the Śudras. The implication is that the four Varṇas in society have functions corresponding to the above four limbs of the human body. In the hands of the Smṛiti-writers, the analogy becomes an argument to justify the superiority of the Brāhmaṇas over the rest and the superiority of the twice-born over the Śudras. The four Varṇas are described as having been created by the primeval Purusha "for the sake of the prosperity of the world."[75] To this end, the Brāhmaṇas were assigned the duty of teaching and studying the Veda, sacrificing for their own benefit and for others, giving and accepting of alms. The duties of the Kshatriyas, the Vaiśyas as well as the Śudras were similarly laid down.

The scheme of the division of labour evolved here really shows a profound appreciation of the importance of this principle. It reminds one of the similar scheme Plato had in view. He proposed to inculcate, with the help of a myth, the idea in the minds of his citizens that some of them had the power of command, that some were fit to be auxiliaries and the others husbandmen and craftsmen.[76] Division of labour is quite essential for the progress of society. But in a truly functional society, every man must have the opportunity to find out, by a process of experimentation, to what particular function he is most adapted. It is only when he thus discovers his true station in life that he can express himself in his work and so fulfil the purpose that is his as well as the society's. To assign functions to men according to the mere chance of birth is to violate this fundamental principle of social justice.

---

74. X, 90; cf. *Atharva-veda*, XIX, 6.

75. *Manu*, I, 31; see also *Śānti Parva*, XLVIII, 67.

76. *Republic*, p. 104.

To determine one's function by the accident of birth is only to provide for the constant frustration of the creative urge in man. The personality of man is a unique thing that blossoms forth, not when it is rigidly channelised, but when it has before it the possibilities of finding out its own proper expression. The recognition of this principle involves what may be called the 'right to go wrong,' and the Hindu authors would never for a moment admit it. Every detail of a man's life and actions is scrupulously laid down and one irresistibly feels that there is hardly any opportunity left for the individual to exercise his judgment at all.

True to this tradition of Hindu authors, Manu, in this case, goes on to say that "man is stated to be purer above the navel than below; hence the self-existent (Svayambhu) has declared the purest (part) of him (to be) his mouth;"[77] and as Brāhmaṇas sprang from his mouth, the inevitable conclusion follows that they are "the lords of this whole creation."[78] This wedge of inequality was pushed in at a very early stage in the development of society. If the four Varṇas were created by the Purusha to carry on functions, corresponding to those of the mouth, the arms, the thighs and the feet, we should expect that each Varṇa is indispensable for its own functions. We should further expect that all these Varṇas would be co-operating for the realisation of a definite common end. There is no place in such a view for the superiority of one class over the rest. Such superiority, however, becomes the key-note of our ancient works from the *Dharmasūtras* onwards. Whatever exists in the world is said to be the property of the Brāhmaṇas.[79] The king is enjoined to honour the Brāhmaṇas,[80] to make them gifts,[81] and to exempt them from taxation.[82] These and other privileges to Brāhmaṇas might be contrasted in detail with the disabilities imposed on the Śudras. They are to serve

---

77. *Manu*, I, 92.
78. *Ibid.*, 93 and 99.
79. *Ibid.*, 100.
80. *Ibid.*, VII, 88.
81. *Manu*, 82-84.
82. *Ibid.*, 133.

meekly the other three castes.[83] "A Śudra," says the text, "whether bought or unbought, he (i.e. the Brāhmaṇa) may compel to do servile work; for he was created by the self-existent (Svayambhu) to be the slave of a Brāhmana."[84] We need not discuss here at great length such and other disabilities attached to the position of a Śudra. It is sufficient at this stage to point out that all possibility of the conception of the State as a moral organism, such as underlies the thought of political philosophers like Plato and Aristotle, Hegel, Green, Bradley and Bosanquet, is ruled out because of the stigma of inherent inferiority attached to certain sections of the body politic.

This criticism applies as well to the earlier Hindu works as to the Smṛitis and the later literature. From the earliest times, the Hindu thinkers seem to have conceived of society as an aggregate of different classes, sometimes competing, sometimes co-operating as the relations of the first two classes show, but never as a moral organism, where the parts are themselves conscious of being animated by a common purpose. The *Śatapatha Brāhmaṇa* states that the priesthood and the nobility are established upon the people.[85] A hiatus is thus created between the first two classes on the one hand, and the people at large on the other. The mutual relations of the Brāhmaṇas and the Kshatriyas do not directly concern us here. But it may be pointed out that in the *Brāhmaṇas* and even in the *Mahābhārata*, there seem to be divergent opinions about the matter. The Buddhist theory frankly looks upon the Kshatriya as the highest class.[86] Ultimately, however, the Brāhmaṇas were successful, it seems, in getting their claims recognised; for, the *Dharmaśāstra* authors are all agreed in giving the Brāhmaṇas the first place of honour in society. The *Agni Purāṇa*[87] holds that half of the revenue collected by the king should be distributed among the Brāhmaṇas. The Brāhmaṇas are never to be taxed and

83. *Manu*, VIII, 413.

84. XI, 2, 7, 16.

85. cf. *Yāj.*, XIII, 334; *Nārada*, XV-XVI, 20; 22; 25; *Brihaspati*; XXVII, II.

86. *Dīgha Nikāya*, III, 1, 15.

87. Beni Prasad: *Theory of Govt. in Ancient India*, p. 190.

are never to be hurt or punished even though leading the most wicked life. The *Bhāgavata Purāṇa* also stresses the supremacy of the Brāhmaṇas.[88] Śukra is on the right track when he maintains that "not by birth are the Brāhmaṇas, Kshatriyas, Vaiśyas, Śudras and Mlechhas separated but by virtues and works."[89] Such a view involves, implicitly at least, the recognition that the worth of all men is the same to start with. It also implies the possibility of a free choice of one's vocation in life. But Śukra does not carry forward this line of reasoning. He is a believer in the doctrine of Karma. The course of the present life of a man is determined, according to him, by his actions in the past birth. "According to the effects of works in previous births the mind of man is inclined to virtues or vices. It is not possible to do otherwise."[90] This fatalistic note leads him to take it for granted that in spite of what he has said above, the birth does determine one's nature and actions and so one's place in the Varṇa system. The old, traditional view asserts itself once again. The Brāhmaṇas are to be treated by the king with greater leniency than the lower orders.[91] Their offences are to be condoned, nay, if a Brāhmaṇa steals wealth, it is a blessing; for the wealth so stolen brings good hereafter. On the other hand, the wealth given to a Śudra leads only to hell.[92]

We thus see how the myth of the Purusha-sūkta could not lead to an organic conception of society. The undue emphasis on the superiority of certain classes and hence on the cleavage between these, with the intrusion of the hereditary principle, proved the enemy of the organic conception. But for these factors, we should certainly have appreciated the great intuitive insight of the Vedic seers in being able to visualise a condition of society, which may have perhaps reflected "the ideal of a social organism with differentiation of functions and activities to be discharged by each class according to its capacities, the place of every individual

---

88. *Ibid.*, p. 200.
89. I, 75-76.
90. 89-90.
91. II, 568, 569.
92. *Śukra* II, 811-812; III, 448-451.

in society to be determined not by birth or wealth or rank but by worth and every class linked to the rest by the law of mutual service."[93]

We see thus that the conception of the State as a moral organism is not really present in Hindu thought. It is only in this sense that the organic theory of the State has a significance for the problem of political obligation. The statements of some of our scholars which we have referred to above use the phrase "organic theory" in a very loose sense. When, therefore, they speak of the idea of the State as an organism as having been realised in ancient India, their statements are only misleading. The truth as we have noted above is that we get only a few attempts to compare the various elements of governmental organisation to the limbs of the human body. The conception of the State as a moral organism can hardly be expected to appear when there is no adequate conception of individuality at all. Such organic or organismic metaphors as we find in Hindu works may be picturesque but they throw no light on the fundamental problem of the relation of the State to the individual. Thus, we have to conclude that the organic theory that harmonises the authority of the State and the liberty of the individual, that bridges over the gulf between the ruler and the ruled, such a theory cannot be traced in our ancient works. There are significant attempts to see that in practice, the interests of the rulers and the ruled are identical and that good and beneficent government is secured for the people. However, even the most paternal government with the most conscientious ruler at the head cannot make the State really organic unless the very nature of individuality is explored and understood and the State is viewed as resting on the common will.

We shall see in the next chapter how the conception of *Dharma* as equated to Svadharma places an undue emphasis on the separateness of the individual from his fellowmen and precludes, therefore, the possibility of visualising the State as the instrument for the realisation of a *common social* good.

---

93. See Wadia and Joshi: *Wealth of India,* pp. 125-126.

Chapter V

The End of the Hindu State

We have discussed in the foregoing chapters whether and in what sense we can speak of the divine right theory or the contract theory or the force theory or the organic theory in Hindu political thought. We have seen that though we get hints here and there which suggest different theories, it would be incorrect to take up any one set of these hints and label it down as the Hindu theory of political obligation. The task of arriving at the Hindu view is much more difficult inasmuch as the Hindu solution of the problem is not given us readymade or completely worked out. The Hindu State, we must remember, is necessarily the product of the Hindu view of life. The one cannot be dissociated from the other. The fundamental question for political thought is: What is the purpose of the State? What does the State stand for? What, in other words, is the place of the State in the whole scheme of life?

Thus we have now to find out what the end of the Hindu State is. And this means necessarily that we have to relate this to the goal of life itself as understood by our ancients. Then only can we see what the State stood for; then only can we see what purpose the State objectified, what promise it held out to the individual, what, in short, was the principle to which the individual was called upon to be loyal. In the light of the end of the State so understood, we could look at the various hints about the problem of political obligation that we have so far considered. We could then have an idea of the nature of the Hindu State and the nature of the relation between the State and the individual.

The question as to the end of the State has been of considerable importance in the history of political thought. As Aristotle points out, some good or supposed good is the end of every action. The activities of men are certainly purposive. It may be that every moment of their lives, men are not conscious of being guided by a purpose. The play of instinct, the force of habit, the activities arising out of the unconscious are yet great problems for psychologists to solve. The last world-war seems to have left the general impression that reason, after all, plays a very small part in human life. Tarde, in the seventies and eighties of the last century, made us familiar with the "laws of imitation." And Graham Wallas, for example, would tell us that human nature in politics is something entirely different from what the political theorists—intellectualists—are wont to believe. Bertrand Russell would lay stress on impulses. A philosopher like Bergson would explain all human activity in terms of the *elan vital.* It is possible to say there are more things in actual political life than are dreamt of in the political philosophy of academic thinkers. And yet, there is no doubt that reason is the distinguishing mark of man. Man alone can think ahead, can plan ahead, can correlate means and ends. We may not speak of purpose as something always in front of man leading him forward as carrot the donkey. But we must admit that there is a scheme of values implicit in every man's life.[1] There is the inner yet powerful recognition of a central purpose, a cardinal principle which determines one's conduct. It is in this sense that we may take Aristotle's dictum that some good or supposed good is the end of every action.

Thus, the problem of the end of the State does not lose any of its importance in spite of different criticisms.[2] A social institution

1. cf. Green: *Principles of Political Obligation,* pp. 31-32.

2. The real service which Social Psychology has done cannot be ignored. As Hetherington and Muirhead admit (*Social Purpose,* pp. 43 ff); "it has broadened our conception of the elements that any true social ideal must find room for if it is adequately to reflect the fullness of human life." Still, the fact remains that social psychology has inherited from its founders an attitude of hostility to philosophy in general. "It has as a whole shown a singular indifference to questions of meaning and validity," so that "so far as political theory is concerned it is an elaborate begging of the question." (*Ibid.*) Compare also Barker's remarks on 'Political and other studies' in *Political Thought in England,* pp. 13-14.

is the embodiment of the purpose of its members. It is through such institutions that the purposes of men in society are, in the first instance, expressed and then fostered and furthered.[3]

What, then, should be the end of the State? Is the State merely to maintain order? Is the end of the State none other than the maintenance of peace and security? Is the State to guarantee the various "natural rights" of man? Is it to be just an adjusting and correcting mechanism? Or, is it, on the other hand, to make possible what the philosophers would call "good life"?

Judging from history, we may say that the functions of the State have gone on increasing with the lapse of time. The greater complexities of life call for more complex and more comprehensive State-action. But, in the history of political thought, the view of the end of the State has not always been favourable to the extension of the sphere of the State. The end of the State, as we find it expressed in the *Republic*, is by no means narrow. The environment of the city-state may have had its influence on the speculations of Plato but the theory he has given us has a validity irrespective of the immediate environment. To Plato and Aristotle the end of the State was no less than the good life of the citizens. Neither Plato nor Aristotle had a distrust of State-action. While this view finds favour even to this day with some thinkers, there are others who stand aghast at the idea that the State may be the institution of institutions which reconciles the various loyalties of the individual. To Green, the State is the sustainer and harmoniser of social relations.[4] It is an institution for the promotion of the common good. The same view is expressed by Bosanquet, when he says that "the ultimate end of the State as of the individual is the realisation of the best life."[5] On the other hand, imaginative pictures of a past golden age have led some thinkers to conclude that the State, along with various other institutions such as private property, is the result of man's fall from the idyllic condition in the remote

3. For a lucid treatment of this subject, reference may be made to the section on "Purpose in Institutional Life" in *Social Purpose*, Hetherington and Muirhead, pp. 122 ff.

4. *op. cit.*, p. 148.

5. *Philosophical Theory of the State*, p. 169.

past. Spencer regards government as a relic of the predatory state and its great duty is, therefore, to efface itself for the sake of the law of freedom, by admitting the right of the citizen 'to ignore the State.'[6] With this we may compare Bentham's dictum. "It is with government as with medicine; its only business is the choice of evils. Every law is an evil, for every law is an infraction of liberty."[7] Mill's idea of individuality and the proper function of the State is biassed by the Benthamite tradition that law is an evil. Thus, individuality, according to Mill, is not nourished and evoked by the varied play of relations and obligations in society. It lies in a sort of inner self, to be cherished by enclosing it, as it were, in an impervious globe.[8] At the same time, Mill had a deep sense of social solidarity and he saw clearly that absolute, unrestrained liberty was a hopeless chimera. He therefore invented the distinction between "self-regarding" and "other-regarding" actions and declared that "to individuality should belong the part of life in which it is chiefly the individual that is interested; to society, the part which chiefly interests society."[9] The thin end of the wedge was thus driven in. Mill justifies the legislation after the pattern of factory acts; he feels, it is just to interdict marriage to those unable to show the means of supporting a family and he considers it right for the State to have a system of examinations by way of enforcing the parental duty of educating children. From administrative nihilism, he seems to have jumped to administrative absolūtism. This inevitable result has a significance about it but we are not concerned with it here. What we note here is that for the so-called individualist, the State is at best a necessary evil and its sphere of action must be rigorously circumscribed in the interests of liberty. More extreme—and more logical—than the individualist is the anarchist, in whose scheme the State has no place at all.[10]

---

6. cf. Barker: *op. cit.*, pp. 99 ff.
7. *Principles of Legislation*, p. 48.
8. cf. Bosanquet: *op. cit.*, pp. 56 ff.
9. *On Liberty*, Ch. iv.
10. Refer, for general information on the subject, Gide and Rist: *Hist. of Econ. Doctrines*, pp. 614 ff.; the article on "Anarchism" in *Ency. of Social Sciences*, Vol. II, and also the article on "Anarchism" in *Ency.Brit.*, Vol. I.

Zeno the founder of the Stoic school is generally accepted as the first systematic exponent of anarchism. All anarchists cannot, indeed, be said to hold exactly identical views. There is a kind of gross anarchism such as Stirner's which would deny the reality of the social fact, would recognise only the personal interest of the individual and would bluntly assert: "The crouching tiger is within his rights when he springs at me, but so am I when I resist his attacks."

This position is obviously untenable and so it need not be criticised. But there is another kind of anarchism the appeal of which is more dignified and subtle. Proudhon's anarchism for example was not a contempt of laws but an almost religious attachment to eternal laws. Thus, Bakunin tells us that "all morality is founded on human respect, that is to say, upon the recognition of the humanity, of the human rights and worth in all men, of whatever race or colour, degree of intellectual or moral development." He recognises, again, that "liberty is not an isolated fact" but "is the outcome of mutual good-will," "a principle not of exclusion, but of inclusion, the liberty of each individual being simply the reflection of his humanity or of his rights as a human being in the conscience of every free man, his brother and equal." And yet, this does not lead him to consider how this equal liberty for all would be actually realized. He does not see that there is bound to be a conflict between men and men, between loyalties and loyalties, in the absence of a co-ordinating principle. The very name of authority is to him anathema. The State is an agent for exploitation and oppression, "a flagrant negation of humanity," "the grave where every trace of individuality is sacrificed and buried." Into the merits and demerits of these views we need not go.

Anarchism is an obvious impossibility except to cranks and visionaries. The State is not an obnoxious institution that has somehow made itself indispensable to us. It is not a necessary evil, a clever trap out of which we should heroically exert to extricate ourselves. The basis of the State is nothing else than human nature. It is essentially a moral institution—at bottom, an expression of the view of the good life for man. Recently, however, thinkers have shown a distrust of the State. The political pluralists see in the State a Leviathan, absolute and irresponsible, above morality, swallowing up the individual and also all the other institutions in society.[11] They are out to demolish the 'metaphysical theory of the State,' which is to them but a facile and dangerous reconciliation of liberty and authority. They feel that the all-absorbing Hegelian State is a grave menace to the liberty of the individual. They therefore demand a 'responsible' or a 'democratic' State. The end of the State is to these thinkers none other than the aim which the rulers in any particular society set before themselves. Hence arises the need for a constant scrutiny of the purposes of the State, which merely means the government, according to them. The functions of the State in this view would be the adjustment of social relationships but an adjustment which may be called just 'keeping the ring.' Duguit, Laski, Hobhouse, Cole have thus enunciated a view which 'discredits the State,' demolishes its 'sovereignty' and makes it but one among many associations.

Tempting though the field is, it would be out of place here to enter into a discussion of the genesis of this attack and the element of truth in it. Briefly, we may say that political theory has divided itself into two schools: that which, starting more or less from the point of view of the Greeks, thinks primarily in terms of the State and attempts to make it the synthesis of all institutions; and that which, by way of reaction from the first, thinks primarily of the institutions and regards the State mainly as a contrivance for providing individuals and societies with certain external conditions within which they may best fulfil their function in the development of individual and social character.

The obvious conclusion is that it is difficult to define the end of the State. There is no single word which would express the idea adequately. The great initial difficulty is to sift the essential

---

11. Compare for example Laski's statement of the monistic theory and his criticism of the same in his *Studies in the Problem of Sovereignty,* Ch. I. Laski here as Hobhouse in his *Metaphysical Theory of the State* protests against implications which the so-called monistic theory does not really have.

from the accidental, the necessary from the incidental functions of the State. It would be enough if we recognize that the State is an organic whole vitalised by the idea of the common good of its members. The end of the State, as Mazzini put it, is "the fullest possible development in all its citizens of the forces and faculties of man."[12]

With this background, let us turn to Hindu political thought and see what the end of the Hindu State was.

It is evident that we cannot expect to find in our ancient works a theoretical discussion of this problem. The main aim of Hindu thinkers was to lay down practical rules of statecraft in the interests of what seemed to them to be the necessary conditions of sound administration. The Hindu view of the end of the State has therefore to be arrived at by interpreting the significance of the maxims laid down for the guidance of the ideal king and so getting at the conception of kingly office underlying them.[13]

We might begin our survey of the Hindu ideas of kingship with a reference to their view of the importance of the king's office. This comes out very clearly from their account of the state of affairs that would result in the absence of this office. The Hindu thinkers have a great dread of anarchy, which is assumed to be inevitable in the absence of monarchy. The possibility of any other form of government taking the place of monarchy is not at all considered by them. In the absence of the king, it is said, there would be a subversion of the social order. The only law in operation then would be the *matsyanyāya*. The weaker being at the mercy of the stronger, chaos would reign supreme. The

12. Quoted by Sir Henry Jones: *The Principles of Citizenship*, p. 91.

13. We do not indeed ignore the fact that monarchy was not the only form of government in ancient India. At least down to the fifth century A.D. a succession of what Jayaswal takes to be republican constitutions of different types can be traced existing side by side with monarchies (See *Hindu Polity*, Vol. I). The *Mahābhārata* (*Śānti Parva*, CVII, 6-32), the *Arthaśāstra* (Bk. I, Ch. XVII) and the account of Megasthenes (Fragments I and LVI) all these speak of the existence of some kinds of non-monarchial polities in ancient India. All the same, monarchy is the predominant type of government in Indian History and it is monarchy in the main that the Hindu authors have in view in their works.

castes and orders would cease to perform their respective duties. The whole scheme of *Dharma* would be wrecked, and according to the Hindu authors, a situation worse than this could hardly be imagined. The scheme of *Dharma* has been taken to be divinely ordained. The disappearance or mutilation of this scheme would thus mean the violation of the divine purpose; and so it would send terrible repurcussions all over the universe. The absolute necessity of the maintenance of *Dharma* is thus emphasized: this being granted, the equally absolute necessity of having a king becomes obvious. The office of the king is the necessary condition of ordered society. So thoroughly are our thinkers convinced of this that they elevate the science of kingly duties to the level of the highest science.[14] According to the *Mahābhārata,*[15] Rājadharma is the refuge of the whole world. On it, we are told, depends the performance of the threefold duties, pertaining to Dharma, Artha and Kāma; nay, salvation too depends on it. As compared with the duties of the other classes in society, the duties of the king are the highest; for, these other duties are all dependent on Rājadharma.

Kauṭilya[16] also speaks of the great importance of *Daṇḍa-nīti* in view of its being the necessary condition of the proper development of the rest of the 'Vidyās'. He even mentions a view to the effect that Daṇḍaniti is the supreme science, while all the rest are included in it. Kāmaṇḍaka[17] probably re-echoes Kauṭilya when he observes, "if Daṇḍa-nīti were to be disturbed the other three sciences would be evil, even if they could exist."

May we not express this view by saying that the science of kingly duties is of unique importance because it is the State

14. The importance of Daṇḍaniti thus inculcated cannot be looked upon as involving a positive approach, as some of our modern scholars have tried to make out. The great emphasis placed by our ancient lawgivers and statesmen on this point is due really to the association of kingly duties with *Dharma.*

15. *Śānti Parva,* LVI, 3-5.

16. *Arthaśāstra,* Bk. I, Ch. 2.

17. *Nītisāra,* III, 8.

that sets the perspective of other institutions in society and so determines their claim to the loyalty of the individual? This would mean that the State is the institution of institutions and that there is no aloofness on the part of the State so far as the various institutions in society are concerned. This point, however, will have to be discussed later.[18]

The importance of the king's office can be seen also by considering the duties he was expected to discharge. The functions of the king in the Vedic times were simple. Leading the people in war and administering justice and punishing the wicked in times of peace constituted the royal duties at that early stage.[19] There is a considerable difference of opinion as to whether Vedic kingship was elective or hereditary; we cannot say definitely what exactly was the principle governing the king's accession to the throne.[20] It is clear that the duty of the subjects was to obey the king and to make contributions for the maintenance of royalty. The king was considered to be himself immune from punishment (*adaṇḍya*)[21] for, he could not be constitutionally responsible to any authority in the State.

---

18. Sec Chapter VII, infra.

19. *Vedic Index*, Vol. II.; see discussion under "Rājan."

20. Jayaswal maintains that Vedic kingship was 'a human institution;' that it was 'elective;' that it was 'a contractual agreement,' and that it was a 'trust' for the purpose of promoting the prosperity of the people. He maintains further that kingship was 'not above the law but under it,' and was 'primarily national and secondarily territorial' (Sec *Hindu Polity*, Vol. Il, pp. 38-39). Our discussion of the divine right theory and the contract theory in the earlier chapters shows how misleading it is to call Hindu kingship 'a human institution,' and 'a contractual agreement.' It is equally hazardous to assert that the Hindu kingship in Vedic times was 'elective,' although Shama Sastri also maintains that it was elective (*Evolution of Indian Polity*, pp. 38-39). The authors of the *Vedic Index* are of opinion that it was sometimes hereditary and sometimes elective. Even if it was elective in some cases, we do not know whether the king was "elected" from among the whole people or from a certain family. There is uncertainty about the constitution and functions of the Sabhā and the Samiti. It is better, therefore, to avoid any generalisation on this point. (cf. Basu: *Indo-Aryan Polity*, p. 55 and Richard Fick: *Social Organisation*, pp. 123 ff.).

21. *Vedic Index*, Vol. II, pp. 210-215.

In the *Śatapatha Brāhmaṇa*, we are told,[22] the king is the upholder of the sacred law (*dhṛitavrataḥ*), for, he speaks and does only what is right. Kingship is thus the embodiment of a philosophic idea.[23] We have here an anticipation of the later more explicit idea that the king's office is meant for the maintenance of *Dharma*. Nay, the *Śatapatha Brāhmaṇa* itself refers elsewhere to the king as the protector of *Dharma* (*Dharmapati*).

In the *Dharmasūtras*, the functions of the king are dealt with at greater length. The king is a Kshatriya 'par excellence.' As such, his supreme duty is to 'protect' the people. According to Gautama, the king must not only protect all 'created beings' and inflict lawful punishments but also support needy students, śrotriyas, all who are unable to work and all who are free from taxes.[24] With strict impartiality, he is to promote the interests of all.[25] Baudhāyana observes that "the king must protect his subjects receiving as his pay one-sixth of their incomes."[26] Āpastamba lays down that no one in the kingdom should suffer from hunger, cold or heat. The king must punish the wicked and those who violate the rules of their caste or order. Similar injunctions are given by Vasishṭha, who lays down that the king must govern according to the principles laid down by the Brāhmaṇas.[27]

The main duty of the king is said to be 'protection.' This does not, however, mean that the State was to confine itself to discharging only the police functions. Protection is a term used in a comprehensive sense, as the above statements clearly bring out. Under 'protection,' we have to include "the departments of what we should now call the church, education, poor relief, the police, criminal and civil justice, legislation, medical relief, public

---

22. V, 4, 4, 5.
23. cf. Ghoshal: *History of Hindu Political Theories*, p. 24.
24. *Gautama*, X, 7-12.
25. *Ibid.*, XI, 5-6.
26. *Baud.*, I, 10-8-1.
27. I, 45.

works, the army and the navy, and the consular and diplomatic services."[28]

What is the principle that determines these functions? What, in other words, is the end, to secure which these functions of the king are ordained? The answer is suggested by the very title of these sacred works. The *Dharmasūtras* are works dealing with *Dharma*; and this includes, as their contents show, private as well as public life together. Domestic ritual as well as the rules to be observed in social life are found together in these works. All these are treated as laid down in the eternal scheme of *Dharma*. The scheme of the four Varṇas and the four Āśramas is, according to these authors, a necessary part of this eternal order. The duty of the king is to see that this scheme is not wrecked. The king is the guarantee of the maintenance of the castes and the orders in their proper sphere. In this duty, the Brāhmaṇa is his help-mate and the two together are said to be the upholders of the moral order of the world[29] (dhṛitavratau). In a word, the king is the maintainer or preserver of *Dharma*. To put it differently, the end of the State is the maintenance or preservation of *Dharma*. It is to this end that the functions of the king are directed.

The same idea underlies the various maxims and rules laid down for the guidance of the king in the *Arthaśāstra* of Kauṭilya, in the *Mahābhārata*, in the *Manu-smṛiti* together with the other *Dharmaśāstras* and even in the later works. Kauṭilya,[30] at the very outset, speaks of the four Varṇas and the four orders. He describes the duties of each of these and also the duties common to all of these. The duty of the king is never to allow people to swerve from their respective duties; for these are duties laid down in the

28. K.V.R. Aiyangar: *Ancient Indian Polity*, 67.

29. *Gautama*, viii, 1-3.

30. *Artha.*, Bk. I, Ch. 3; cf. "This obligation of the State to maintain *Dharma* has been urged, not only by writers with transparent sacerdotal inclinations, like the author of the *Manu-smṛiti*, but even by those, who, like Kauṭilya, viewed politics from a secular stand-point," (K.V.R. Aiyangar: *Some Aspects of Ancient Indian Polity*.) In fact, as we have already pointed out, there is no ground for taking Kauṭilya's approach as being positive.

Vedas which are the final authority as to the righteousness or otherwise of acts. Kauṭilya's position is briefly this: the adequate discharge of the duties of these castes and orders means *Dharma*; and the king's duty is to see that these are duly discharged. That means, the king's duty is to maintain *Dharma*.

The *Mahābhārata* lays down numerous rules for the guidance of the king. The functions of the king cover a very wide field. The king is to protect the people; if he fails to afford protection, he must be shunned like a leaky boat on the sea.[31] He should make his subjects happy, should observe truth and should act sincerely.[32] The four castes must be maintained in the performance of their duties.[33] The king earns eternal merit in whose kingdom there is no wickedness, dissimulation, deception and envy.[34] The king is to maintain *Dharma* as laid down by the Vedas.[35] He must cause all people to consider *Dharma* as the foremost of all things.[36] Sometimes, the king is even identified with *Dharma*.[37]

The *Dharmaśāstras*[38] are all agreed that the duty of the king is to maintain the castes and orders in the performance of their duties. Barring a few points of difference as regards the exemptions and privileges to *Brāhmaṇas* and other matters comparatively of little importance for our purpose here, they agree in the main as to the functions of the king. Further, there is at the back of all these injunctions a profound conviction on the part of these authors that what they are expounding is *Dharma*.

And finally, Śukra also accepts the standard classification of castes and orders and regards the king as the preserver of the social edifice. He says that the king must make the people habituated

31. *Śānti Parva*, LVII, 43-44.

32. *Ibid.*, 11.

33. *Ibid.*, 13.

34. *Ibid.*, 37.

35. *Ibid.*, LIX, 106.

36. *Ibid.*, 135.

37. *Ibid.*, LXXII, 25.

38. cf. *Manu*, VII, 24, 35, 203; VIII, 41, 42, 46
Yāj., XIII, 361; *Vishnu*, III, 13.

to performing their respective duties and that he himself must perform his duty.[39]

Any further details are hardly necessary. We can confidently maintain that the end of the State according to Hindu authors from early times down to comparatively modern times is the maintenance of *Dharma.* We have now to see what the exact significance of this term is. What exactly do we mean when we say that the purpose of the State is the maintenance of *Dharma*? What is *Dharma*?

The term *Dharma* is one of the most comprehensive and important terms in the whole range of Sanskrit literature.[40] It has various meanings. Sometimes it stands for sacred law, sometimes for duty, sometimes for custom. It may signify religion or religious merit. There is no single word in the English language to express the idea of Dharma adequately. We must therefore determine the correct significance of the term by taking into consideration what the Hindu authors themselves say about it and how they interpret it when they look upon it as the end of the State.

The word 'Ṛita' is used in the *Ṛig-veda* to convey somewhat the same sense which the word *Dharma* conveys later on. From early times, men must have observed the regularity and orderliness of the phenomena of nature. They must have noted that the rising and setting of the sun, the moon and the stars, the march of the seasons and the ebb and tide of the ocean, these are not phenomena happening at random. They are not mere freaks. There seems to be an underlying order that they follow, a law that they observe. This idea of a law, governing the phenomena of nature, is expressed in the *Ṛig-veda* as Ṛita. Thus, we are told:

> "The flowing of the flood is Law, Truth is the sun's extended light."[41]

---

39. *Śukra,* I, 50-51.

40. Jolly: Article in *Ency. of Religion and Ethics,* Vol. 4.
cf. also: "*Dharma* is the meeting place of the individual and society, of religion and philosophy, of here and hereafter, of man and God. It is the cement of society, the bond of love, the means of attainment of God."
K.S.R. Sastri: *Hindu Culture,* p. 93.

41. Bk. I, Hymn 105. cf. Griffith's translation, p. 137, foot-note.

Elsewhere, it is said:

> "To Law belong the vast deep earth and heaven; milch-kine supreme, to Law their milk they render."[42] The regular, or rather regulated, arrival and departure of the Dawn is said to be in obedience to the reign of Law Eternal.[43] The Fathers have placed the sun in heaven according to Ṛita, the sun is the bright countenance of Ṛita. The year is spoken of as the wheel of Ṛita with twelve spokes.[44]

This, then, is one sense in which the term Ṛita is used—Ṛita meaning the Law that governs all the phenomena of nature. It is used in another sense also, as denoting the norm which men here must follow. This sense of the word comes out in connection with its uses with reference to the gods, Mitra and Varuṇa, who are declared to be "lovers and cherishers of Law."[45] These two are invoked, as "those who by law uphold the Law, Lords of the shining light of Law", to protect and enrich men.[46] It is believed that in their capacity as guardians of Ṛita, they could not only shelter men, chasing their enemies away, but could also influence the forces of nature. Hence, it is said:—

> "The winds waft sweets, the rivers pour sweets for the men who keep the law; so may the plants be sweet for us. Sweet be the night and sweet the dawns, sweet the terrestrial atmosphere; sweet be our father Heaven to us."[47]

The moral character of Varuṇa is expressed repeatedly in the most emphatic manner. "What, Varuṇa, has been my chief transgression?" goes forth the cry;[48] and his forgiveness is prayed for.[49] It is interesting to note that this Law of Varuṇa is regarded as something external to and therefore imposed from without on

---

42. *Ibid.*, Bk. IV, Hymn 23.
43. *Ibid.*, Bk. I, Hymn 123.
44. Keith: *Religion and Philosophy of the Veda*, pp. 83-84.
45. *Rig-veda*, Bk. I, Hymn 2.
46. *Ibid.*, 23.
47. *Ibid.*, 90.
48. *Rig-veda*, Bk. VII, Hymn 86.
49. *Ibid.*, 88, 89.

man. Its breach is to some extent looked upon as unavoidable. What is prayed for, thus, is not the will to avoid such pitfalls, but only immunity from the consequences thereof.[50] All the same, the conception of Ṛita as a norm of conduct for men to follow is certainly traceable in the *Ṛig-veda.* This may also be seen from the reply of Yama and Yami, to the effect that the marriage between a brother and a sister is contrary to the Law of Varuṇa.[51] Ṛita thus refers not merely to natural phenomena but also to human conduct.[52]

And there is a third sense in which the word Ṛita is used and that is "the right order of the sacrifice."[53] As Keith observes, "Ṛita applies to all aspects of the world, to the sequence of events in nature, to the sacrifice and to man's life."[54]

In the *Brāhmaṇas,* the term, 'Ṛita' is less important; and the term *Dharma* takes its place.[55] The king is hailed as the guardian of *Dharma* and to him who has the power, men resort in matters of *Dharma.*[56] In the *Ṛig-veda* the word Dharman was used in the same sense as Ṛita; and we find that the word *Dharma* enters here into its legacy. *Dharma* comes from the root "dhri" which means "to hold." It therefore means the principle that holds

---

50. cf. *Ibid.,* Bk. I, Hymn 25.

51. *Ibid.,* Bk. X, Hymn 10; see Keith: *Religion and Philosophy of the Veda,* Vol. I, Ch. 16, p. 247.

52. cf. "We see in Ṛita a development from the physical to the divine. Ṛita originally meant "the established route of the world, of the sun, moon and stars, morning and evening, day and night." Gradually, it became the path of morality to be followed by man and the law of righteousness observed even by the gods." Radhakrishnan: *Indian Philosophy,* Vol. I, p. 79.

    Also cf. "It (i.e. Ṛita) meant originally the firmly established movement of the world, of the sun, of morning and evening, of day and night—its manifestation was perceived in the path of the heavenly bodies—and that right path on which the gods brought light out of the darkness became afterwards the path to be followed by man, partly in his sacrifices, partly in his general moral conduct"—Max Muller: *Hibbert Lectures,* 1878—pp. 244-245.

53. cf. *Ṛig-veda,* Bk. I, Hymns 41 and 68, and Mckenzie: *Hindu. Ethics,* pp. 5-6.

54. *Religion and Philosophy of the Veda,* p. 249.

55. *Ibid.,* p. 479.

56. *Śatapatha Brāhmaṇa* V, 3, 3, 9; and V, 4, 4, 5.

together the whole universe, physical as well as moral. Hence, the word *Dharma* comes to mean, firstly, the cosmic order and secondly, the law governing human society. In this latter sense, as we have seen, it was looked upon as something external to man, existing independently of man's volition. Its breaches were therefore regarded as almost inevitable. The Ṛig-vedic seers thus fail to see how this law, which governs the physical universe, is to be applied to the problems of life in society. In the example of Yama and Yami, indeed, we have noted that Ṛita is regarded as enjoining certain acts and forbidding others. But the problem is: how are we to determine which acts are really enjoined and which prohibited? We may grant for the moment that the same law which reigned supreme in the realm of nature has a sway in human relationships also; that, if the orderly procession of the sun, the moon and the stars reflects the working out of the purpose of a divine mind, the lives of men here must also be similarly regulated with reference to the divine purpose. Still the difficulty remains. In the case of natural phenomena there is no will or purpose on the part of those forces which are said to be moving in accordance with Ṛita. It is otherwise in the case of man. He has his will and he makes his choice between various alternatives every moment of his life.[57] It is little consolation for him to know that the principle of the natural order is reflected in the social world too. The problem is to find out what the dictates of such a law would be. For, it must be accepted as law by men, if it is to govern human relationships. The difficulty is well-nigh insuperable, unless the conception of Ṛita or *Dharma* is related to the teleological springs of man's being.

---

57. There is, as Caird points out, an "apparent opposition between the ordinary conception of the world, as a system of causally connected objects in space and time, which is presupposed by physical science, and what seem to be the fundamental ideas of morality and religion, the ideas of God, freedom and immortality." The problem is: "If man, like all the other objects of our empirical knowledge, is merely one part of the world of objects which act and react upon each other, according to fixed general laws, what room is left for the assertion of his moral freedom, or for any higher destiny which distinguishes him from the other creatures?" This is the problem which Green endeavours to solve. See Green: *Prolegomena to Ethics,* Preface by Caird, pp. iii-v.

In the *Brihadāraṇyaka Upanishad,*[58] there occurs an important passage which describes how the four Varṇas came into existence and how *Dharma* was created. Verily, we are told, in the beginning this was Brāhmaṇa, one only. That being one was not strong enough. "It created still further the most excellent Kshatra (power), viz. those Kshatras (powers) among the Devas,—Indra, Varuṇa, Soma, Rudra, Parjanya, Yama, Mrityu and Iśāna. Therefore, there is nothing beyond the Kshatra, and therefore, at the Rājasuya sacrifice, the Brāhmaṇa sits down below the Kshatriya...... But Brahman is (nevertheless) the birth-place of the Kshatra. Therefore, though a king is exalted, he sits down at the end (of the sacrifice) below the Brahman, as his birth-place. He who injures him, injures his own birth-place. He becomes worse because he injured one better than himself."

We see that the Brāhmaṇa is clearly regarded here as superior to the Kshatriya in the world of the Devas. The two other Varṇas were also created in order that Brāhmaṇa may be strong enough. But even this was not enough. "He created still further the most excellent Law (*Dharma*). Law is the Kshatra (power) of the Kshatra, therefore there is nothing higher than the Law. Thenceforth even a weak man rules a stronger with the help of the Law, as with the help of a king. Thus the Law is what is called the true. And if a man declares what is true, they say he declares the Law; and if he declares the Law, they say he declares what is true. Thus both are the same."

This passage has important implications. Moral authority embedded in law is said to be metaphysical in character. Law-givers are called the declarers of truth, law and truth being characterised as the same.[59] *Dharma* is declared to have been created by the Brāhmaṇa finally, in order that he may feel strong enough. And *Dharma* is associated with Kshatriya. It carries its own sanction with it; for there is nothing higher than *Dharma.* In the world of

58. *The Upanishads*—tr. by Max Muller, Pt. II, pp. 88-89.

59. J.N.C. Ganguly: Article on "Philosophy of *Dharma*" in the *Indian Historical Quarterly,* Vol. II, 1926.

the Devas, then, the four Varṇas are to be found, with *Dharma* as the guiding principle above them all. From this follows the similar scheme for this world also. As the text puts it,[60] "Among the Devas that Brāhmaṇa existed as Agni (fire) only; among men as Brāhmaṇa, as Kshatriya through the (divine) Kshatriya, as Vaiśya through the (divine) Vaiśya, as Śūdra through the (divine) Śūdra......" There seems to be a little confusion here. Brāhmaṇa is said to have existed as Agni only among the Devas. If that is so, it is difficult exactly to see the meaning of the phrases 'through the (divine) Kshatriya, through the (divine) Vaiśya' and 'through the (divine) Śūdra.' But the general trend of the passage is clear. It represents an attempt to justify the division of society into four Varṇas by regarding it as a replica of the social order among the Devas. Further, *Dharma* is conceived as the power or the sanction behind the authority of the Kshatra in the world of Devas. The suggestion is that the established order of society is also similarly backed by *Dharma*. The question may indeed be asked on what grounds we could hold that among the Devas such a scheme of social organisation really prevailed. To that our authors have no answer to give. In the *Ṛig-veda*, we have seen, the moral order underlying social phenomena was conceived of as perhaps mysteriously related to the physical order of the universe—or rather, the one was not clearly distinguished from the other. Here we find that the division of society into four classes is said to be the replica of the pattern in the world of the Devas. The underlying idea in this case too is that the Law which governs the physical universe, the universe of the Devas (if we may call it so) and the human world is fundamentally the same.[61] It is an assumption indeed—an assumption that is clouded by the mythological setting in which it is placed. What concerns us in the main is how the Hindu thinkers instead of relating the conception of *Dharma* to the purpose of man in society take an entirely different path and come to the comfortable conclusion that the existing social order is itself the manifestation of *Dharma*.

---

60. *Brihad Upa.*, I, 4, 15.

61. See Hopkins: *Ethics of India*, pp. 37-38.

In the *Śatapatha Br.* already the four classes in society are assumed to be rigid and the idea that the Śudras and even the Vaiśyas are impure is already present. Thus, it comes about that the Brāhmaṇa and the Kshatriya never go behind the Vaiśya and the Śudra... in order to avoid a confusion between good and bad.[62] A confusion of these classes is looked upon as evil; for this particular order of society alone is looked upon as 'the proper order.'[63]

Once the existing order of society, together with the hierarchical arrangement, comes to be looked upon as *Dharma*, the way is opened out for further increasing its scope. The concept of *Dharma*, because of its associations, has a halo around it; so that, if a law-giver wishes to sanctify any custom or usage, he has merely to put it down as *Dharma*. That was the only feasible way of bringing the lives of the actual men and women in a definite relation to *Dharma*. All the criticism that has been levelled against the conception of an eternal Law of Nature, carrying its own sanction with it, could well be directed against the conception of *Dharma*. It is noteworthy, however, that while the Law of Nature became in Europe a phrase to prop up the pet theories of philosophers of opposite schools of thought, a peculiar sanctity has always been associated with *Dharma* in India; and probably this is so because there is a remarkable unanimity among the Hindu thinkers about the principles of social organisation. They all agreed that the social organisation, as represented by the four Varṇas and Āśramas, with the king to preserve its equilibrium, was in accordance with *Dharma*. That need not, however, blind us to the fallacy involved in their attitude. They must have come to the conclusion that a particular course of conduct was proper by the same process of thought which we generally employ in respect of all questions. Then, they must have put it down as being in accordance with *Dharma*. It is interesting in this respect to compare their method, with the method adopted by the Utilitarian philosophers in Europe. These latter maintained that the highest good is a matter of mere calculation. You have only to measure

62. *Śata. Br.*, VI Kanda, 4 Adhyaya, 4 Brāhmaṇa.

63. *Ibid.*, V Kanda, 4 Adhyaya, 4 Brāhmaṇa, 13, 19.

the pleasure and the pain involved in the action and find out the greatest good of the greatest number.[64] About the fallacy of identifying good with pleasure and the difficulty of classifying pleasures, we need not say anything here. What strikes us as similar to the faith of the Hindu authors in the conception of *Dharma* is the equally firm faith of the Utilitarian philosophers in the efficacy of their calculus of pleasure and pain as the unfailing test of every action. And the result in both cases is similar. Like the Hindu authors, the Utilitarians seem to have come to the same conclusions which thinking men would come to in respect of various social problems of the day. Probably, they employed the same processes of thinking as ordinary men. But they would insist that their only test was by means of that infallible touchstone, the calculus of pleasure and pain.[65] To resume our point, we are not suggesting that any custom could be treated as *Dharma*, if a law-giver out of sheer fancy chose to look upon it as such. What we emphasize is the idea that the scope of *Dharma* is so very comprehensive because in it come to be incorporated all the rules and regulations concerning all aspects of life. Secondly, this practice of embodying in the sacrosanct scheme of *Dharma* a healthy rule or precept makes it possible for law-givers to introduce changes necessary, due to time and place, without challenging the validity of the conception itself. The conception of *Dharma* thus goes on adding to its content until its scope defies definition. If a work on *Dharma* may include the discussion of the duties of the castes and the orders, it may also include instructions as to the proper way of appeasing certain deities. This, we may say, is in keeping with the spirit of Hinduism, which can accommodate within its system the crudest forms of animism as also the most subtle speculations on the nature of the Absolute.

We may now return to our point. We noted the tendency in the *Śatapatha Brāhmaṇa* and the Upanishads to identify the established

---

64. cf. Bentham: 'Nature has placed man under the empire of *pleasure* and *pain*. We owe to them all our judgments, and all the determinations of our life.' (*Principles of Legislation*, p. 2)—and '...legislation thus becomes a matter of arithmetic.' (p. 32.)

65. See Dickinson: *The Meaning of Good*, pp. 70-71.

order of society with the scheme of *Dharma*. The *Dharmasūtras* carry forward this method. Thus, Āpastamba maintains that there are four castes, Brāhmaṇa, Kshatriya, Vaiśya and Śudra, and amongst these, each preceding (caste) is superior by birth to the following.[66] The functions of each of these are also definitely laid down. Not only are there specific duties for the four castes but there are also equally obligatory duties for the four stages into which a man's life is divided. All these are said to be in accordance with *Dharma*, which also lays down definite duties for the king. The same in essence is the scheme followed by Gautama, Baudhāyana and Vasishṭha. The authors of the *Dharmaśāstras* or *Smṛitis* also continue the same procedure and discuss the various duties of castes and orders, of the king in his manifold relationships, of the guilds and corporations—all under the broad title of *Dharma*. With their injunctions on these topics we are not for the moment concerned. What interests us at this stage is the development in the conception of *Dharma*.

These works imply that *Dharma* is not only the Law that governs the phenomena of nature; it is not merely the Law which somehow mysteriously governs human conduct. The concept of *Dharma* comes to be more definitised here. Out of the vague conception of the Law, holding together the whole universe, animate and inanimate, emerges the concrete conception of Svadharma, which means one's own *Dharma*. Thus, the Brāhmaṇa has his Svadharma, the Kshatriya has his Svadharma, the Vaiśya and the Śudra have their Svadharma; there is a definite scheme of Svadharma for the Brahmachārin, the Gṛihastha, the Vānaprastha and the Sannyāsin. Further, Svadharma lays down duties for ordinary times as well as duties for times of distress. An elaborate classification of *Dharma* thus springs up and there is a scheme of Svadharma for the king also. So far as the individual is concerned, his highest duty is conceived to be the fulfilment of his Svadharma in all aspects of life. That really is the purport of the discourse to Yudhishṭhira by Bhīsma, when the former was so touched by the carnage of the great war, that he thought of retiring to the forest. The teaching of

66. Prasna I, Patala I, Khanda I, 3, 4.

the *Bhagavad-gīta* on this point is to the same effect. "Better one's own duty (Svadharma) though without excellence, than the duty of another well performed."[67] It is by faithfully discharging the duties with respect to one's Svadharma, that one obtains the '*summum bonum.*' To quote the *Bhagavad-gīta* again, "Every man intent on his own respective duties, obtains perfection (eligibility for the path of knowledge)."[68] The Buddhist *Dhammapada*[69] expresses the same view when it says: "Let no one forget his own duty for the sake of another's, however great; let a man after he has discerned his own duty be always attentive to it."

Kauṭilya, who is often looked upon as having divorced politics from religion and having built it up on a positive basis, does not really stand apart from the line of the authors of the *Dharmasūtras* and the *Smṛitis.* He too regards the fulfilment of Svadharma as obligatory on all: "The observance of one's own duty leads one to Svarga and infinite bliss. When it is violated, the world will come to an end owing to a confusion of castes and duties."[70]

This emphasis on one's own duty illustrates the Hindu view of *Dharma. Dharma* signifies a certain harmony, divine and eternal, which pervades the whole universe and which therefore covers the world of man—the rulers and the ruled alike.[71] The violation of Svadharma therefore would bring about nothing less than chaos and confusion throughout the universe. That shows how supremely important is the discharge by everyone of the duties of his station in life.

When *Dharma* is thus translated into or equated to Svadharma, it is brought into a definite relation with man's life. It is at this stage that the conception of *Dharma,* which so far appeared to be unrelated to the individual, is so interpreted that in the due discharge of one's *Dharma,* the ultimate end of human life—viz.

---

67. XVIII, 47.
68. *Ibid.*, 45.
69. XII, 166.
70. *Artha.*, Bk. I, Ch. 3.
71. Beni Prasad: *Theory of Govt. in Ancient India*, p. 347.

moksha—is assured. In this way, Svadharma leads ultimately to moksha; it is thus a means to an end. From the point of view of the empirical existence, however, Svadharma may even be regarded as an end in itself; for man's duty here can be no more than performance of duties laid down by *Dharma*, in the expectation of its due reward in the realization of the ultimate end of existence.

We thus get a clue to the solution of our problem. We can now see what is meant by saying that the end of the Hindu State is the maintenance of *Dharma. Dharma*, as we have seen, reduces itself ultimately to Svadharma, which in turn is the way to salvation. The ultimate end of the Hindu State, then, is to see that each individual observes his Svadharma and is thus enabled to realise emancipation or final release, which is the goal of all existence. The State in Hindu thought is the instrument to secure the highest good for the individual. We must, however, not be misled by appearances. The highest good of the individual is conceived of in a particular and peculiar way, and the State is an instrument to secure the highest good as conceived in that particular way. We must thus see what the highest good is, according to Hindu ideas: for that alone will enable us to see the bearing of the end of the State (as represented by *Dharma*) on the problems of citizenship and the true nature of individuality.

And here we come across a peculiar characteristic of Hindu thought. The beyond and the hereafter have always had a peculiar fascination for the Indian mind. From the earliest times, the Indian seers speculated on the nature of the ultimate Reality behind and beyond the passing, changing, perishable phenomena of the empirical world. The result of the great quest have been embodied in the various systems of Indian Philosophy. These systems, while differing *inter se* on certain fundamental issues, are however agreed on the postulates, aims and conditions for a realisation of the religious purpose of life.[72] The doctrine of Karma, which fixes the responsibility of all his actions on the individual, the fruits of which

72. This part of the argument is based on Dasgupta's *History of Indian Philosophy*, Vol. I, pp. 71 ff.

accrue to him in a series of births is accepted by all the Indian philosophical systems, and in Buddhism in particular, the law of Karma becomes, as it were, the highest principle of the universe. This doctrine of Karma explains the endless cycle of births and deaths, which an individual has to pass through. The problem was how to break through this endless cycle. Different answers were given by different philosophers. To some, the only path of salvation was through knowledge, to some through various intellectual and spiritual exercises, while to others Bhakti or devotion offered itself as the proper solution. All of them, however, were agreed that this empirical existence was a source of misery.[73] The individual has no hope of finding his true nature except by cutting off the various worldly ties. In all the philosophical systems and more particularly in Sānkhya, Yoga and Buddhism, the belief that this world is full of sorrow is strongly emphasized. If the Āśrama Dharma imposed on all the duty of passing through the Gṛihastha stage, it was recognised that the last stage in life here must be one of complete detachment from the world. The life of the contemplative forest-dweller had a peculiar fascination for the Hindus,[74] for, it seemed to be the nearest approach to the ideal condition of blessedness in which the soul would be quite unaffected by joy or sorrow, by happiness or misery, by friendship or enmity, by the feeling of hot or cold, in short, by all the pairs of opposites. It may be true to say, with Dasgupta, that this pessimistic view loses all terror as it closes in absolute optimistic confidence in one's own self and the ultimate destiny and goal of emancipation.[75] What we have to observe, however, is that such a view generates a feeling of indifference, if not actual loathing and hatred for this world. And this profoundly influences the Hindu conception of the State and human relationships. In India, it has been truly said, philosophy has never been merely an intellectual exercise in vain hair-splitting. It has always been a matter of realisation.

---

73. cf. A.S. Geden's Article on 'salvation' in *Ency. of Rel. and Ethics*, Vol. XII.

74. cf. "We see everywhere in the history of man that the spirit of renunciation is the deepest reality of the human soul." Tagore: *Sannyasi*, p. 151, also Sādhanā, p. 4.

75. *op. cit.*, p. 77.

Once the truth dawned upon the seeker, he generally made an attempt to translate it into practice. The *Gītā* and the Upanishads, the teaching of the Buddha, of Mahāvīra and of Śankara, all illustrate this peculiar comradeship between religion, philosophy and social life in India. It is on account of this comradeship that the influence of metaphysical speculation has been so great on the conception of the Hindu State. Underlying the doctrine of moksha—final release—is that deep-rooted conviction of the essential poverty and wretchedness of earthly existence, which according to A.S. Geden[76] is so characteristic of every variety of Eastern thought.

The goal of human existence, then, is moksha. There are differences of opinion as to what this exactly means. Moksha literally means release, but release from what? And answers to this question are really the subject-matter of the deepest philosophy. We may not probe into the mysterious intricacies of metaphysics to find out the correct answer. Our concern is essentially with the scheme of life laid down in our ancient works. If moksha is the goal of life, if moksha, in other words, is the highest good which man must strive to attain, let us see how, by what means, by what kind of conduct, he may hope to attain it. Whatever the exact meaning of moksha be, if we can say that the means laid down for the attainment thereof are such as can be the foundations of a truly ethical life, it should be enough for our purpose. That is to say, we must only know what scheme of life and values is laid down as obligatory for the State to maintain in order that the "highest good" may be attained.

Who is, then, "the good man" according to our ancient thinkers? The good man is really he who discharges his Svadharma. *Dharma* is the central principle, loyalty to which is to be expressed by each observing his Svadharma. If this Svadharma is so conceived that it inculcates the real nature of personality as expressing itself in the pursuit of the common good, we should have a satisfactory basis for the State. Unfortunately, this is not the case. The Indian

76. Article on "Salvation" in *Ency. of Religion and Ethics.*

mind, dwelling on the most difficult metaphysical problems, has not cared to develop a true conception of ethical life. Not that there are no ethical ideas in Hindu thought. What we mean is, the Hindu view of life—the goal of life as well as the means for the attainment thereof—leaves no scope for a strenuous ethical life, a life in the pursuit of the common good. Thus, we noticed above that in the *Ṛig-veda,* Varuṇa is taken to be the god in charge of the moral law. But the question of the nature of right action was never seriously attended to by our philosophers. In the *Brāhmaṇas,* there is no theory of ethics, the ideas of the prevalence of the moral order and the punishment of sin occurring in the *Ṛig-veda* cannot be found in living force any longer in the *Brāhmanas.*[77] Somehow, the de-ethicizing process has manifested itself. "In the *Ṛig-veda,* the most impressive figure is Varuṇa, the up-holder of Ṛita," in the *Atharva-veda,* he sinks into comparative insignificance, and in the *Brāhmaṇas,* "through the correct performance of sacrifice one can attain one's end," "the divorce between religion and morality is almost complete."[78] Similar remarks have been made regarding the Upanishads. "The problem of the Upanishads is not primarily that of human conduct;" it is essentially a religious quest—a quest after Reality.[79] And what the Upanishads give us for the solution of the problem of human conduct is, after all, that "good and evil exist only for him who is in the state of avidyā;" "he who has attained deliverance is beyond good and evil."[80] The possession of knowledge makes a man independent of all morality, he would be excused for the slaying of an embryo, the murder of a father or of a mother.[81] We come across similar ideas in the *Bhagavad-gīta* where it is said, "He who knows this to be the killer and he who believes this to be killed, both these do not know that

77. See Keith: *Religion and Philosophy of the Veda,* pp. 468-69.

78. McKenzie: *Hindu Ethics,* pp. 18-20.

79. McKenzie: *op. cit.,* pp. 67-68.

80. *Chandogya Upa.,* iv-14-3; *Brihad Upa.,* iv-4-23; *Kausitaki Upa.,* iii-1.

81. Keith: *op. cit.,* pp. 584-585.

this neither kills nor can be killed."[82] "The highest good of the Upanishads," as McKenzie remarks, "is at its best a state of being in which all ethical distinctions are transcended."[83] The Buddha did a great service by cutting at the root of rites and ceremonies. He largely ethicized Karma. The *Dhammapada* lays stress on the duty to love in return for hatred and to do good in return for evil. The Buddha laid down the mutual duties of parents and children, of pupils and teachers, of husband and wife.[84] And yet the logical foundation of a truly ethical life, viz. the conception of individuality, could not be provided for by the Buddha, for to him there was neither the individual soul nor the universal soul. The *Bhagavad-gīta* marks a definite advance inasmuch as morality here takes to itself a content far more definitely positive than it has had in the other writings. But even here, the question of the sanction behind man's *Dharma* is not discussed; ultimately, *Dharma* is *Dharma.* God has willed things as they are. This again is not a satisfactory basis for morality.[85]

Further, the six systems of Indian Philosophy, differing profoundly in their implications regarding questions like the state of the emancipated soul, have one feature in common. They all alike involve the same attitude to the phenomenal world. For him who has attained to the philosophical stand-point the ethical is transcended.[86] Further elaboration is not necessary. We may well conclude that logically, there is no scope for ethics in the philosophical ideas and theories of the Hindus. Actually, as a matter of practice, various virtues of an ethical nature may be recognised, but these cannot be deduced from the postulates of their philosophy. Thus, bold and sublime in the depth and comprehensiveness of their metaphysical speculations, these sacred works tend to ignore morality here, the necessary objective counterpart of a truly religious life.

---

82. II, 19.

83. *op. cit.*, pp. 79, 91, 95.

84. *Ibid.*, pp. 107-109.

85. McKenzie: *op. cit.*, pp. 133 ff.

86. *Ibid.*, p. 157.

The Hindu view of the ultimate goal of life precludes the possibility of due attention to the development of that aspect of our life which seeks satisfaction only in comradeship with fellowmen. The world of ordinary experience is thought of as a barrier blocking the way to Reality. The love of kinsmen, the family ties, the manifold social relationships into which man necessarily enters, are so many obstacles in the path of the attainment of moksha. The performance of various duties is at best a mere discipline.[87] We see thus that the conception of Svadharma as leading to the ultimate end of life implies the separateness of the individual from his fellows. There is no place in this view for a common life of endeavour to attain the goal. Each one doing his duty attains the final goal, which it seems can be realised even apart from one's fellowmen. It may be that this insistence on the absolute necessity of everyone doing his own duty irrespective of the consideration as to whether others are doing the same was intended in the main to facilitate the practical working of the whole social structure. The danger of such an emphasis is, however, obvious; for, such a view fosters particularity and exclusiveness.

Now, let us look at the scheme of Svadharma as actually worked out to see the ethical significance of the code of conduct as laid down by various Hindu law-givers. If we are right in maintaining, as we have done so far, that there is no scope for a truly ethical life on the basis of our ancient thought, we should find that the duties laid down as Svadharma must necessarily lay emphasis on each individual achieving the final goal. We should like to see if

87. Ganganatha Jha in *The Philosophical Discipline* (Kamala Lectures 1928) has tried to refute the view that there is no room for morality in Indian Philosophy. But even he has succeeded in showing only that there is a course of discipline which every aspirant after Jnana must go through, before he can reach the highest state. This discipline, he says, is not merely physical but intellectual, ethical and spiritual as well. But is this really the point? The defect we noted above is that Hindu thought does not reconcile the ordinary duties of life with the demands of the ultimate good. Can we say that in the very performance of certain duties, in the very discharge of even the smallest obligations in life, we actually realise ourselves, that there is our moksha? If we admit, as Jha does, that when the goal is reached, all distinctions are negated, in other words, the supreme good is not an ethical good, do we not create an unbridgeable gulf between the duties in life here and the goal of life?

Svadharma is so planned as to enable man to seek his good in the company of his fellowmen.

Dharma, that is, Svadharma, may be classified under six heads:[88] (i) the Varṇa-dharma, (ii) the Āśrama-dharma, (iii) the Varṇāśrama-dharma, (iv) the Guṇa-dharma, (v) the Nimitta-dharma, (vi) and the Sādhāraṇa-dharma.

The Varṇa-dharma refers to the duties of the individual as a member of his Varṇa or class. Of the four Varṇas, the Brāhmaṇa, the Kshatriya and the Vaiśya, are entitled to initiation, the study of the Veda and the kindling of the sacred fire, whereas the Śudras are not.[89] The duties of the Brāhmaṇa are said to be six: studying the Veda, teaching, sacrificing for himself, sacrificing for others, giving alms and accepting gifts. The duties of a Kshatriya are: studying, sacrificing for himself, bestowing gifts and protecting the people. A Vaiśya must study, sacrifice for himself and bestow gifts like the Kshatriyas; his special duties are agriculture, trading, tending cattle and lending money at interest. And the Śudra must serve the other three classes. In times of difficulty, men of the higher castes might take to the occupations of the next lower, but in ordinary circumstances, a man must stick to the occupations fixed for him according to the Varṇa-dharma scheme.[90]

This briefly is the scheme of Varṇa-dharma; and the duty of the State would be to secure conformity to it. The difficulties of such a scheme being rigorously followed in practice are evident; but they do not concern us; for, our aim is to examine the *ideas* of the Hindu thinkers on matters connected with our main problem. It may yet be remarked that the Hindu authors do not devote equal attention to finding the solution of the problem of the duty of the State to the mixed castes, such as for instance are referred to by Manu.[91] They would probably be allowed to follow their own customs and practices, it appears. As regards the

88. cf, *Yaj. Smṛiti:The Mitākshara,* pp. 3-4.

89. See *Āpastamba,* Prasna, I, Patala 1, Khanda 5; *Gautama,* Ch. I; *Vasishtha,* Ch. II, 3; *Baudhāyana,* Prasna, I, Adhyaya 2, Khandika 3-6.

90. *Vas.,* II, 14; *Manu,* I, 88; also X, 1-5; *Śānti Parva,* LX, 8-29.

91. *Manu,* X, 6 ff. also cf. *Yāj.,* I, 90; *Vishṇu,* XVI, I.

intrinsic merits and demerits of the scheme itself, firstly, it may be stated that it involves a denial of equal opportunity for every individual to realise the best that is in him. Division of labour in the interests of society as a whole is indeed a laudable plan; but when certain types of work are branded as inferior and therefore relegated to a certain class of people only, the resulting system cannot be looked upon as in any sense healthy. It would not be too much to say that such a system involves a violation of the most elementary principles of social justice.[92] We shall have occasion to discuss this point later in connection with the Hindu conception of citizenship.

As regards the ethical implications of the Varṇa-dharmas, it may plausibly be maintained that they inculcate co-operation. The duties of the Brāhmaṇas to teach and to sacrifice for others, the duty of the Kshatriyas to protect the people, the duty of the Vaiśyas to look after agriculture and trade and the duty of the Śudras to devote themselves to the service of others seem to teach the individual to be helpful to others. It would seem that these duties are not primarily directed to the interest or the good of the individual as apart from others. Rather, it might be suggested, these are duties which ask the individual to forget himself in the service of others. Nothing can be farther from the truth. It may at once be admitted that the Varṇa-dharma inculcates certain common duties; but we shall be sadly mistaken if we take this to signify that the individual realises himself only in and through society. Nor does it mean that the individual was ever advised to observe the Varṇa-dharma, because he would thereby be contributing to the common welfare. In the oft-quoted Purusha-sūkta in the *Ṛig-veda,* some scholars have read a very profound meaning. They have taken it to imply the organic view of society where each limb contributes to the welfare of the whole.[93] But it may as well have been no more than an attempt to justify or at

---

92. S.V. Venkateswara's defence of the social inequality of Varṇa-dharma scheme as indicating the moral claim of all to have equality of opportunity entirely fails to carry conviction. See his *Indian Culture through the Ages*, pp. 38-40.

93. cf. Dikshitar: *Hindu Administrative Institutions*, p. 51.

least to explain away the established order by interpreting it as divinely ordained. So long as the individual is not asked to identify himself with the whole, which is society, so long there cannot be an idea of genuine co-operation. Dr. Radhakrishnan maintains that "the institution of caste illustrates the spirit of comprehensive synthesis characteristic of the Hindu mind with its faith in the collaboration of races and the co-operation of cultures."[94] We must admit that the hierarchy of classes is an excellent arrangement to provide a framework for different natures and aptitudes. It may also be true that if the Śudras were not to be excluded from the civilizing influence of the Āryas, the only place for them could be on the lowest rung of the social ladder. These, however, are explanations of a historical nature. They may enable us to understand the problem; but they are not justifications for the same. Historically speaking, the Varṇa-dharma scheme may have been inevitable. But the moral implications of the same need not therefore be accepted as sound. The Hindu authors nowhere speak of the unity of purpose as between the various social groups. The idea that each by performing his allotted function in the Varṇa scheme contributes to the good of the whole does not come out clearly in any of the sacred works. Hence, though the Varṇa-dharma scheme has social bearings, it does not relate the individual to society. It does not bring out the nature of man's relation with the other members in society. It only links him up with the ultimate goal of life.

Let us pass on to the consideration of the Āśrama-dharma. The scheme of Āśramas seems to have been of great antiquity. According to Deussen, the theory of the four Āśramas was in course of formation in the older Upanishads. Prof. R. Davids maintains that the four stages of life came into vogue after Buddha, while Prof. Jacobi would regard them much older than both Jainism and Buddhism.[95] Any way, it is relevant to note here that Āśrama-dharma divides the life of man into four stages: the Brahmachāri, the Gṛihastha, the Vānaprastha and the Sannyasta.

---

94. *Hindu View of Life*, pp. 93 ff.

95. cf. N.N. Law: *Studies in Indian History and Culture.*

The initiation ceremony of a Brāhmaṇa takes place in the eighth year after conception, of a Kshatriya in the eleventh year after conception and of a Vaiśya in the twelfth.[96] Thus commences the Brahmachārin stage. The student must approach a Guru and receive instructions from him in the Veda. The Brahmachārin is to live in the Guru's Āśrama, observe scrupulously various rules of personal purity and decorum, beg his food, control his senses and obey the teacher in all matters. It is in this stage of life that his outlook on life is moulded under the guidance of his teacher. The Epic summarises the duties of the Brahmachārin as follows:

> "Always studying the Vedas, silently reciting the mantras obtained from his preceptor, worshipping all the gods, O Yudhishṭhira, dutifully attending upon and serving his preceptor with his own body smeared with clay and filth, the person leading the Brahmacharya mode of life should always observe rigid vows, and with senses under restraint, should always pay attention to the instructions he has received. Meditating on the Vedas, he should live, dutifully serving his preceptor and always bowing to him. Unengaged in the six kinds of works, never doing with attachment any kind of act, never showing favour or disfavour to anyone and doing good acts even to his enemies—these, O Son, are the duties of a Brahmachārin."[97]

What is the type of citizen that such a training would produce? There can hardly be any doubt that the discipline for a Brahmachārin is intended mainly to fit him, not for the Householder's stage, not for a life dedicated to the cause of the community, but rather for the realisation of the ultimate goal of all existence. The emphasis laid on the control of the senses, on the simplicity of life and on the duty of always obeying the Guru, would necessarily develop in the student the ascetic bent of mind. From the very earliest stage of his life, he would develop a sense of the unreality of this world and would cultivate the habit of looking to something beyond for things of lasting value. The

---

96. *Manu,* II, 36; also *Gautama,* I, 57, II; *Vasiṣṭha,* XI, 49-51; *Vishṇu,* XXVII, 15-17. *Yāj.*, I, 14.

97. *Śānti Parva,* LXI, 18-21.

matters spiritual would always have a special fascination for him and it is probably such training which one generation after another must have received that explains the remarkable achievements of ancient Indians in the realms of metaphysical speculation. One of the main causes of the stability and vitality of the Indian culture through the ages may well have been the sound system of imparting instruction to pupils in the Brahmachārin stage, from which they would come out strongly imbued with a faith in the divinely ordained nature and the essential soundness of the existing social organisation and the traditional cultural ideals. It is certain, however, that the sort of training imparted to a Brahmachārin was not meant, at least explicitly, to qualify him for the next stage in life. He would indeed be taught that the Householder's stage *must* be gone through. The Hindu authors often speak of the great importance of the Gṛihastha stage. Thus, according to the *Mahābhārata*,[98] "the highest religion as sanctioned by the scriptures, consists in the duties of a householder." The Hindu authors certainly realised that the production of wealth in order to sustain the whole society was the duty of the Householders only. The other orders were dependent on the Gṛihastha—nay, the gods, pitṛis, guests, servants and the birds and beasts all were supported by the Gṛihastha.[99] Thus, the Householder's mode of life is declared to be the root of all the others.[100] And yet, the Brahmachārin's life is one continuous round of discipline and studies. The healthy questioning spirit that would challenge the traditional order would not be fostered in such an environment. And it requires no argument to show that the scheme of instruction would emphasize philosophical studies but not social problems. That is why we find India has had philosophers, she has had 'law-givers' but she has hardly had any social philosophers, studying social phenomena and trying to relate these in terms of cause and effect.

---

98. *Śānti Parva*, XXIII, 2-7.

99. *Ibid.*, 4-5; *Manu*, III, 77-80; *Vasishṭha*, VIII, 14-16; *Vishṇu*, LIX, 27-28.

100. *Ibid.*, CXCI, 10.

Then comes the Gṛihastha stage. The duties of a Gṛihastha may be summarised as marriage, begetting children, the performance of various daily rites, including the Śrāddhas and earning wealth by fair means.[101] According to Praśastapāda,[102] the duties of a 'Kṛitadāra Gṛihastha,' are comprised in the five sacrificial ceremonies or Yajnas every morning and evening. These five Yajnas are: (I) Bhutayajna or sacrifice to Bhutas, (2) Manushyayajna or the serving and entertaining of guests, (3) Devayajna or the offering of incense to the sacred fire, (4) Pitṛiyajna or paying respect to the dead through Śrāddhas etc. and (5) Brahmayajna or the reading of the sacred texts, the Vedas. This is the traditional list of the duties of a Householder repeated in different ways by different works. Kauṭilya, too, gives us in essence the same list. "The duty of a householder," he says, "is earning livelihood by his own profession, marriage among his equals of different ancestral Ṛishis, intercourse with his wedded wife after her monthly ablution, gifts to gods, ancestors, guests and servants, and the eating of the remainder."[103]

Studying the above list we see that the holy duties which have a direct reference to society are those which Praśastapāda calls 'Manushyayajna,' or the duties of entertaining guests. The other duties have reference to Pitṛis and gods and Devas, with which we are not here concerned. The duty of hospitality to guests is certainly looked upon as important by Hindu authors. One of the injunctions to a Snātaka is "Treat the guest as a god." It would seem that here at least we come across an injunction which speaks directly of the individual's duty to others in society. If, however, we set about analysing the treatment to be given to guests, we find that the hierarchical idea has entirely vitiated it; for who is the guest, in the first place? Manu starts by saying that one must offer to a guest who has come (of his own accord) a seat and water, as well as food, garnished (with seasoning) according to

---

101. *Manu,* III and IV; *Śānti Parva,* XC, 1-10.

102. S.K. Maitra: *The Ethics of the Hindus,* pp. 13-16.

103. *Artha.,* Bk. I, Ch. 3.

his ability.[104] But this rule is soon modified; for, we are told, "A Kshatriya (who comes) to the house of a Brāhmaṇa is not called a guest, nor a Vaiśya, nor a Śūdra, nor a personal friend, nor a relative, nor the teacher."[105] Further, such a Kshatriya may be fed after the Brāhmaṇas have eaten; and the Vaiśyas and Śūdras may be allowed to eat *with his servants,* showing (thereby) his compassionate disposition."[106] This injunction, then, rules out the duty of hospitality to others as such. The Atithidharma does not mean that we have duties to one another, as we are all intimately related. Vishṇu agrees with Manu. "By honouring guests," we are told, "he (i.e. the householder) obtains the highest reward." Heaven is declared to be the reward of one who honours the guest. But, "a guest" (atithi) is defined as "a Brāhmaṇa who stays for one night only." A Kshatriya may indeed be entertained, but he is not "a guest" strictly speaking and so he must be entertained only after the Brāhmaṇa guests have eaten. The Vaiśyas and Śudras may be given food with his servants.[107] The differential treatment[108] to be given to guests takes away from the merit of hospitality by itself. The kind of hospitality recommended by these law-givers does not at all open out the path for realisation of one's best self in the company of or in the service of fellowmen. As the reward of this so-called hospitality accrues to the host the merit of the gift of a cow. If a guest is not properly treated, it is not a breach of social decorum; it is not a failure to observe a rule of social conduct. It has a magical significance. The sins of the uncared-for or ill-treated guest are visited on the defaulting host! This also points unmistakably to the fact that it was not the duty to fellowmen, which interested the law-givers as much as the spiritual reward involved in this hospitality. Thus, even in the Gṛihastha's duties

104. *Manu,* III, 99.

105. *Ibid.,* 110.

106. *Ibid.,* 11-112. *Mine.*

107. *Vishṇu,* LXVII, 2-46.

108. 3 cf. 'Even as regards the highly lauded and essential duty of a householder, viz. hospitality, the Brahmin has his privileges. He need not treat a non-Brahmin as his guest unless he comes on the occasion of a sacrifice'—Dr. Ghurye: *Caste and Race in India,* p. 54.

the social implications are not brought out; the truly social aspect of man is not emphasized. The Gṛihastha stage is particularly important because man has to repay the three-fold debt. The great value of the Gṛihastha stage lies in the fact that its end is the begetting of a son; and so discharging the debt to Pitṛis. Perhaps, the basic fact that the institution of family is the coping-stone of the whole social arch and that therefore the interests of family-life must be looked after seems to have proved too strong to be ignored. But even then, such a life was only the second best; for, it is said, 'knowing this (the self) people of old did not wish for offspring ...... for desire of son is desire for wealth, and desire for wealth is desire for worlds.'[109]

The duties of a Vānaprastha and a Sannyāsin need not detain us long. The Vānaprastha stage is to begin when "the householder sees his body wrinkled and hair white on his head" and "when his children get children.'[110] This period is to be passed in the performance of severe austerities. In the summer, the hermit must expose himself to five fires; during the rains he must sleep in the open air; in winter he must wear wet clothes. The recitation of the Veda and the five sacrifices are not to be given up.[111] The fourth stage is the Sannyāsin's. "In merit" says the *Mahābhārata*, "it reigns supreme over the three other modes of life," and is therefore declared to be 'the refuge of all.' The Sannyāsin must cut himself off from all society. He must not stay for more than one night in one village.[112] His main endeavour now must be to free himself from every kind of attachment. Such a person is shorn of anger and error. He regards equally a clod of earth and a lump of gold. He has neither friends nor enemies. Praise and blame, the agreeable and the disagreeable, are all the same to him.[113] As Manu puts it, "Let him not desire to die, let him not desire to live; let him wait for (his appointed) time as a servant

---

109. *Brihad. Upa.*, iv-4-22.

110. *Manu,* VI, 2; *Mahābhārata, Mokshadharma Parva,* CCXLIV, 4; *Vishṇu,* XCIV, 1-2.

111. *Manu,* VI, 2-30; *Vishṇu,* XCIV, 1-13; *Mokshadharma Parva,* CCXLIV, 4-30.

112. *Vishṇu,* XCIV, 6; cf. *Manu,* VI, 61 ff.

113. *Mokshadharma Parva,* CCXLV, 36.

(waits) for the payment of his wages...... Let him patiently bear hard words, let him not insult anybody, and let him not become anybody's enemy for the sake of this (perishable) body."[114] This sort of stolidity is to be attained by reflecting on the transitoriness of the passage through mundane existence and on the impure nature of the body, upon the destruction of beauty by old age, upon the pain arising from diseases, bodily and mental, or due to an excess (of the bile etc.), upon the pain arising from five naturally inherent affections (viz., ignorance, egotism, love, wrath and dread of temporal suffering), on his having to dwell in an embryo covered with everlasting darkness, on his having to dwell between urine and faeces, on the manifold anxieties arising from the study of the Veda, on the anxieties in youth from not obtaining the objects of pleasure, on the union of those whom we hate and the separation from those we love[115]...... In short, the Sannyāsin must constantly remind himself that life is all suffering and what seems to be pleasure is no more than delusion. Thus, when he becomes indifferent to all objects, he obtains eternal happiness both in this world and after death.[116]

The last two stages of one's life are thus to be given to withdrawing oneself from all the attachments of the world. It may be noted that even a good act should not be done by the Sannyāsin, for that will bring in good fruit, which will necessitate a new birth. As far as possible, the Sannyāsin and even the Vānaprastha must lead a life of isolation. Attachment is 'bandha' or bondage. The story of Bharata, the sage, who had to be born again for the only crime of having dearly loved a little deer, is well-known. The *Gīta* indeed points the true way, when it commends the performance of acts without the desire of fruit. Acts, the *Gīta* rightly maintains, are inevitable, so long as one lives. The real Sannyāsa is not the abandonment of acts but the abandonment of or non-attachment to the fruit thereof. In other words, once you are convinced of the rightness of a certain act, you must do it at

---

114. *Manu,* VI, 45-47.

115. *Vishṇu,* XCVI, 25 ff; cf. *Manu,* VI, 61 ff.

116. *Manu,* VI, 80.

all cost, you must do it for its own sake, letting the result take care of itself. But that does not seem to be the view involved in these injunctions of our ancient lawgivers. The Vānaprastha and the Sannyāsin are not enjoined to lead a selfless life of active social service, to set themselves to repair some of the evil in this world, to take up the cross of suffering on behalf of humanity. If they were asked to renounce the family ties and the other narrow ties of the Gṛihastha stage in order to feel and act as members of a larger family, in order to place themselves at the service of a larger circle, where all are brethren, in other words, if the Vānaprastha and the Sannyasta stages were but opportunities to transcend narrow loyalties in the interests of higher ones, such a scheme would be really commendable. That, however, is never the idea behind the scheme of Āśrama-dharma. On the other hand, all worldly affections are looked upon as so many ties that bind a man down to the misery of this world. The Vānaprastha and the Sannyasta stages are meant for giving the individual an opportunity to cut off these ties. Society is thus denied the contribution of these men out of the richness of their experience. It is exactly when men are fit to be the leaders of new thought, capable of advising the younger generation on the basis of their experience in life, that they are required to withdraw into the solitude of the jungle. Even if we admit that the Gṛihastha stage was regarded as the most important, it was not the final stage. Towards the end of his life, the individual must come to a stage where there would be no worldly ties. The Āśrama-dharma scheme is, thus, not only not social in its implications; it even fosters a spirit of indifference to the needs of society by its emphasis on the necessity of "renouncing the world" by undergoing the discipline laid down for the Vānaprastha and Sannyasta stages.

The third category of Dharma in our classification above is the Varṇāśrama-dharma. It refers to the duties of a man in a certain stage or Āśrama of life, with special reference to his Varṇa. For instance "a Brāhmaṇa student of the Vedas should carry a staff of palāśa wood etc." The Guṇa-dharmas are special duties; for instance, the protection of subjects incumbent on the king who has been anointed according to scriptures and possesses other qualities. The Nimitta-dharmas are secondary duties, such as "penances which are occasioned by omitting to perform what is commanded or by committing what is forbidden."[117]

These duties are thus laid down for particular occasions for particular men or classes. They need not, therefore, detain us. Far more important are the Sādhāraṇa-dharmas, which mean duties which are common to all.

Let us, then, consider the significance of Sādhāraṇa-dharmas, the duties which are obligatory on all people, irrespective of distinctions of caste and order. They are thus to be distinguished from the Varṇa-dharmas and the Āśrama-dharmas which are obligatory only with reference to particular Varṇa or Āśrama.

The Sādhāraṇa-dharma scheme, according to Manu, comprises the following ten duties:-

(1) Firmness of purpose in the discharge of one's duties (dhriṭiḥ).

(2) Forgiveness (kshamā).

(3) Self-control (damaḥ).

(4) Non-appropriation (or avoidance of theft).

(5) Cleanliness (śaucha).

(6) Restraint of the senses and sensibilities (Indriya-nigrahaḥ).

(7) Wisdom (Dhīḥ).

(8) Learning (vidyā).

(9) Veracity (satyam).

(10) Abstention from anger (akrodhaḥ).

Elsewhere he gives us a summary of the same: (I) Abstention from injuring, (2) veracity, (3) non-appropriation, (4) cleanliness and (5) control of the organs are declared to be "the summary of the law of all castes."[118]

---

117. *Yaj. Smriti*, I, 1, *Mitāksharā*, pp. 3-5.

118. It is not quite clear whether these duties are meant for four castes as well as the four orders. Perhaps, they refer to the four castes only and the list of ten-fold duties noted above apply only to the four orders of the twice-born. The Śudras, then, would be excluded from this scheme of Sādhāraṇa-dharma. However, this does not necessitate any alteration in our criticism of the scheme.

A glance at the above list shows, as S.K. Maitra rightly points out,[119] that all the duties have reference to the attainment of the individual's own perfection. There is no implication of positive social service in this scheme. Forgiveness (kshamā), avoidance of theft (chauryābhāva) and even veracity have the autonomy of the individual in view. Self-control, cleanliness, the restraint of the senses and abstention from anger definitely inculcate a certain attitude of mental equilibrium, which, however, need not issue out into active social service. No one indeed can deny the great value of attaining to a well-balanced state of mind, unruffled by the passing gusts of passion and desire. A man, who is not a sovereign of himself, who has not the capacity to harmonise his impulses and instincts, and who, therefore, lives from moment to moment, without attempting to see life as a whole, is certainly not the man to be of service to society. Service to society—and therefore to oneself—does require at least something of the state of a 'sthitaprajna,' which the Gītā so well describes. The "samatva," which is said to be the essence of "Yoga" is thus a very essential part of the equipment of a man to enable him to realise himself. Where Manu errs is in his emphasis exclusively on duties which aim at the autonomy of the individual, leaving society out of consideration. The Sādhāraṇadharmas are common to all, but do not involve a conception of the community as one whole.

According to Yājñavālkya,[120] the Sādhārana-dharmas are the following:-

(I) Harmlessness.

(2) Veracity.

(3) Non-stealing.

(4) Purity—internal and external.

(5) Controlling of the organs, i.e. employment of the intellect and the organs of action in lawful objects.

---

119. *Ethics of the Hindus,* p. 8.

120. *Yāj.*, V, 122. See Mitāksharā commentary on the same.

(6) Liberality, i.e. removal of the pain of living creatures by giving them food and water.

(7) Self-control, i.e. repression of the internal organ, the mind.

(8) Mercy, i.e. protecting the afflicted.

(9) Forgiveness, i.e. non-emotion of the mind under injury.

The list is somewhat different from Manu's but it is evident that the duties even here are primarily with reference to the individual's self-sufficiency.

Vishṇu[121] has amplified the traditional list. He enumerates the common duties as under:-

> "Forbearance, veracity, restraint, purity, liberality, self-control, not to kill (any living being), obedience to one's Guru, visiting places of pilgrimage, sympathy (with the afflicted), straightforwardness, freedom from covetousness, reverence towards gods and Brāhmaṇas and freedom from anger."

Let us turn to the list of "eternal duties" for all Varṇas as enunciated by the *Mahābhārata.* These are[122]:-

> "The control of anger, truthfulness, justice, forgiveness, begetting children upon one's own married wives, purity of conduct, avoidance of quarrel, simplicity and maintenance of dependants."

It is hardly necessary to point out that the spirit behind these different lists of duties is essentially the same and one looks through these in vain to find a provision for duties of positive social service. In this respect also Kauṭilya agrees with the authors we have already noticed. The common duties according to him are:-

> "Harmlessness, truthfulness, purity, freedom from spite, abstinence from cruelty and forgiveness."

Further references are hardly necessary. We might only mention the list of Sāmānya duties according to Praśastapāda, for,

---

121. II, I6 and 17. cf. *Vasishṭha,* IV, 4 and X, 30.

122. *Śānti Parva,* LX, 7.

as we shall see, it seems to strike a new note in some respects. The Sāmānya duties, according to him are[123]:-

"Moral earnestness (Dharme Śraddhā), Regard for the Spiritual (Dharmé manaḥprasādaḥ).
Refraining from injury to living beings (ahimsā).
Seeking the good of creatures (bhūtahitatva).
Speaking the truth (Satyavachana).
Refraining from theft (asteya).
Sexual continence (brahmacharya).
Sincerity, purity of motive (anupadhā).
Renouncing or restraining anger (krodha varjana).
Ablution, personal cleanliness (abhishechana snāna).
The eating of linseeds and other specified substances on special occasions for the object of the purification of the body (suchi-dravya sevana).
Devotion to the Deities recognised by the Vedas (viśishta devatā bhakti).
Fasting on special occasions (upavāsa).
Moral watchfulness (apramāda) i. e. the unfailing performance of the unconditional duties (nitya-naimittikānām karmāṇam avashyambhavena karanam).

The noteworthy feature of this classification is the inclusion of 'bhutahitatva' along with 'ahimsā.' These two represent, as Dr. Maitra rightly points out,[124] the positive and the negative aspects of a moral inclusive and humanitarian ideal of life in which the individual can achieve his moral end only by going beyond himself instead of remaining confined within the stone walls of independent neutrality. We only wish the ideal of 'bhūtahitatva' had been explained more fully. It is true, indeed, that Praśastapāda seems to be striking out a new path by laying down "seeking the good of creatures" as an essential duty of every man. It is possible, however, to exaggerate the importance of this injunction. For, if it means merely seeking the good of others just out of sympathy, as it were, without feeling the identity of our good with their good,

---

123. S.K. Maitra: *Hindu Ethics,* p. 10; it is not clear that "Dharme Śraddhā" really can mean "moral earnestness;" but we follow Maitra here.

124. *Ethics of the Hindus,* p.17.

then, we are not after all very far from the spirit which lies behind Manu's "forgiveness," Kauṭilya's "forgiveness" and "abstinence from cruelty," or the injunction of the Epic to maintain dependants. And this meaning does not seem to be quite unlikely. The word "bhūta" refers to all living beings. "Bhūtahitatva" thus would mean seeking the good of all creatures—human and animal alike. This conception of the duty of man to see his self everywhere and to cultivate a feeling of compassion for all created beings is by no means foreign to Hindu authors.[125] It does not, however, imply that it is only in and through society, striving for a common end, that true self-realisation is possible.

The scheme of Sādhāraṇa-dharma, thus, does not really view the individual as a member of society determined by the conception of a common good. The Sādhāraṇa-dharmas are duties for all, irrespective of Varṇa and Āśrama. In that sense alone they are common duties. They are not common duties in the sense of duties which are obligatory on all members of society, striving after a common end. The emphasis on a common end is absent in Hindu works; and as Maitra concludes from a survey of various classifications of Sādhārana-dharma, "Hindu morality primarily aimed at self-autonomy. Even the communal duties have in fact this end of self-autonomy in view."[126] As we had occasion to point out earlier, the duties which have or seem to have a social and therefore genuinely ethical import are said to be obligatory only because they are "Svadharma" and so lead on to the ultimate goal of existence.[127]

We have thus examined the import of *Dharma.* The end of the Hindu State is, as we said, the maintenance of *Dharma.* And *Dharma* is a conception that determines the whole Hindu view

---

125. cf. *Bhagavad-Gītā,* VI, 32; XII, 4, 13; XVI, 2.

126. *Ethics of the Hindus,* p. 25; cf. *Bhagavad-Gītā,* III, 17-18.

127. Performance of such duties is said to bring its due reward only after death. Man is not realising himself here and now while performing his duties. cf. *Gautama,* XI, 29 (S. B. E., Vol. II, p. 235). "Men of several castes and orders who always live according to their duty, enjoy after death the rewards of their work and by virtue of a remnant of their merit they are born again in excellent countries, castes, families, endowed with beauty, long life, learning in the Vedas, virtuous conduct," etc.

of life. While *Dharma* is an eternal verity, an unchallengeable principle to which the whole universe is subject, it is at the same time the norm of conduct for men. As such, it is translated into Svadharma. The concept of *Dharma* as thus explained is broad enough to embrace all aspects of life. Economic, political, social as also religious topics are included under *Dharma*. The State is an institution—a very essential institution—to enable its members to realise the ultimate goal of life. This ultimate goal of life can be realised only if all the activities of life here are regulated in accordance with *Dharma*. In Hindu thought, there is no clear differentiation as between economic institutions, religious institutions or political institutions. Institutions, whatever their immediate purpose, are related to the ultimate end of life. There is thus an affinity of purpose between various institutions.[128] The caste, the family, the guild, the State—all these—have their value inasmuch as they provide the proper milieu for the individual to observe his *Dharma*. In this sense, all institutions in society are means to realise the same end in different ways. This does not, however, mean that the State is only one among many institutions; nor does it imply a division of sovereignty.[129]

We emphasize this point because it enables us to say what the place of the State in life is, according to Hindu authors. The end of the State or the purpose objectified by the State has an intimate bearing on the end of human existence itself. The State is not mere police; its sway extends over the whole sphere of *Dharma*. In the absence of the State, *Dharma* would be violated. Since the proper maintenance of *Dharma* is conceived to be the pathway to salvation, *Dharma* may even be looked upon as an end in itself, so far as empirical existence is concerned. There can thus be

---

128. As J.N.C. Ganguly points out, "The unity of *Dharma*, thus enunciated connected ethics with politics and sociology in the Hindu philosophical thought of the time and allowed religion to operate in spheres where it is said to be out of place, unfortunately, according to the tendencies of the modern day infused probably by the new-born scientific spirit." See article on "Phil. of *Dharma*", *Ind. Hist. Quarterly*, Vol. II, 1926.

129. See Ch. VII, Infra.

no doubt that the State has an important function to perform in the Hindu scheme of life. The remark of Bloomfield[130] to the effect that in the Hindu scheme of life there is no provision for the interests of the State cannot, therefore, be held to be wholly justified. We must however add that the conception of *Dharma* profoundly influences the Hindu view of the relation of the State to the individual. The State that emerges out of this association of *Dharma* is peculiar in several respects.

The proper criticism to make would rather be along a different line. That the State has its own place in the Hindu scheme cannot be denied. Only, the end of the State, as visualised by Hindu authors, is open to criticism. As has been pointed out earlier, the conception of *Dharma* has been taken to sanctify the existing social order with all the iniquity that is implied in the hierarchical arrangement. The existing social order is looked upon as *Dharma* objectified. This means the apotheosis of the 'status quo'. If the concept of *Dharma* were interpreted to mean that the ideal social order would be concretised *Dharma*, such a conception would indeed be healthy. The justification of the actual social order would be sought with reference to such an ideal. Then it would be an elevating influence even as Plato's "city which is in heaven" is meant to be. Unfortunately, however, the Hindu authors have always taken the actual to be the ideal. Instead of making an attempt to actualise the ideal and translate the ideal in institutional terms, the actual has been idealised. Such an attitude makes inevitably for conservatism[131] and kills the spirit of critical examination. There is to be no analysis of the very foundations of the social order.[132] By connecting the State with *Dharma*, the distinction between the actual and the ideal is ignored; and the State is placed beyond the range of criticism.

---

130. *Religion of the Veda*, pp. 4-5.

131. "The end of law is the preservation of the 'status quo,'" is also the conclusion Mr. Pal comes to after an examination of the Hindu conception of *Dharma*. See *The Hindu Philosophy of Law*, pp. 123, 134 and 139.

132. cf. also: "*Dharma* implies...... in short the maintenance of the established order"—Hopkins: *Ethics of India*, p. 92.

Further, the analysis of the concept of *Dharma* has showed us that it places undue emphasis on only one aspect of life—one which aims at self-sufficiency. Thus, there is no incentive left for the individual to look beyond himself. *Dharma* can be realised by leading a self-centred and contemplative life, mechanically conforming to the rules and regulations of the Varṇa-dharma and Āśrama-dharma. Hence, we come to the conclusion that the State is based not on the mutual need for protection, not on the common need for an institution to hinder the various hindrances to the fullest development of the members. It is made to rest rather on the exclusiveness of men, on the differences between man and man. It does not embody a common purpose. There is nothing to be realised as the common good by society as a whole. The individual does not feel that he is unreal apart from membership of society. In brief, the Hindu theory fails to observe that the various social relationships into which man enters determine his individuality. Apart from these relationships, the individual is an abstraction. To the Hindu thinkers, however, the individual is what he is, even apart from society, that is to say, even without his willing himself as one among others (or many), all ennobled by the common purpose. For him, self-realisation must come only through the disinterested performance of the prescribed duties. The sanction behind these duties, the validity of these rules and regulations it is not for him to question or challenge. The failure to grasp the real nature of individuality is always fraught with danger. "An un-criticised individualism," as Bosanquet rightly observes,[133] "is always in danger of transformation into an uncritical collectivism." Hobbes started with "free" individuals and ended with the unrelieved gloom of abject slavery to the great Leviathan. Spencer similarly failed to reconcile the two ideas of the State as an organism and the State as a joint-stock protection company for mutual assurance. Political obligation can be adequately understood only by a proper appreciation of the nature of individuality, which political thinkers in the west from Plato and Aristotle down to Green and Bosanquet have tried to

133. *Philosophical Theory of the State,* p. 66.

expound. The Hindu thinkers do not indeed postulate or start with an antithesis between the individual and society. In fact, the problem does not at all present itself to them in that light.[134] The individual is looked upon as realising his end in life by performing various duties according to *Dharma.* In practice, this performance must certainly have necessitated the maintenance of those social conditions which alone can make the due discharge of these functions possible. And this means, the Hindu State, in practice, must have maintained a definite system of rights and obligations. That, indeed, cannot be denied. Only, looking to the end of the State and the goal of human existence as visualised by Hindu authors, we must say that they fail to develop a correct theory expressing the right relation between the individual and society. The individual has a definite set of duties to discharge but its significance he does not know. He is only to conform to the particular scheme, because that is his Svadharma. The idea of a common purpose vitalising the life of all members of society does not emerge at all. As a result, the individual has to be constantly looking to the distant future when he will attain his true freedom. The proper discharge of his duties here and now becomes, in this view, a mere discipline, perhaps a necessary evil, which one has to submit oneself to, in order to attain the higher goal. The kingdom of God accordingly seems to be somewhere afar in the clouds and not on this earth. In other words, the end of the State does not relate man to his fellow beings aiming at the realisation of social good here and now; the State does not represent a co-operative endeavour. "The ideal of the State as set forth in the Epics and later Sanskrit literature is," as Dr. N.N. Law profoundly observes,[135] "the attainment of the *summum bonum* 'moksha' through Dharma, Artha and Kama." Let us not, however, forget that the State is to maintain conditions in which each individual by himself may work out his own salvation. The effort to attain salvation is only

---

134 Barker suggests that a realization of the apparent antithesis between the individual and the State is in fact necessary in order that a real synthesis may be ultimately possible. *Greek Political Theory,* p. 4.

135. *Aspects of Ancient Indian Polity,* p. 144.

individually made. It is not collective at all.[136] The members of the State are not asked to realise that together they stand and together they fall. Each is asked to mind his Svadharma. The idea that each minding his Svadharma contributes to the good of the whole and that it is only with reference to the good of the whole that Svadharma has value does not occur in any of the Hindu works. Hence, we cannot accept the statement that "the State is the machinery for the *collective* attainment of salvation by the people under its care."[137] That is why, as we pointed out in an earlier chapter, the conception of the State as a moral organism, realising, in the words of Aristotle, individual virtue in the common good cannot be found developed in Hindu thought.

To conclude, the end of the State as visualised by Hindu thinkers is defective from various points of view. The State comes to be looked upon as the agency for the perpetuation of the "status quo." It aims, not at attaining the good of the whole but merely at maintaining an equilibrium in society, which involves the denial of the equal worth of all persons, the elevation of the higher classes in society and the degradation of the lower. There is, thus, injustice at the very root of the Hindu conception. The goal of human existence, as visualised by them, is, again, imperfect. Man is not, in their view, a member of a moral and spiritual organism. He seems to be an entity by himself, capable of realising himself apart from his membership of society. Thus, the Hindu State which sought to translate this ideal in institutional terms was bound to be defective and imperfect. We shall see in the next chapter how this conception of *Dharma* which determines the end of the State determines also the place of the individual in the ordering of the State.

---

136. cf. Pal: *The Hindu Philosophy of Law*, p. 169; he is right in the main, though his phraseology is rather confusing.

137. *Aspects of Ancient Indian Polity*, p. 144

CHAPTER VI

THE STATE AND THE INDIVIDUAL IN HINDU THOUGHT

"On the one side, in fact, inequality harms by pampering; on the other by vulgarizing and depressing. A system founded on it is against nature, and, in the long run, breaks down."

—MATTHEW ARNOLD—Quoted by Tawney: *'Equality'*, p. 24.

The end of the Hindu State is, as we have seen, to maintain *Dharma.* This means that the State must maintain conditions in which each individual may fulfil his Svadharma. We must try to see now more definitely the nature of the relation of the State and the individual involved in such a view; we must consider, in other words, the place assigned to the individual in the ordering of the State.

Political theory in the west begins with the Greeks. The Greek mind dared to wonder about things and to raise questions about them. The religious motive appealed but little to the Greeks. They were thus free from the sense of the littleness of human thought and endeavour. On the other hand, they were imbued with a strong sense of the value of the individual. The individual was thus placed over against the State in the works of the Sophists and a reconciliation of the antithesis was the achievement of Plato and Aristotle.[1]

This reconciliation must be related to the conditions of life in the Greek city-state. These conditions of life form the background of Greek political theory. The Greek city was peculiarly suited to

1. Barker: *Greek Political Theory*, p. 4.

the work of unifying the interests of men. It was the home of all occupations and of all classes. Life within common walls drew men together into a natural intimacy. Its market place, its gymnasium and its colonnades gave men an opportunity for a common life. The city, thus, was a club as well as a "unit of government."[2] The spirit of the city became a solvent for the more "instinctive forms of social unity."[3] The family tie was subordinated to the feeling of community resulting from the common life in the city. The Greeks thus identified their very civilization with this process of incorporation in the city and thus became "citizens." The ideal of the ancient city-state thus came to be "a partnership in all science; a partnership in all art; a partnership in every virtue and in all perfection."[4] This explains Plato's saying in the *Laws* that "all one's family and all one's wealth belong to the city." The life of the citizen was conceived as being fulfilled in the city; the good man and the good citizen were identical, for man was looked upon as essentially a "political" animal. His activities as a member of the city-state were calculated to lead to the development of his various faculties and to the blossoming of his personality.[5]

The beginnings of political life in Italy were similar to those in Greece.[6] The Greeks and the Romans were not far distant from each other in ethnological descent; their languages were really and obviously related; there was a close relation between their religious practices. Thus, on the whole, there was a close relation between their civilizations. Their environmental conditions, too, were largely similar. The two peoples developed the same kind of polity—that which the Greeks called the "Polis" and for which

---

2. Barker: *Greek Political Theory,* pp. 17-19.
3. Mac Iver: *The Modern State,* p. 73.
4. cf. *Delisle Burns: Pol. Ideals,* ch. on "Athenian Liberty".
5. As Hobhouse remarks, "the history of liberty as a principle of high social organization begins only with the emergence of the civic state." Liberty, to the Greeks, he observes, meant not merely the autonomy of the city-state as against subjection to any other power, it meant within the State the rule of law; it also implied a positive share in self-government, the power to rule and to be ruled with a view to life at its best—*The Elements of Social Justice,* pp. 91-92.
6. What follows is based on the discussion of the subject in Ward Fowler's *The city-state* and in Mac Iver's *The Modern State.*

the nearest equivalent Latin name was "Urbs." The form of the State, then, was, to start with, similar in Greece and Rome. And yet Rome's contribution lay, not in developing and perfecting the democratic city-state like Athens, but in building up a fabric of Empire with all its problems of organisation. By the year 300 B.C. the first great revolution in Roman history was completed; 'patrician' exclusiveness was broken and every department of government was thrown open to 'plebeians.' The people were clearly sovereign in the legislative assembly of tribes, presided over by the tribunes of plebs. The executive was under control, each magistrate being liable to impeachment and popular trial after his year of office. Yet democracy in the Athenian sense this was not; for the actual work of government was not done by the people. A new hereditary nobility, not indeed of patrician descent, but resting on service done to the State, acquired the virtual monopoly of high office. The Senate gradually grew in power and became foreign minister, financial minister and war minister responsible to no other person or assembly. Rome thus developed into an oligarchy. The citizenship in Rome thus did not mean that universal partnership which is associated with the Greek polity. From early times, as Mac Iver[7] points out, the Romans distinguished between civil rights—rights of equality before the law—and political rights—rights of membership in the sovereign body. In her career of conquest and expansion in Italy, Rome conferred civil rights on a number of towns and thus admitted them to partial citizenship. The principle of empire, however, soon proved incompatible with the city-state ideal.[8] The idea of representation did not occur to the Roman Senate. It fell back on the doctrine of power. The sense of citizenship, the basis of political order, was destroyed by the lack of opportunity for its exercise. To sum up, the problem of citizenship could not adequately be solved by Rome to meet the requirements of the Empire. The conception of citizenship, as involving active and constant participation in the affairs of the State, could develop

7. *op. cit.*, p. 97.

8. Mac Iver: *op. cit.*, p. 99; cf. Ward Fowler: *op. cit.*, pp. 318 seq.

only when the size and population of the State were strictly limited. In one respect, however, Rome did distinct service. To the Greek, the alien and the slave were outside the body politic. They could not claim the protection of the law. Rome brought about a healthy change in this respect. The traditional law of Rome, represented by the Twelve Tables, was, it must be admitted, to be applied only to her citizens. The "jus gentium" was originally a vindication and reservation of the peculiar right and privilege of the Roman citizen; but it gradually came to be the basis of justice for aliens and Romans alike. Out of this conception developed the idea of the universality of law, and herein lies the distinctiveness of the contribution of Rome.[9] However, what concerns us more here is the fact that by distinguishing between civil and political rights, the Greek ideal of citizenship was compromised and the perfect reconciliation of the State and the individual was thus out of the question.

With the downfall of Rome, the "State" as a unified institution, actually disappeared from Western Europe.[10] So far as political organisation was concerned, the achievement of the great classical evolution of citizenship was as if it had never been.[11] Feudalism was a polyarchy. It was the rule of the individual rather than of law. Not the claim of the State, not the welfare of the whole, but the claim of a lord and the right of a master maintained the obligation of men to one another. "Decentralisation, doubtful sovereignty, conflicting laws, union of church and State, and the association of landholding, political power, and personal allegiance—these characterised the politics of the Middle Ages."[12]

From the break-up of feudalism, there emerged the centralized monarchies of early modern Europe. Monarchy alone could save the people from the iniquity of feudal privileges. It only could solve also the intolerable conflicts of religion. The emergence of the national state is thus associated with absolute monarchy; and

9. Mac Iver: *op. cit.*, p. 115.

10. D. Burns: *Political Ideals*, p. 57.

11. Mac Iver: *op. cit.*, p. 155 ff.

12. Gettell: *Introduction to Political Science*, p. 61.

in the doctrine of the divine right of kings were reconciled, as it were, the claims of Caesar and of God.[13] This was, however, a temporary solution. The very influences which had exalted the king worked for his downfall or his reduction to the status of the "constitutional monarch." With the growth of intelligence and wealth the mass of the people demanded more political rights. The advent of the industrial age and the consequent diminution of the importance of agriculture in the economic life of nations made the working classes more and more self-conscious and articulate. As a result of these forces, the State moved towards democracy, creating new and complex problems which demand our most careful consideration to this day.

It is, then, with the rise of the modern nation-state that the old problem of the right relation between the State and the individual once again assumes importance. In the interval between the disappearance of the independent city-state and the rise of the modern nation-state, men's thoughts about life and conduct were cast, as Dr. Bosanquet[14] points out, in the mould of moral theory, of religious mysticism and theology, of jurisprudence. Up to about the sixteenth century, people in Europe were content to be governed from above. The Reformation prepared the ground for the new order. It triumphantly asserted the claim of the individual to the right of private judgment and thus opened a new era in the political life of Europe.[15] The French Revolution attempted to work out this idea but with many misconceptions and extravagances. To correct these and to evolve out a correct theory may be said to be the mission of the thinkers of the next century.[16]

The realisation that every political whole presents the same problem as was presented by the Greek city-state must be credited to the insight of Rousseau,[17] who revived the Platonic tradition by

---

13. J.S. MacKenzie: *Fundamental Problems of Life*, p. 123.

14. *Philosophical Theory of the State*, p. 8.

15. Vaughan: *History of Political Philosophy*, Vol. I, p. 10.

16. *Ibid.*, Vol. I, p. 16.

17. Bosanquet: *op. cit.*, p. 12; See also Barker: *Greek Political Theory*, pp. 388-389; and Vaughan: *Introduction to Rousseau's Social Contract*.

thinking of the State as a moral organism, although under the garb and in the vocabulary of the contract theory. In the works of Hegel, Green, Bradley and Bosanquet we see this tendency fully developed. The idealist theory of the State, thus, refuses to worship a supposed individual liberty which Mill, for instance, stood for. It rather emphasizes the moral well-being and betterment of the whole community and conceives of each of its members as attaining his own well-being and betterment in and through the community.[18]

Citizenship, in this view, is essentially an ethical function. It consists in the individual's identifying himself with the end of the State and contributing out of the richness of his own experience towards the furtherance of this end. In so determining himself by the conception of the common good, he realises his best self and respects only the law which he would consider obligatory on himself if he made up his mind rationally about the matter, taking into consideration all its aspects.

It must be noted, however, that the idealist theory of the State always has in mind the ideal State. The perfect reconciliation of the State and the individual which the theory postulates cannot be said to have been actually achieved in practice. How far the government of any particular State actually expresses the general will is quite a distinct question and the Idealist would certainly be prepared to accept the divergence between the ideal and the actual. When, therefore, the critics identify the actual with the real—in other words, when they thus implicitly reject the validity of the ideal—and still, when they criticise the "metaphysical" theory, much of their criticism, we must say, is really beside the mark.[19] The value of such criticism lies in the emphasis that it lays on the

18. Barker: *Political Thought in England* (1848-1914), p. II.

19. For instance, Hobhouse vehemently criticises Hegel's identification of freedom and law; but he does not take into consideration what we have said above, viz., that according to Hegel, freedom would be identified with obedience to the law in the *ideal* State (See pp. 32 ff. *Metaphysical Theory of the State*)—So, also, on p. 45, criticising Bosanquet's conception of the real will, he tells us that the actual alone is the real. "The man's will is in short just what it is with all its limitations, and not what it might be if these limitations were removed."

necessity of evaluating the actual achievement of institutions. Laski is thus right when he maintains that we must obey the State, not because its theoretic purpose is a splendid one, but because of our conviction that it is genuinely seeking to make that purpose valid in events.[20] This does not, however, make it unnecessary to enquire whether its theoretic purpose is really a splendid one, whether the ideal that it seeks to achieve is really a worthy one.

To revert to our point; the citizen obeys the law because, ultimately, he feels he is the author of the law. This involves active interest on the part of the individual in the work of legislation. It postulates also the eligibility of every citizen to help to carry on the work of administration by discharging executive and judicial functions. No man can be a good citizen unless he thus interests himself in the affairs of the State. It is in order to secure this sort of personal and active interest in the administration that political philosophers have often proposed to limit the number of citizens in the State. Thus, one of the conditions of a sound system of government, according to Rousseau, is that the State must be so small that the people can be easily brought together and may know with ease all the rest.[21] The problem before us today is the problem of maintaining the active interest of the large number of citizens in the working of the modern State. The point we seek to emphasize here is that the citizen must have "the will to will the common will." It is only by willing the common will and by thoroughly identifying himself with the good of the whole that he realises his true self. A citizen is the State in miniature and the State is the fulfilment of his personality. The consummation can be achieved by a process of integration, whereby the State would express the collective will in which the individual wills are all harmonized.[22]

We thus visualise citizenship as an ethical function and interpret it as a quest after the realisation of the common end—the end of

20. *Grammer of Politics*, p. 27.

21. *Social Contract*, Bk. III, Ch. IV.

22. Miss Follett: *The New State*, Chs. V and XIII.

the State. In such a view, the antithesis between the individual and the State disappears; for, it is the State in which the personality of the citizen is realised in its completeness. The cleavage between the rulers and the ruled also similarly vanishes; for, the citizens are really the rulers in their collective capacity. We have only to understand more fully the secret of the group process in order to be able to translate this conception in institutional terms. Much of the distrust of democracy that has of late been often evinced, is traceable to the realisation that our institutions today do not really make possible the genuine expression of the true citizen-spirit. By our present method of the counting of heads, we are, perhaps, not getting at the general will at all. This, however, is a problem in the technique of the organisation of democracy; it does not reflect on the nature of democracy as such. We would only point out that in the ideal State, there would be "the closest of moral bonds between the citizen and the State," for, "the State is the condition of the organised good life for its members."[23]

Such a conception of citizenship could not emerge in India. Various factors seem to have combined to prevent such a consummation. The vastness of the country itself would naturally make it impossible for the citizen to aspire to have an effective share in the administration of the State. There could not, in such circumstances, be any possibility of the intense, common life for the people such as was possible in the Greek city-state. Further, the unsettled condition of society on account of the continuous struggles between different tribes must have necessitated a strong executive. In times of conflict, the capacity of leadership and personal bravery comes to be highly prized. Such conditions would strengthen the power of the king. The cleavage between the ruler and the ruled may also have been the result of the racial

23. Bosanquet: *Philosophical Theory of the State,* pp. 266 ff.

cf. also: "For us, therefore, the citizen is not merely enfranchised. He is not a good citizen merely because he votes...... The concentric circles of his obligation and responsibility are, as the surface of a pond, ever widening. The State is the people functioning jointly in governance of themselves and the citizen is the individual thus functioning." Newman: *Citizenship and Survival of Civilization,* p. 57.

differences between the conquerors and the conquered. The Aryan conquerors came into contact in their new home with people who were different from them in respect of language, religion, usages and physical type. There could evidently be no question of associating with them in the work of government in the true citizen spirit. The only problem could have been: should these conquered tribes be exterminated or should they be somehow assimilated to the new culture? Complete extermination would be a manifest impossibility. The new settlers were after all very few in numbers as compared with the native people. There is little doubt that the Aryans had to do a good deal of fighting with them. Before long, however, the necessity of extending the Aryan fold so as to admit the native peoples must have been felt. To this end probably the Śudra class must have been recognised as an integral part of society.[24] The fusion of various cultural types in India was made possible by the inclusion of various gods and goddesses of different tribes into the corpus of Hinduism.[25] It must not be forgotten, at the same time, that the Aryans had a strong sense of racial pride. Though the Śudras were recognised as members of the body politic, they were never to be treated as equals; and various disabilities were therefore imposed on them. The Śudras thus were excluded from a share in political power. These various conditions are unfavourable to the growth of a democratic form of government. The only alternative would be the aristocratic and the monarchic types; and of these the former alternative was ruled out probably because of the recognition of the important position of the priestly class in the State. The story of the struggle between the Brāhmaṇas and the Kshatriyas has been handed down to us in the Vedic legend of Visvāmitra and Vasishṭha. The Brāhmaṇas as a class do not, however, seem even to have aspired to be kings themselves. On the other hand, the

---

24. cf. "The former (i.e. Brāhmaṇas, Kshatriyas and Vaiśyas) are conquering Aryans; the latter (i.e. the Śudras) are subject Dasyus." *Cambridge History of India,* Vol. I, p. 54. See also, Ragozin: *Vedic India,* pp. 282-283.

25. Vide Radhakrishnan: *Hindu View of Life,* pp. 37-40. *Ency. of Religion and Ethics,* Vol. V, Article on *Dravidians.*

theory of the "joint lordship" of the Brāhmaṇa and the Kshatriya is found developed even in the *Śatapatha Br.* where, it is said, the priesthood and the nobility are set upon the people.[26] This does not mean that the Brāhmaṇa rules along with the Kshatriya. The Brāhmaṇa can exercise his influence only indirectly through the king. In practice, the Brāhmaṇa may have dictated the policy of the king. In theory, however, his functions are clearly differentiated from those of the Kshatriya.[27] At the same time, the precedence of the Brāhmaṇa over the other classes in society is recognised. Thus, a Brāhmaṇa may be without a king but it is quite improper that a king should be without a Brāhmaṇa.[28] In the words of the *Mahābhārata*, "whatever exists in the world is the property of the Brāhmaṇa...... The Brāhmaṇa eats but his own food, wears but his own apparel, bestows but his own alms, for the Brāhmaṇa is the chief of all castes, and the greatest and the best."[29] There seems, thus, to have been a sort of an 'entente cordiale' between the king and the Brāhmaṇas, whereby though the privileges of the latter are recognised, political power is really vested in the king. Thus, the monarchical element in the State gained greater strength. It is not surprising, then, that monarchy has been the predominant type of government in ancient India.

On account of the operation of factors enumerated above, the masses were excluded from the exercise of political power. Various other factors seem to have operated in the same direction. The vastness of the country and the other factors noted above may have made impossible the development of an active civic sense, such as would be fostered by means of intimate contacts with fellowmen within the limits of a city-state. The influence of the natural environment which probably brought home to man his insignificance as compared to the magnitude of the forces of nature may also to some extent account for the absence of the strong sense of individuality favourable to the growth of an

26. XI, 2-7-19.
27. *Ibid.*, IV, 1. 4. 1-6.
28. Vide Dutta: *Origin and Growth of Caste in India*, p. 5o.
29. *Śānti Parva*, LXXII, 9-12; cf. also *Manu*, 100-101.

active civic consciousness.[30] The lines along which the Indian polity could develop were thus determined by the various forces which moulded Indian history from early times.

But these environmental forces cannot be regarded as the complete explanation of the absence of the true democratic spirit. This can be explained only with reference to the Hindu view of life with all that it implies. This means, we must study more closely the conception of *Dharma*; for it is the conception of *Dharma* that determined the right relation of the State and the individual.

Dharma, as we have already seen, has not been visualised as a common quest after the realisation of a common good. This is the initial difficulty. The State is not a co-operative endeavour in which all are alike interested. The function of the State is no more than to prevent a confusion between the *Dharmas* of the different classes and orders in society. The State is thus made to rest on the exclusiveness of men. It may be said that everyone is interested to see that the performance of Svadharma is possible by one and all. In that sense, the State has a purpose in which all are interested. But that is not the same as saying that the State is an institution through membership of which alone man can be what it is in him to be. Thus, the very motive for the true citizen-spirit is absent because of the conception of *Dharma* summed up as Svadharma. So long as one quietly performs one's duties, the interactions of one's life and actions with those of the other members of society are ignored. In a word, the end of the State is the maintenance of a condition of equilibrium and not the harmonisation of the interests and loyalties of the members with reference to the conception of a common good, which has a meaning for all of them.

Further, *Dharma* differentiates between the worth of persons. Just as *Dharma* does not give us the idea of a common good to be realised by us in and through the membership of society, so, too, it ignores the potentially equal worth of persons for contributing to the common good. Thus, not only are the people at large excluded

30. cf. R. Davids: *The Origin and Growth of Religion*, pp. 21-22.

from political power, but there is not even the recognition of the equality of all before the law.[31]

We saw in the last chapter how as early as the period of the *Brāhmaṇas,* the hierarchical idea had already emerged. The development is continuous since then. According to Manu, the Brāhmaṇa is by right the lord of the whole creation.[32] Whatever exists in the world is his rightful property.[33] He has a special claim to be honoured if he goes as a guest to any householder.[34] He has thus various privileges in society. But that is not all. Even the king must give him preferential treatment. While emphasizing the king's duty to act with justice, he enjoins him to be lenient towards Brāhmaṇas.[35] One of the best means for the king to secure happiness is said to honour the Brāhmaṇas.[36] Though dying (with want), a king must not levy a tax on Śrotriyas, and no Śrotriya residing in his kingdom must perish from hunger.[37] It is the privilege of the Brāhmaṇa to investigate law-suits and the Śudra is explicitly debarred from settling the law.[38] In the matter of eliciting true evidence, the Brāhmaṇa is only to be asked to 'speak;' a Kshatriya to 'speak the truth;' a Vaiśya is to be admonished by mentioning his kine, grain or gold, while a long list of threats and imprecations is regarded as necessary in order to get correct evidence from a Śudra.[39] Thus virtue is assumed to be the possession of the Brāhmaṇa, while the Śudras are looked upon as essentially sinful. It is this attitude that reveals itself in the graded punishments prescribed for the four Varṇas for the same offence.

---

31. cf. P.N. Banerjea: *Pub. Admn. in Ancient India,* pp. 170-71.
32. *Manu,* I, 93; it seems the Brahmanical profession had begun to set up claims of superiority and sacredness for itself even in early Ṛig-Vedic times. Refer Dutt: *Beginning and growth of caste in India,* pp. 45-46.
33. *Manu,* I, 100.
34. *Ibid.,* III, 109-110.
35. *Ibid.,* VII, 32; cf. also *Vishṇu,* III, 96 and Yājñavālkya, I, 334.
36. *Manu,* VII, 88. Yājñavālkya, I, 333.
37. *Manu,* VII, 133; cf. *Āpastamba,* II, 10, 26, 10; *Gautama,* X, 9; *Vasishṭha,* XIX, 23.
38. *Manu,* VIII, 9, 21.
39. *Manu,* 88 ff. *Vishṇu,* VIII, 19 ff.

Let us take, for instance, the offence of defamation.[40] If a Kshatriya defames a Brāhmaṇa, he is to be fined one hundred 'panas;' for the same offence, a Vaiśya must be fined one hundred and fifty or two hundred; whereas, a Śudra must suffer corporeal punishment. On the other hand, a Brāhmaṇa would be fined fifty 'panas' for defaming a Kshatriya, twenty-five for defaming a Vaiśya and only twelve for defaming a Śudra. Further, for offences of twice-born men against those of equal caste, the fine would be twelve 'panas;' but if, a Śudra were to mention the names and castes (jātis) of the twice-born with contumely, 'an iron nail, ten fingers long, shall be thrust red-hot into his mouth.' The punishments for adultery are also similarly graded,[41] the Brāhmaṇa being always shown leniency. He may even take the law into his own hands, without bringing the offence to the notice of the king; for, by his power alone, he may punish his foes.[42] He always has the privilege of compelling a Śudra to work for him; for, the Śudra was created by the Self-existent to be the slave of the Brāhmaṇa. Further, the Śudra can have no property and a Brāhmaṇa may confidently seize it, if there is any with him.[43] The Brāhmaṇa is exempted from capital punishment; instead, it is said, tonsure has been prescribed for him. The killing of a Brāhmaṇa is looked upon as a grievous sin and the king must not even think of such a thing as capital punishment for the Brāhmaṇa. As the text puts it, 'Let him never slay a Brāhmaṇa, though he has committed all (possible) crimes; let him banish such an offender, leaving all his property (to him) and (his body) unhurt.'[44]

In the *Mahābhārata*, Yudhishṭhira is advised to "wait humbly upon the gods and the Brāhmaṇas," for the Brāhmaṇas are "the foremost of human beings on earth."[45] They are always to be

40. *Manu*, VIII, 267-284. cf.; *Vishṇu*, V, 23-25; 100-103. Also *Brihaspati* XX, 5-15; Nārada, XV, XVI, 22, 25; *Gautama*, XII, I.

41. *Manu*, VIII, 374-378; cf. *Vasishṭha*, XXI, 2-5; Yājñavālkya, II, 288.

42. *Manu*, XI, 31-32.

43. *Manu*, VIII, 413, 417.

44. *Manu*; VIII, 379-381; *Vishṇu*, V, 8; *Bṛihaspati*, XXVII, II.

45. *Śanti Parva*, LVI, 12, 22 (p. 78); LXXII, 10-12.

shown mercy, even when they deserve punishment. Thus, "if a Brāhmaṇa becomes guilty of Brahmanicide or of violating the bed of his preceptor, or other elders, or of causing miscarriage, or of treason against the king, he should be punished with banishment. No corporeal punishment is laid down for him."[46] In what may be called his coronation oath, Pṛithu is made to promise the Brāhmaṇas exemption from punishment.[47] In the *Mahābhārata* it is said, "Even the Brāhmaṇa who is destitute of knowledge is a god,...... learned, or unlearned, he is always a great deity...... So even if the Brāhmaṇa is always engaged in evil deeds, he is still considered as deserving of honours."[48] The penalty for Brahmanicide is the most severe; for killing a Vaiśya, it is distinctly less severe but a Śudra's life matters no more than the life of a dog, a bear or a camel.[49]

It is remarkable that even the *Arthaśāstra* of Kauṭilya is not free from this obsession by the hierarchical idea. Kauṭilya is in this respect also in line with the traditional Brahmanical works. Thus, we are told, "if among Brāhmaṇas, Kshatriyas, Vaiśyas, Śudras and outcastes, any one of a lower caste abuses the habits of one of a higher caste, the fines imposed shall increase from three 'panas' upwards (commencing from the lowest caste). If any one of a higher caste abuses one of a lower caste, fines imposed shall decrease from two 'panas.'[50] A Brāhmaṇa witness, before examination, is only to be enjoined to "tell the truth;" a Kshatriya or a Vaiśya witness is to be threatened with the loss of his sacrificial and charitable deeds; whereas a Śudra is to be admonished as follows : "Whatever thy merits are, in thy former birth or after thy death, shall they go to the king, and whatever sins the king may have committed, shall they go to thee if thou

46. *Ibid.*, 32-33, pp. 78-79; cf. *Gautama,* XII, 46, *Baud.*, I, 10, 18, 17.

47. *Śānti Parva,* LI X, 108.

48. *Anuśāsana Parva,* CLI, 20-23.

49. *Śānti Parva,* CLXVI, 52-56. cf. "Murder is only 'real murder' when it is committed on the person of a priest. The priest is exempt from capital punishment and from oppression. None may insult or hurt him."—Hopkins: *Ethics of India,* pp. 59-60.

50. *Artha.*, Bk. III, Ch. XVIII.

utterest falsehood; fines shall also be levied on thee, for facts as they have been heard or seen will certainly be subsequently revealed."[51] The law regarding adultery is similarly harsh on the Śudras. "A Kshatriya, who commits adultery with an unguarded Brāhmaṇa woman shall be punished with the highest amercement; a Vaiśya doing the same shall be deprived of the whole of his property and a Śūdra shall be burnt alive wound round in mats."[52] And the Brāhmaṇa is to be treated leniently. "Whatever may be the nature of the crime, no Brāhmaṇa offender shall be tortured." Banishment seems to have been the maximum punishment for him. "After having thus branded him and proclaimed his crime in public, the king shall either banish a Brāhmaṇa offender or send him to the mines for life."[53] Thus, according to Kauṭilya also, law is a respector of persons, inasmuch as the punishment for the same crime differs for persons of different castes. It is really surprising in the face of this evidence to be told that caste distinctions and undue partiality to Brāhmaṇas are assigned no prominence in the *Arthaśāstra*.[54]

The *Śukranītiśāra* does not deal specifically with the punishments to be meted out to offenders of different castes. There is evidence, however, to show that the author did not seek to attack caste privileges. Thus, the ten advisers of the king were to be Brāhmaṇas. In their absence, Kshatriyas could be appointed. In the absence of Kshatriyas, even Vaiśyas might be appointed; but "Śūdras are never to be appointed even if they be qualified."[55] The appointment of other officers was also to be determined with reference to the caste (varṇa).[56] It is further laid down that "one should not desire

---

51. *Arthaśāstra*, Bk. III, Ch. XI.
52. *Ibid.*, Bk. IV, Ch. XIII.
53. *Ibid.*, Bk. IV, Ch. VIII.
54. *Ibid.*, Foot-note by Shama Sastri, p. 220. Shama Sastri tries to make out a case for regarding what he calls "an abnormally high punishment for a minor offence" on the part of a Śudra, the result of interpolation. This need not necessarily be so for it is not inconsistent with the general spirit of the *Arthaśāstra* as reflected above.
55. *Śukra*, II, 859-861.
56. *Ibid.*, II, 862-867.

equality with gods, cows and Brāhmaṇas ...... One should always worship, respect and serve these. It is not known how much of the divine spirit is implanted in them."[57] Judging from the spirit of these sayings, it might safely be said that the author of this work had nothing to say against the differential treatment of offenders on the basis of caste. It is interesting to note here that Alberuni's account of India also bears witness to the fact that punishments were graded according to caste.[58]

The privileges of the Brāhmaṇas and the disabilities of the Śudras are asserted with great vigour in the *Agni Purāṇa.* Giving presents to Brāhmaṇas is regarded as one of the duties of the king. The king is enjoined to "worship, protect and supply the Brāhmaṇas with the necessaries of life."[59] The Brāhmaṇas are not to be taxed, even if the king is in dire distress.[60] A Kshatriya assaulting a Brāhmaṇa should be punished with a fine of hundred 'panas,' a Vaiśya found guilty of a similar offence should be liable to a fine of two hundred 'paṇas,' while a Śudra should expiate his guilt by losing his life. On the other hand, a Brāhmaṇa having used criminal force on a Kshatriya should be punished with a fine of fifty 'panas,' but the fine should be only twenty-five and twelve 'panas' for assaulting a Vaiśya and a Śudra respectively. Abusive language addressed to a Brāhmaṇa is to be severely punished. A Brāhmaṇa, however, is exempt from capital punishment, banishment being the "ultima ratio" for him.[61] "A Brāhmaṇa leading the most wicked life and guilty of the most heinous crimes, should not be hurt or killed, as the killing of a Brāhmaṇa is the deadliest of all sins."[62]

It is not necessary to multiply such statements. The Hindu State has from the earliest times been dominated by the hierarchy of the Varṇas, and the Brāhmaṇas have always claimed privileges for

---

57. *Ibid.*, III, 448-451.

58. *Alberuni's India*, Vol. II, pp. 161-162.

59. *Agni Purāṇa*—Translated by Dutt, Ch. CCXXII, 15.

60. *Ibid.*, Ch. CCXXIII.

61. *Agni Purāṇa*—Ch. CCXXVII.

62. *Ibid.*, Ch. CCXXII, 17-18.

themselves to the detriment of the other classes in society. Our ancient thinkers, thus, could not realise the necessity of securing the equality of civil and political rights.[63]

To such a development, even Buddhism did not prove a hindrance. It is a mistake to suppose that Buddhism was against the institution of caste as such. Considerable misunderstanding as to the real nature of this institution in the time of the Buddha has arisen because of the failure to take into account the fact that the home of Buddhism was in the north-east of India.[64] The stronghold of Brahmanism was in the Madhyadeśa. As it spread eastwards, its social rules became lax. Secondly, the authors of the Buddhist texts were unsympathetic if not hostile to the Brahmanical rules of life. Many of them were Kshatriyas prior to becoming monks. This accounts for their insistence on the precedence of the Kshatriya class over the rest. Really speaking, as Richard Fick has ably shown,[65] the Buddhist writers never cared in the least to contradict the caste theory as such. They never thought of introducing a better organisation of society. The Buddha was, indeed, "the first to establish his universal brotherhood (Sanga) of coenobite monks, open to all persons of all ranks."[66] This order of monks was not a hierarchy, but a brotherhood dominated by the one idea that all life is misery. This brotherhood opened its arms to all corners of all ranks. The Buddha, however, was not a champion of social equality or a denouncer of all distinctions of rank and ancient traditions.[67] The caste idea was so deeply rooted in the minds of the great majority of monks that even as members of the brotherhood some thought that one who was a Kshatriya or

---

63. For an account of the civil and religious disabilities of the lower castes, reference may be made to Dr. Ghurye's book: '*Caste and Race in India*', pp. 10 ff. Even under the Peshwas, the lower castes were more harshly punished than the higher ones—*Ibid.*, p. II.

64. R. Davids has tried to show that in Buddhist times, "The caste system, in any proper or exact use of the term, did not exist." (See *Buddhist India.*, p. 62.) This view is, however, inadmissible. (*Vide Camb. History of India*, Vol. I, p. 294).

65. *Social Organisation in North-East India in Buddhist Times*, pp. 17-31.

66. M. Williams: *Buddhism*, pp. 72 ff.

67. *Ibid.*, p. 71.

a Brāhmaṇa before initiation deserved the best quarters, the best water and the best food.[68] The ideal of a true Brāhmaṇa is highly spoken of, not only in Brahmanic literature but even in Buddhist writings.[69] It is remarkable that even the *Dhammapada* declares that a true Brāhmaṇa goes scatheless, though he has killed father and mother and two valiant kings, though he has destroyed a kingdom with all its subjects.[70] In the Pali Canon and in the Jātakas, the division of society into four castes, Khattiya, Brahmana, Vessa and Sudda is taken for granted as something self-evident. The insistence of the Buddhist works on the worthlessness of caste has reference to the eligibility of a man for attaining emancipation. "Khattiya, Brāhmaṇa, Vessa, Sudda, Chāndāla, Pukkusa will be all equal *in the world of the gods,* if they have acted virtuously here." "Of no value are the Vedas, of no value is birth or caste for the future world," runs a Jātaka text. So far as life here is concerned, the caste distinctions are taken for granted, with all their implications. Thus, we have it on the eminent authority of Fick that the castes continued after the spread of the Buddhistic doctrine quite as well as before, and that the social organisation was not in the least altered by Buddha's appearance.[71]

Thus, Buddhism is not a gospel of social equality. The equality in the world of the gods, referred to in the Jātaka texts quoted above, does not lead to the conception of social equality here. Hence, the Buddhist teaching could not lead to the development of the idea of the equality of civil and political rights. On the other hand, the Brāhmaṇas were free from taxes even in the eastern lands, in spite of the undisputed fact that the greater portion of the land was in their hands. Whether they also claimed immunity from capital punishment in these parts of the country, we cannot say with certainty.[72] We can be certain, however, that the iniquity of the hierarchical scheme of Varṇas was not destroyed—was not

---

68. *Tittira Jātaka*, I, 217, quoted by Fick, p. 33.
69. Dutt: *The Origin and. Growth of Caste in India*, p. 261.
70. Ch. XXI.
71. *op. cit.*, p. 32.
72. *Ibid.*, pp. 211-212.

sought to be destroyed—by the teachings of the Buddha. The condition of the lower classes in society was on the other hand far from satisfactory. The lower castes such as the Chāṇḍālas were considered impure. Their very sight would cause pollution. They had therefore to be segregated from the rest of society and they were required to stay outside the town.[73] Taking these factors into consideration, it may well be pointed out that it is hardly correct to speak, as Shama Sastri does, of "the stupendous change in her (i.e. India's) social, religious and political institutions......brought about by the magic wand of a skilful wizard."[74]

We conclude, then, that the Hindu thinkers have never risen to the perception of the value of the individual personality as contributing to the common good. The hierarchical ordering of society lies at the very basis of the Hindu State. Thus, firstly, as we have seen in the last chapter, there is no recognition of a common good as the end of the State, to be attained by cooperative endeavour. And secondly, the State does not recognise the individual, apart from the class or caste to which he belongs. As Dr. Banerjea rightly remarks, "Individuals had rights and duties not as component parts of the body politic but as members of estates or classes in society."[75]

Let us see more closely the significance of the Varṇa scheme. Let us not mistake the Hindu position for Bradley's conception of the right relation between the individual and society, visualised in his chapter entitled "My Station and its Duties," in his *Ethical Studies.* There may seem to be at first sight a resemblance between the Hindu doctrine of Varṇa-dharma and the Bradleyan insistence on the performance of one's duties as determined by one's station. In reality, there is an important distinction between the two. All that Bradley wants to convey is that it is possible to realise true freedom by performing the duties of one's proper station in society. Each member of society can realise himself truly in the

---

73. Fick: *op. cit.*, Ch. XII.

74. *Evolution of Indian Polity*, p. 113.

75. *Public Administration in Ancient India*, pp. 39-41.

moral whole which society represents. Apart from this moral whole he cannot find the function which makes him himself.[76] We must remember that Bradley is here trying to counteract the fallacies of the so-called "individualist" theory. His aim is to show that "the individual" man, the man into whose essence his community with others does not enter, who does not include relation to others in his very being, is a fiction.[77] Man is rather a social being; "he is real only because he is social and can realise himself only because it is as social that he realises himself."[78] Bradley's insistence on the moral whole must be understood in the light of this aim. He emphasizes the conception of the State as a moral organism because he is contending against the view that it is a heap or a machine. In this moral organism, it seems as if the individual is swallowed up; it seems as if all that he counts for is the work he is doing in his allotted place. Truly speaking, the theory seeks to "break down the antithesis of despotism and individualism, while preserving the truth of both."[79] All that it says is that there is scope for every man to realise his best self in society by fulfilling the duties of his proper place. This proper place, however, is not the place determined for the individual by the sheer accident of birth. It is always necessary to see that "the stations, duties and equipments of different individuals should correspond to their fitness."[80] The social organisation ought always to provide opportunities for every man to qualify himself for the duties of his proper station. A division of society into "natural" masters and "natural" slaves is subversive of social justice.

The Varṇa-dharma scheme is defective in two ways. Firstly, it leaves no scope for the individual to find out by a process of trial and error his proper station in life. The mere fact of birth is taken to determine his whole course of life. In a society based on Varṇa-dharma a man cannot rise from a humble position to a

---

76. *op, cit.*, p. 163.
77. *Ibid.*, p. 168.
78. *Ibid.*, p. 174.
79. *Ibid.*, p. 187.
80. J.S. Mackenzie: *Fundamental Problems of Life*, p. 109.

position of eminence. The Varṇa determined by birth comes in the way of his rising to the full stature of his mental and moral manhood. Secondly, having thus determined a man's vocation and place in society, apart from his aptitude and fitness, the Varṇa-dharma brings in invidious distinctions between the members of the different classes in society. As a result, the Brāhmaṇas become the most privileged class, the Śudras little more than beasts; and the Vaiśyas also are too far below to take an intelligent interest in the affairs of the State.

And yet we find that the Varṇa-dharma scheme is some times defended as fundamentally sound. It is asserted that there are four distinct orders of the active nature or four fundamental types of the soul in nature, Svabhāva; and the work and proper function of each human being corresponds to his type of nature.[81] The Brāhmaṇa, then, is one who is characterised by "calmness, self-control, askesis, purity, long-suffering, candour, knowledge and acceptance of spiritual truth." The Kshatriya is one who is possessed of "heroism, high spirit, resolution, ability, not fleeing in the battle, giving and lordship (Iśwarabhāva)." "The natural work of a Vaiśya consists of agriculture, cattle-keeping and trade, inclusive of the labour of the craftsman and the artisan." Finally, all work of the character of service falls within the natural province of the Śudra.

We do not know for certain if really there are four fundamental types of nature. But even granting that there are, all that such a statement implies is that it is possible to classify humanity into four classes as above: it means that in an ideal society, given perfect freedom and due opportunity for each man to select his function, there will arise these four classes corresponding to the four fundamental types of nature. The nature of a man, then, would lead him inevitably to select the kind of life which is suitable to him. By the choice he makes we should be able to judge his innate nature. A man would be a Brāhmaṇa or a Kshatriya, a Vaiśya or a Śudra according to the type of life he chooses, which his

81. Aurobindo Ghose: *Essays on the Gīta*, pp. 371 ff. (second series.)

nature prompts him to. This evidently presupposes the provision of equal opportunity to every man to choose the kind of life which suits his nature best. Given this opportunity, there is, indeed, nothing truer than the assertion that "one's own natural work is better than another's, even if it looks defective from some other point of view." Given this necessary condition, we can certainly say that one does not incur sin when one acts in the true spirit of the work and in agreement with one's own law of nature.[82] Only, we must add, this law is not given to us as a datum; we have to arrive at it by experimentation.[83]

It must be asserted emphatically that Varṇa-dharma, as laid down in our sacred works, cannot be interpreted as above. On the other hand, it is birth alone which makes a man a Brāhmaṇa or a Kshatriya, a Vaiśya or a Śudra, as the case may be. Even in Vedic times, "the priests and the nobles practised hereditary occupations and either class was a closed body into which a man must be

---

82. cf. Ghose: *op. cit.*, p. 372.

83. Mr. Venkata Rao gives us a thought-provoking and interesting comparison between Bradley's doctrine summed up in *My Station and its Duties* and the doctrine of Svadharma as inculcated in the *Bhagavad-gītā*. He points out how "both point to one's station in society and the duties flowing therefrom as the path of realization." Bradley, however, does not say clearly how one is to discover one's station in life. He is content merely "with pointing the finger of scorn at empty-headed enthusiasts who pine for a life above their station." This is a great defect in Bradley's presentation of the doctrine, in spite of "the depth and reach of his idealism." The *Gītā* goes a step further than Bradley in this respect. "With its theory of Guṇas or threefold qualities it carries us a step further in social analysis and points out that one's station is to be determined by one's own inner nature." And yet the problem is not completely solved; for, the question that now arises is: How are these Guṇas acquired? The *Gītā* is very vague on this point. "It implies," as the writer rightly remarks, "the theory of Karma and rebirth," and Svadharma is thus liable to be interpreted merely in terms of conventional social divisions and ranks current in societies in different epochs. The same criticism applies to Bradley's doctrine as well, says the writer. There is thus a similarity between "the European idealism as represented by Bradley and Hindu Dharma Śāstra as represented by the Bhagavad-gītā"—a similarity "both in strength and in limitation." What we must emphasize, therefore, is that a healthy and progressive society must provide the necessary institutions—the proper 'milieu'—for the discovery and culture of the 'guṇas' or the aptitudes of its members.

(See Article by M.A. Venkata Rao on "Bradley and the *Bhagavad-gītā*" in *The Aryan Path*—October 1931).

born."[84] These two Varṇas, therefore, were organised almost as castes on a hereditary basis. There could be no question of choice in the matter on the part of the individual. The Vaiśyas also formed a distinct class by themselves, separated on the one hand from the Brāhmaṇas and the Kshatriyas, and on the other hand from the Śudras.[85] In the *Rig-veda*, inter-marriages between the three classes were not uncommon. There were no rules explicitly prohibiting marriages with the Śudras. Perhaps, such rules were not still necessary because the Śudras came into contact with the Aryans as hated enemies or despised slaves. The differences of colour and culture between them must have been a sufficient barrier against regular marriages between the two.[86] In the period of the *Brāhmaṇas*, the marriage with a Śudra girl comes gradually to be disliked, as may be inferred from the example of Kavasha Ailusha in the *Aitareya Brāhmaṇa*.[87] The elaborate regulations about the loss of caste that we come across in the *Dharmasūtras*[88] leave not the slightest doubt that heredity alone was the main determinant of caste. The rules regarding mixed castes which are laid down in the *Manu-smṛiti* also point to the fact after all that the caste of a man was determined by his birth.

It must be admitted that our ancient thinkers have often tried to give us their idea of a true Brāhmaṇa and a true Kshatriya, in terms of the mental and spiritual equipment of each of these. According to the *Mahābhārata*, a true Brāhmaṇa is he "who is self-controlled, has drunk the soma in sacrifices, is of good conduct, has mercy for all creatures and patience to bear everything, has no desire of improving his position by acquisition of wealth, is frank and simple, mild, shorn of cruelty and forgiving of sinful deeds."[89] A true Kshatriya must have learning activity (samutthānam),

---

84. *Vedic Index*, Vol. II, p. 264.
85. *Ibid.*
86. Dutt: *Origin and Growth of Caste in India*, pp. 68-69.
87. *Aitareya Brāhmaṇa*: translated by Keith, ii-19, p. 148.
88. cf. *Gautama*, XXI; *Vasishṭha*, I, 20-23.
89. *Śānti Parva*: LXIII, 8.

ambition, dreadfulness (ugratvam), good conduct and strength.[90] It is these attributes which are considered as the distinctive marks of a Brāhmaṇa or a Kshatriya as the case may be. A Brāhmaṇa who is not well-versed in the Vedas is thus compared to "an elephant made of wood, an antelope made of leather," and to "grain without kernel and a well without water."[91] Likewise, a Kshatriya, incapable of protecting the people, is considered perfectly useless, therefore deserving of no respect and to be shunned like a leaky boat on the sea.[92]

The *Bhagavad-gītā* enumerates very lucidly the distinctive qualities of the four Varṇas. "Tranquillity, restraint of the senses, penance, purity, forgiveness, straightforwardness, also knowledge, experience and belief (in the future world)"—these are the proper qualities of a Brāhmaṇa. The characteristics of a Kshatriya are: "Valour, glory, courage, dexterity, not slinking away from battle, gifts, and exercise of lordly power." A Vaiśya finds the satisfaction of his nature in agriculture, in tending cattle and in trade; and a Śudra in service.[93]

The enumeration of these necessary qualities of the four Varṇas need not mislead us as to the real significance of the Varṇa-dharma. It cannot be taken to mean that the possession of certain attributes really determines the Varṇa of a man. All that it really signifies is that a man, born in a particular Varṇa, must try to develop the proper qualities of that Varṇa; for, it is only by developing these qualities that he can discharge his Svadharma. That this is the correct interpretation is seen from the tenor of the verses following those quoted above.[94] The *Bhagavad-gītā* recognises that the duties of the four Varṇas must be based on the essential nature of men on whom the Varṇa-dharma is to be obligatory. It assumes, however, that the essential nature of a man is itself to be judged from the fact of his birth. The

---

90. *Ibid.*, XXIII, 9-12.
91. *Śānti Parva,* XXVII, 47-50.
92. *Ibid.*, LXXVIII, 42-43.
93. Ch. XVIII, 41-44.
94. Ch. XVIII, 45-48.

birth of a man in a particular Varṇa would thus be an index to his nature (Svabhāva); and the duties laid down for that Varṇa are in accordance with the needs of that nature! Only such an explanation as this can explain Kriṣhṇa's exhortation to Arjuna to fight "in view of his Svadharma" (Svadharmam api cha āvekshya na vikampitum arhasi).[95]

It is possible to multiply references from the *Dharmasūtras*, the *Dharmaśāstras* and also from the *Nīti-śāstras*. It is not necessary for our purposes, however, to add to the evidence we have considered above. What we seek to emphasize is that we must once for all get rid of the idea that the Varṇa-dharma could at any time mean the *dharma* determined by the law of our being, by our

---

95. The issue which perplexed and confused Arjuna was this: Was it proper to fight the unscrupulous and sinful Kauravas, thus incurring the inevitable sin of the extinction of the family? "Nought of good," says Arjuna, "can spring from mutual slaughter!" Would it not be better to be killed at the hands of the enemies and so to prevent the destruction of the family? (Vide Ch. I, 28-46). In reply, Kriṣhṇa first expounds the real nature of the soul. "There is no existence for that which is unreal; there is no non-existence for that which is real." (II, I6). "These bodies appertaining to the embodied (self) which is eternal, indestructible and indefinable, are said to be perishable" (II, 18); but so far as the Self is concerned, "He who thinks it to be the killer and he who thinks it to be killed, both know nothing. It kills not and is not killed" (II, 19-20). Here, then, is one line of argument for urging Arjuna to fight. "O Pārtha, how can that man who knows it (i.e. the Self) to be thus indestructible, everlasting, unborn and inexhaustible, how and whom can he kill, whom can he cause to be killed?" (II, 21).

It is not difficult to see that this is, by itself, a weak argument. If, in the ultimate, there is no killer and no killed, then why take the trouble of destroying the bodies, doomed to decay and death? Or, the argument may even be construed to justify evidently anti-social conduct as well.

Having said this, Kriṣhṇa adopts another line of argument. He points out that it is the duty of the Kshatriya to fight. "Nought better can betide a martial soul than lawful war ......" Fighting was thus put forward as the natural duty of Arjuna as a Kshatriya. "Having regard to your Svadharma also, you ought not to falter," (II, 31-32) is the exhortation. Does this leave any doubt that Svadharma was to be determined by one's birth? It may be added here that it would be unfair to judge the value of the teachings of the *Gītā* from their implications as to the duty of fighting. After all the war and the mental conflict of Arjuna must be taken as an occasion for the Lord to deliver his precious message, as to the meaning of Reality. It is in the depth of its philosophical significance that we can realise the truth of considering the *Gītā* as one of "the five Jewels," with all its "lofty declarations," "sublime aspirations" and "pure and tender piety" (see E. Arnold's *The Song Celestial*, Preface).

Svabhāva, unconnected with birth. The doctrine of Karma is too strongly embedded in the Hindu mind to allow it to conceive of one's nature and functions as being determined by anything save birth. As Tagore rightly points out, "India laid all her emphasis upon the law of heredity, ignoring the law of mutation, and thus gradually reduced arts into crafts and genius into skill."[96]

To sum up, the conception of the hierarchical scheme of Varṇas creates a hiatus between the different classes in society. The large mass of the people is thus placed in an unfortunate and unjust position.[97] The Brāhmaṇas and Kshatriyas are the only classes who could exercise an influence on the working of the State-machinery. Even these, however, would enjoy their privilege as a class, not as individual citizens of the State. The Vaiśyas and the Śudras as also the border-tribes mentioned in the *Mahābhārata* have merely to "accept orders." They could have no opportunity to take an active and constructive interest in the work of the State. Evidently, therefore, they could not feel themselves as related to the whole; they could not really identify themselves with the State—and so become the State.

Besides these lower classes in society, who were excluded from political power, were the women, whose position was also such as to make impossible the development of the true citizen-spirit on their part.

Let us look at this point a little closely. The position of woman in ancient India has often been regarded as highly satisfactory. "The general Hindu view of woman," says Dr. Radhakrishnan, "is an exalted one."[98] Similar is the opinion of Prof. S.V. Venkateswara, who maintains that, "the social history of women in ancient India directly disproves the hypothesis of social tyranny."[99] If, however, we study this history, if we critically study the statements of our

---

96. *Nationalism,* p. 117.

97. cf. Radhakrishnan: "The confusion of birth and qualities has led to the undermining of the spiritual foundation of caste."—*Indian Phily.,* Vol. I, p. 591.

98. *Hindu View of Life,* pp. 88-89.

99. *Indian Culture through the Ages,* pp. 18-22.

ancient thinkers on this subject, we cannot help feeling that the position of woman was far from exalted.

In the *Ṛig-veda,* there is no ritual contempt or ceremonial impurity for women. The wife could take an active part in the religious ceremonies as an equal partner of her husband and could offer joint libations to the gods (cf. 1, 83, 3; 131, 3; viii, 31, 5). Ladies like Visvavara could not only compose verses but could even officiate as priests at a sacrifice (cf. v, 28). Ghosha, Apala, Lopamudra also composed hymns and rose to the rank of Rishis (cf. x, 39; viii, 8o and 1, 170 respectively). The high value placed on marriage comes out clearly from the long and striking hymn (x, 85) which accompanied the ceremonial.[100] And yet we find in the *Ṛig-veda* the evidence to show the slow development of the inferiority complex, which was to characterise woman in later times. Thus, the birth of a male was regarded as preferable to that of a female (vi, 61, I). A woman was supposed never to be able to take care of herself. After her father's death she had to live under the guardianship of her brother till her marriage, lest she should go astray[101] (i, 124, 7). With women, it is said, there can be no lasting friendship; their hearts are like those of hyenas (x, 95, 15). "The mind of woman brooks not discipline, her intellect hath little weight" (viii, 33, 17). Moreover, women were not recognised as independent persons in the eye of the law, whether married or not. They could not take an inheritance and lived with their parents and brothers or relatives[102] (iii, 31, 2). The position of women seems to have declined after the Ṛig-vedic times.[103] In the *Śatapatha Brāhmaṇa* a woman and a Śudra are grouped together as embodying impurity (xiv, I, 131). In the Maitrayani Samhita, it is so said, "Woman is Nirṛiti" (i.e. evil

100. See *Cambridge History of India,* Vol. I, pp. 88-89.

101. See *Cambridge History of India,* Vol. I, pp. 88-89, and cf. also *Vedic Index,* Vol. II, pp. 485-486.

102. Dutt: *Origin and Growth of Caste in Ancient India,* pp. 74 ff.

103. *Ibid.*, pp. 119 ff. A good deal of what follows is based on this book. cf. also Hopkin's Article on "The position of the Ruling Class in India"—with its appendix on the "Status of Woman", *Journal of the American Oriental Society,* Vol. XIII.

personified). She is forbidden to go to assemblies and take part in public life (iv, 7-4). The birth of a daughter is looked upon as an occasion for sorrow. In the words of the *Aitareya Brāhmaṇa*, "the daughter is a sorrow, while the son is light in the highest regions of heaven to his father" (viii, 13-18): The *Śatapatha Br.* requires the wife to take her meals after her husband (I, 9, 2, 12; x, 5, 2, 9). Woman was of course excluded from inheritance and she had no property of her own. If her husband died, she passed to his family with the inheritance like the attic epikleros.[104] Her wergeld was equal to that of a Śudra.[105] As Keith observes, "woman in India has always suffered much from all religions but by none has she been so thoroughly despised as by the Brāhmaṇas of the period of the *Brāhmaṇas*."[106]

In the Sūtras we get numerous references to show that women were now reduced quite to the status of Śudras.[107] They are habitually referred to in the same breath with the Śudras. The penance for killing a Brāhmaṇa woman is the same as that for killing a Śudra (*Gautama*, xxii, 17; *Āpastamba*, i, 9, 245; *Baudhāyana*, i, 10, 19, 3). Women are debarred from offering on their own account either the vedic śrauta sacrifices or the gṛhya sacrifices. They are even looked upon as property, as may be seen from the maxim laid down by Vasishṭha: "A pledge, a boundary, the property of minors, an open or sealed deposit, women, the property of a king or of a learned priest are not lost by being enjoyed by others."[108]

The position of woman in the *Mahābhārata* is similar. Woman as such had no value. On the whole, it seems she is regarded

---

104. *Cambridge History of India*, pp. 134-335.

105. *Ibid.*

106. *Religion and Philosophy of the Veda*, p. 475.

107. It is interesting to note that this progressive decline in the position of women has gone hand in hand with the increasing severity of caste rules and ceremonial purity probably because of the large acccession of the black non-Aryan female element into the households of the Vedic Aryans. Vide Dutt: *op. cit.*, p. 119.

108. XVI, 16. Also cf. 'A woman is not independent, the males are her masters' (V, 12).

almost as chattel and "receives only the respect due from a sensible man to potentially valuable property."[109] The *Manu-smṛiti* speaks of the inherently wicked nature of women in view of their ability to seduce even learned men.[110] Woman is enjoined never to do anything independently, be she a girl, a young woman, or an aged one. "In childhood a female must be subject to her father, in youth to her husband, when her lord is dead, to her sons; a woman must never be independent." She has thus no individuality. "Him to whom her father may give her, or her brother with her father's permission, she shall obey as long as she lives, and when he is dead, she must not insult his memory."[111] It is in the same spirit that the text lays down that "though destitute of virtue, or seeking pleasure elsewhere, or devoid of good qualities, a husband must be constantly worshipped as a god, by a faithful wife."[112] We cannot help feeling as we read these maxims that the desire of the ancient Indians to preserve the purity of the race has probably led them to constitute husbands into the moral watchdogs of their wives. Woman by her very nature is looked upon as suspect. What a low view of the character of womankind is involved in the statement that "women do not care for beauty, nor is their attention fixed on age; thinking it is enough that he is a man, they give themselves to the handsome and to the ugly."[113] Strangely enough, along with such statements, there are others which inculcate the duty of honouring women. "Women," it is laid down,[114] "must be honoured and adorned by their fathers, brothers, husbands, and brothers-in-law who desire (their own) welfare;" for, "where women are honoured, there the gods are pleased; but where they are not honoured, no sacred rite yields rewards." Though it may seem some relief to come across these

109. Hopkins: Article on "The position of the Ruling Class in India", in the *Journal of the American Oriental Society*, Vol. XIII.

110. *Manu*, II, 213-215.

111. *Manu*, V, 147-151.

112. *Ibid.*, 154.

113. *Ibid.*, IX, 14.

114. *Ibid.*, III, 55-56.

comparatively rare passages, we shall be sadly mistaken if we take these as a recognition of the personality of woman. Such an interpretation would be quite false to the general spirit of the Law-books. On the other hand woman is always looked upon as inferior to man in all our ancient works. Perhaps, as Bagehot would assert, this is the natural result of the times of conflict. In the passage quoted above, there is an injunction to honour women but what this means comes out clearly in the verses immediately following. "The houses on which female relations, not being duly honoured, pronounce a curse, perish completely, as if destroyed by magic." Hence, men who seek their own welfare should always honour women on holidays and festivals with gifts of ornaments, clothes and dainty food.[115] Thus, after all, they are no more than dolls, to be gratified and pampered, that they might not curse the whole family! Who could say that there is anything like the recognition of the intrinsic worth of the personality of woman anywhere in these maxims?

Other *Dharmaśāstra* works are in agreement with the spirit of Manu's teaching on the subject. Thus, Yājñavālkya lays down that "when a maiden, her father, when married, her husband and when old, her sons should protect her. In their absence, the kinsmen should take care of her. The women are never independent."[116] And in the same spirit as Manu's, he goes on to say that "woman is to be honoured by her husband, brother, father, kindred, mother-in-law, husband's younger brother and the "bandhus," *with ornaments, clothes and food.*"[117] Bṛihaspati lays down that "a woman must be restrained from slight transgressions even by her relations; by night and day she must be watched by her mother-in-law and other wives belonging to the family."[118] The personality of the wife is completely merged in that of her

115. *Manu,* III, 58-59.

116. *Yāj.*, III, 85.

117. *Ibid.*, III, 82. Italics mine.

118. XXIV, 2.

husband.[119] Nārada also repeats the traditional injunctions;[120] and so does Vishṇu, according to whom, it is the duty of a woman "to remain subject, in her infancy, to her father; in her youth, to her husband; and in her old age, to her sons; not to act by herself in any matter and after the death of her husband to preserve her chastity or to ascend the pile after him."[121]

Śukrāchārya's attitude towards woman is also similar. He enjoins the husband to keep his wife in the performance of domestic duties. Generally speaking, woman is looked upon with suspicion, and is therefore to be closely watched. "Living with other persons, speaking with them even publicly, independence even for a moment, and residence in their houses should not be granted to females by the husband, king, son, father-in-law and relatives; nor leisure for anything besides domestic duties be allowed."[122] The duty of the husband is thus to keep the wife to domestic work and to please her by giving her clothing, food, love, and affectionate words.[123] The wife has no existence apart from her husband. "Women," it is laid down, "have no separate right to the use of the means for the realisation of the threefold end, viz., dharma, artha, and kāma."[124] The list of duties prescribed for woman shows that the domestic duties exhaust all her activity.[125] Behaving with her husband as with a great god, she gets fame in this world and heaven in the next.[126] When such is the attitude

---

119. *Brihas.*, XXIV, 8—"That wife is declared to be devoted to her husband who is afflicted when he is afflicted, pleased when he is happy, squalid and languid when he is absent and who dies when he dies." We need not imagine that this only illustrates the ideal of harmonious relations between husband and wife; for no law-giver has any rule to the effect that "that husband is declared to be devoted to his wife who is afflicted when she is afflicted, pleased when she is happy...... and dies when she dies."

120. XIII, 31.

121. XXV, 12-14.

122. *Śukra,* Ch. III, 39-43.

123. *Ibid.*, Ch. III, 48-49; 196-197.

124. *Ibid.*, Ch. IV, and section iv, II.

125. *Śukra,* Ch. IV, Section IV, 12-42.

126. *Ibid.*, 43, 44; 62-65.

to woman, she could evidently have had no interest in the affairs of the State.

The Buddha admitted women to the Sangha. A nun could attain Arhatship. But this does not signify equality; for, it is laid down that she could attain Buddhahood only after being born as a man.[127] The status of woman could not, therefore, have been appreciably modified as a result of the Buddhist teachings.

Besides the lower classes in society, then, women were also debarred from the privilege (or, shall we call it the duty?) of interesting themselves and sharing in the tasks of government.

Further, the ancient Indian State recognised and regulated the institution of slavery. The observation of Megasthenes[128] that "all the Indians are free and not one of them is a slave" is not borne out by other evidence. Slavery seems to have existed in India from remote antiquity. Besides the three higher castes and the Śudras there existed a class of men, who, owing to legal disabilities, suffered loss of status in society. From the evidence from Pali books it seems that even members of the higher castes were made slaves, besides non-Aryans and conquered peoples. Slavery was the result of capture in war and also there was voluntary enslavement or sale of children, slavery for debt and slavery as punishment for heinous crimes.[129]

The founders of Jainism and Buddhism did much to propagate the doctrine of ahimsā but the institution of slavery seems to have been so deep-rooted that hardly any attempt was made in the Buddhist period to remedy the evil.[130]

In the *Kauṭilīya,* we have a definite attempt to regulate this institution so as to make it humane. The author lays down that "those who do not heed the claims of their slaves...... shall be

127. Monier Williams: *Buddhism,* p. 87.

128. McCrindle: *Ancient India as described by Megasthenes and Arrian.* See *Fragments,* XXVI, XXVII, and XLI.

129. See Narayanchandra Banerjea's Article on "Slavery in Ancient India", in *Calcutta Review,* August 1930.

130. See Article referred to above.

taught their duty;"[131] selling of children into slavery is prohibited, particularly for the Aryans, provision is made for restoring freedom to the slaves under definite circumstances and the evils connected with the system are sought to be suppressed.[132] It was perhaps as a result of this strict regulation that the condition of the slaves was such that Megasthenes could not notice the existence of the institution at all. This humane injunction of Kauṭilya does real credit to him, looking to his age—the age, when Aristotle was content to say that some men are by nature free, while others are slaves. In spite of this, it appears that the institution of slavery not only did not die out but it even received a new lease of life perhaps as a result of the contact with the Greek or Central Asian invaders.[133]

The *Manusamhitā*, thus, mentions seven kinds of slaves and declares them to be incapable of holding or inheriting property; and the later Smṛiti writers do not challenge the validity of the institution.[134] The statements of the law books on the subject of slavery are corroborated by the historical records.[135]

This recognition of slavery is, then, another weak point about the ancient Indian Polity, in spite of the fact that slavery was almost universal in ancient societies. However humane the treatment of slaves may have been, it has to be admitted that the very existence of this class would preclude the possibility of the co-operation of all the members of the body politic in order to secure a common end.[136]

We conclude, then, that the social organisation in ancient India was defective in as much as it ignored the vital principle of the equality of the worth of all persons.

---

131. *Artha.*, Bk. II, Ch. I, p. 47.
132. *Ibid.*, Bk. III, Ch. 13.
133. Vide article referred to above.
134. *Manu*, VIII, 413-416; *Nārada*, V, 24-42.
135. See article on "Slavery" by Jolly in *Encyclopaedia of Religion and Ethics.*
136. cf. "A slave is an unassimilated, undigested atom, something which is in the body politic but yet is hardly a part of it."— Bagehot: *Physics and Politics*, p. 71.

This is not to suggest that all inequality is unjustifiable. Inequality in certain respects—that which Rousseau[137] calls "natural inequality"—is unavoidable. Men are not born equal in many respects. There are differences in the physical, intellectual and moral development of persons. Differences in treatment based on such differences do not in themselves constitute a violation of social justice.[138] Very often, however, differences in physical and intellectual development are the result of the inequality of opportunities. The social organisation makes it, often enough, impossible for man to develop his innate capacities to the fullest extent. The creative impulses have often to be repressed on account of the pressure of the social institutions.[139] Man is often crushed by the very institutions he creates. When he is thus denied the opportunity of directing his energies into creative channels, when he is condemned to live his life within certain circumscribed limits which prevent full growth, it is evidently unjust to place him at a further disadvantage by offering less to him by way of reward—in whatever form—than to his more fortunate brother provided with better opportunities.[140] The equality we advocate is certainly not the equality of absolute magnitude, but an equality of proportion. This is the sense in which Aristotle understood the term. "Injustice," he says, "arises when equals are treated unequally. and when unequals are treated equally."[141] Thus, equality, properly understood, does not mean a refusal to give practical recognition to distinctions of intellect and character. It does not mean the

137. *A Discourse on the Origin of Inequality.*

138. cf. Laski: *Liberty in the Modern State,* pp. 16-18.
Also see Tawney: *Equality,* pp. 47-48.

139. Bertrand Russell: *Political Ideals,* p. 25.

140. J.L. Dickinson brings out this point very clearly in his *Justice and Liberty.* He ably exposes the injustice of the system, under which "the son of a rich man," though he be a fool "may be placed in life in a snug position where he may draw ten times or a hundred times the income of a man born of great ability who had the misfortune to be born poor," p. 83.

141. Vide Hobhouse: *Elements of Social Justice,* p. 97. "The simple generalisation that all men have equal rights," the author observes, "would make a hash of social relationships. A convicted murderer would then stand on the same footing as the most harmless citizen, and a child would have no more claim on his mother than on any chance corner," p. 95.

suppression of individual genius and character. It only means that distinctions of physical force, wealth or birth are insignificant when the question of the moral worth of persons is considered. By providing an equality of opportunity genuine distinction of capacity would be brought out all the more clearly. By encouraging this real merit, society would be providing better opportunities for men really capable of rendering service.

In the sphere of politics, then, equality would mean, as Laski rightly points out "the absence of special privilege."[142] It means that every member of the State should have the same opportunity as any other to influence the working of the State in view of the common good.

"Whatever rights inhere in another by virtue of his being a citizen must inhere, and to the same extent, in me also," to quote Prof. Laski again. Thus, the monopoly of political power in the hands of a hereditary class is obviously an unjustifiable privilege. As Green profoundly observes, "We cannot believe that the capacities of man can be fulfilled in a state of things in which any rational man is treated merely as a means and not as an end in himself."[143] The social organisation must provide equal opportunities to all to develop their latent capacities to the full.[144] The translation of this idea in institutional terms is difficult and raises intricate questions. These, however, must be solved if the right of citizenship is to be of value at all. Without this kind of equality, there cannot be liberty; if liberty means the continuous power of expansion or the capacity for continuous initiative, it can rarely be present except in a society based on equality.[145] Equality thus understood is not only not antithetic to liberty, but is a very necessary condition of true liberty.

---

142. *Grammar of Politics*, p. 153.

143. *Prolegomena to Ethics*, p. 217.

144. Laski: *op. cit.*, p. 154; also *Liberty in the Modern State*, pp. 18-19.

145. R.H. Tawney, in his recent book, *Equality*, presents an acute analysis of the problem of economic inequality as affecting the working of democracy. cf. B. Russell: *Political Ideals*, p. 19; and Laski's Essay, 'A plea for Equality' in *Dangers of Obedience*, pp. 211 ff.

The conception of citizenship in virtue of which one feels himself the author of the law he is called upon to obey could not, then, develop in ancient India. With the social organisation as represented by the hierarchical Varṇas and the hiatus that these create between the higher and lower classes, with the inferior position assigned to the members of the fair sex and with the institution of slavery recognised, it is evident that the ancient Indian polity could not be an organic whole with one common life pulsating through all its members. There could only be the rulers on the one hand, and the ruled on the other; the governors on the one hand, and the governed on the other. The king may be so trained up as always to rule according to definite principles, as always to secure good government. The subjects also may be taught to render obedience to the king in view of the importance of his functions. A polity organised on this plan may achieve efficiency and may be really suitable for certain conditions, at a certain stage. It may maintain stability and order but may also suppress variety and departure from the traditional. For the future we must pin our faith to a geniunely democratic government. It is only such a government that can open out to the masses new avenues of creative effort. Any form of government other than the democratic suffers from the fatal defect of preventing the natural expansion of the human spirit. The democratic principle alone offers the plane, where the claims of men to a share in the common good can be regarded as equal.[146] It is in a democratic government that the interest of the sovereign and that of the people would be identical.[147] The problem is colossal. The conferring of the vote and the counting of heads do not solve it. Various solutions are being suggested with a view to making democracy really possible.

---

146. Laski: *Dangers of Obedience*, pp. 208 ff.

147. cf. "I should have wished to be born in a country in which the interest of the sovereign and that of the people must be single and identical, to the end that all the movements of the machine might tend to the general happiness. And as this could not be the case unless the sovereign and the people were one and the same person, it follows that I should have wished to be born under a democratic government, wisely tempered."—Rousseau: *A Discourse on the Origin of Inequality*, p. 158. Also see Laski: *Grammar of Politics*, p. 27.

The great question is to find out how the average man, with all his multifarious activities which seem to absorb his loyalty, and with little opportunity to be able to judge matters rightly, can be made to feel in him the glow of the true citizen-spirit, can be made to take active and sustained interest in the affairs of the State and can be made to realise the value of the higher loyalty to the ideal of the State, wherein are blended and harmonised all his loyalties, and which, therefore, really demands "the whole of him." When the individual is thus integrated into the harmony of the State, the antithesis between the sovereign and the subject disappears. When such a synthesis has been achieved, every man can say with truth, "I am the State."

This, then, is the nature of the problem of the Indian Polity, even as it is the problem before the countries in the west. When we criticise the achievements of our ancients, when we emphasize their shortcomings, we need not forget at the same time that this great problem has still to be solved by humanity. Judged by the standard we have set before us, the institutions of the west would also fall short of the ideal. In fact the thinkers in the west have seen this and have even wondered if democracy could ever be a reality. However, if the ideal of democracy is one where the individual is really in a position to contribute towards the development of what Miss Follett calls the collective will, then, though the task before us may be heavy, there is no ground for repudiating the democratic ideal. The point is, democracy has not yet failed us; we have not yet risen into real democracy. It is, therefore, more of democracy that we want, not less. We have thus to revisualise our *Dharma* in the light of the above remarks. It has to be recognised that ours is a social problem fundamentally; no mere change in the political organisation or in the governmental machinery can wholly solve it. If only we can arrive at an adequate conception of citizenship which will harmonise the diverse elements in the Indian polity, which makes India "a vast ethnological museum" and "a world in miniature," we shall not only have solved our own problem, we shall certainly have contributed not a little to the solution of the problem that is before the west today, where "the man is represented by an octopus of abstractions sending out its innumerable suckers into the far-away future."[148] Let us only keep constantly before ourselves the fundamental idea that the end of citizenship and of all the institutions it creates is the development of individuality.[149]

---

148. Tagore: *Nationalism*, p. 14.

149. Hetherington and Muirhead: *Social Purpose*, p. 210.

Chapter VII

The Nature of the Hindu State

Having discussed the end of the State and the relation of the State and the individual in the light of the concept of *Dharma*, we have now to determine the nature of the Hindu State as a whole. We have seen the shortcomings of the Hindu view of the end of the State; we have also noticed how the conception of true citizenship could not arise in ancient India. What, then, is the nature of the State so ordered? What is its place in the ordering of life? That is now the question before us. And in order to envisage the nature of the State, we must see what its sphere was, what exactly was expected of the king as the head of the State, what were the limitations on the kingly authority and how far these may be regarded as adequate in order to ensure the right relation between the State and the individual.

Let us approach our problem by examining the functions of the State and so determining its sphere.

During the early Vedic times, the duties of the king must necessarily have been but a few. One of the important duties of the king was to lead the tribe in wars, which were only too numerous at the time.[1] Besides offensive war, defence was his chief duty, as his title "the protector of the tribe" indicates. In return for his warlike service the king received the obedience of the people and in particular their contributions for the maintenance of royalty. The *Śatapatha Brāhmaṇa* looks upon him as wielding the rod of punishment, being himself immune from punishment

1. The account of the functions of the king in Vedic times is based largely on that in the *Vedic Index*, Vol. II, pp. 210 ff.

(adaṇḍya). He seems, thus, to have taken an active part in the administration of the criminal law.[2]

With the growing complexity of civilisation, the functions of the king must necessarily have become manifold and complex. We have seen in the last chapter how various factors tended to strengthen the power of the king, thus making monarchy the dominant type of polity in India. The conception of the king as the guardian of *Dharma*, which emerges clearly in the *Śatapatha Brāhmaṇa*[3] and which forms the bed-rock of all our ancient political speculation, necessarily makes the king's functions varied and onerous. As the text puts it: "To thee (i.e. the king) the State is given for agriculture, for well-being, for prosperity, for development" (V, 2, 125).

In the *Dharmasūtras*[4] the main duties of the king are said to be to protect all beings, to keep the four castes (Varṇas) to their respective duties and to punish those who stray away from the path of duty. This statement itself indicates the sphere of the State. The king is to keep the four castes and the four orders to their respective duties. These duties cover necessarily the whole field of life. It is, therefore, over the whole field of life that the jurisdiction of the kingly authority extends. The maintenance of *Dharma*, in other words, involves the supervision over—and the interference in case of need with—all the activities of life.

The *Mahābhārata* gives us more glimpses into the significance of the concept of *Dharma* as determining the functions and the sphere of the State. The primary duty of the king, according to the Epic, is to protect the people by constantly upholding the rod of chastisement.[5] Protection, however, does not mean merely security from foreign danger or internal dissensions; it means the maintenance of conditions in which each and every man may

2. *Cambridge History of India*, Vol. I, p. 132. Also Basu: *Indo-Aryan Polity*, p. 57.
3. V. 3. 3. 9 and V. 4. 5.
4. *Vasishṭha*, Ch. XIX; *Gautama*, XI; *Āpastamba*, p. 166; *Baudhāyana*.
5. *Śānti Parva*, XV; XXXII; LVIII, I; LXIX, 30, 104-105; LXXII, 7.

perform the duties of his station unmolested.[6] The king must punish the offenders and administer justice,[7] following the rules laid down in the sacred works.[8] It is the duty of the king to see to it that there is in his kingdom no thief, no wicked man, no drinker of alcohol, no one neglecting the sacred fire or the sacrifice.[9] Drinking shops, public women, pimps, actors, gamblers and keepers of gambling-houses and other persons of this sort should be checked by him, lest they should afflict and injure the better classes of the subjects.[10] Begging is to be discouraged; for, as the text curtly puts it, "it is only the robbers who give to the beggars."[11] In matters social, the king is to regulate marital relations and to punish the breaches thereof.[12]

The functions of the State are not, however, confined to the negative task of hindering the hindrances in the way of the fulfilment of *Dharma.* The king, in other words, is not merely to punish the breaches of *Dharma.* He is also to promote and further *Dharma.* He is rather to adopt a more active policy of reclaiming the land for cultivation and fertilising it,[13] or excavating large tanks all over the kingdom in order to make agriculture partly independent of rain and of supplying seed and food to the agriculturists. Measures should also be taken against fire, snakes and other destructive agencies. Diseases should be stamped out, and the people must be protected from the Rākshasas.[14] Public

6. *Ibid.*, LVII, 15, 35-36.
7. *Ibid.*, LXV, 5-7; LXIX, 32.
8. *Ibid.*, LIX, 107.
9. *Ibid.*, LXXVII, 8-28.
10. *Ibid.*, LXXXVIII, 14-15.
11. *Ibid.*, LXXXVIII, 24. The statement is significant. Begging may demoralise the beggar and also the giver. The latter, instead of trying to root out the evil itself, takes it as inevitable and feels the satisfaction of having done a good turn to the beggar and so the evil spreads. A wise king—or a wise government—must certainly attempt to discourage begging and apply remedies at the very root.
12. *Ibid.*, CXLV-CXLVI, 63-65.
13. *Śānti Parva,* LXV, 2.
14. B. Prasad: *Theory of Government in Ancient India,* p. 46.

works, like the construction of roads and the provision of water along these, must also be undertaken by the king.[15]

These manifold functions of the king indicate the wide sphere of State action. Clearly there can be no attempt at a limitation of this sphere, when the king is enjoined "not to allow sin to be committed in his kingdom," but rather to "cause virtue to be practised."[16]

The *Arthaśāstra* also starts with the assertion that the king shall never allow people to swerve from their duties.[17] One of the main duties of the king is said to be to "establish safety and security by being ever active" and to "maintain his subjects in the observance of their respective duties by exercising authority."[18] The king, according to Kauṭilya, is the pivot of the governmental machinery. It is he who looks to the interests of the people and averts dangers awaiting or befalling them. It is he who rewards virtue and punishes wrong. His prosperity leads to the prosperity of the kingdom. He imparts his quality to the elements of the State. Progress and downfall depend on him. Hence, he is the head of all other elements.[19] The extent of the king's authority or the sphere of State action comes out clearly from Kauṭilya's injunctions regarding the organisation of the whole administrative machinery and the assignment of various functions to the heads of government departments. The Kauṭiliyan State has, clearly enough, important economic functions. The king, for instance, is to carry on mining operations and manufactures, exploit timber and elephant forests, offer facilities for cattle-breeding and commerce, construct roads for traffic, both by land and water, and set up markets.[20] He is to exercise his right of ownership with regard to fishing, ferrying and trading in vegetables, in reservoirs or lakes.[21]

---

15. *Śānti Parva,* LXIX, 53.
16. *Ibid.,* XXIV, 16.
17. Bk. I, Ch. 3.
18. *Ibid.,* Ch. 7.
19. Bandyopadhyaya: *Kauṭilya,* pp. 58-59.
20. *Artha.,* Bk. II, Ch. I, p. 46.
21. *Ibid.,* p. 47.

He is to protect agriculture from the molestation of oppressive fines, free labour and taxes; and herds of cattle from thieves, tigers, poisonous creatures and cattle disease.[22] Commerce is to be regulated by him through the Superintendent of Commerce, who is to ascertain the demand or the absence of demand for and rise or fall in the prices of various kinds of merchandise. He is also to ascertain the time suitable for their distribution, centralisation, purchase and sale.[23] In fact, Kauṭilya advocates a positive and definite policy on the part of the State towards the economic organisation of the country. Thus, he provides for a Superintendent of Weaving, whose duty is to employ qualified persons and to fix their wages according to a definite plan.[24] The king must also have Superintendents of Agriculture[25] and Liquor[26] and the Slaughter-house.[27] He is also to regulate social relations and to impose a fine for offences like cruelty to women, the contempt of the husband and such other deviations from the norm of orderly behaviour.[28] Punishment is also to be meted out to one who embraces asceticism without making provision for the maintenance of his wife and sons.[29] The king is also to undertake more positive and socialistic functions like the maintenance of the aged, the infirm, the afflicted and the helpless.[30] Into the details of various other functions we need not go; for, in fact, Kauṭilya advocates royal paternalism.[31] "The object of the Kauṭiliyan State," it has been rightly pointed out,[32] "was no mere police." The duty of the political organisation did not end with the protection of

22. *Ibid.*, p. 48.
23. *Ibid.*, Ch. XVI, p. 104.
24. *Ibid.*, Ch. XXIII, p. 124.
25. *Artha.*, Bk. II, Ch. 'XXIV.
26. *Ibid.*, Ch. XXV.
27. *Ibid.*, Ch. XXVI.
28. *Ibid.*, Bk. III, Ch. III, pp. 175-177.
29. *Ibid.*, Bk. II, Ch. I, p. 47.
30. *Ibid.*
31. Bandyopadhyaya: *Kauṭilya,* p. 64.
32. *Ibid.*, p. 49 and p. 279.

life and property. It had rather to cover the whole field of social life. The sphere of the Kauṭiliyan State was, then, coextensive and coterminous with the whole of life and there was no corner of it too sacred for its interference.[33] As Beni Prasad puts it, the State, in fact, was commensurate with society.[34]

The sphere of the State as judged from the functions of the king laid down in the Laws of Manu also covers the various aspects of life without any limitation. The ideas of Manu in this respect agree closely with those of the *Mahābhārata*. The duty of the king to keep the subjects in the performance of their duties is, as usual, emphasized.[35] The doctrine of matsyanyāya is brought in to inculcate the importance of royal duties, which, of course, are the sole guarantee of the social order. One of the important duties of the king is to administer justice with scrupulous care. The punishments for various offences are all indicated in this connection and that gives us an inkling into the scope of State activity. It is the duty of the king to prevent and punish theft, adultery, defamation, violence and assault.[36] The economic life of the people is also to be regulated by him.[37] The followers of various occupations, mechanics, manual workers have all to be under the supervision of the State. The king is to punish physicians or veterinary surgeons who cause injury to their patients. Social morality is also to be guarded by the State. For example, offering presents to a woman, romping with her, touching her dress or ornaments or sitting with her on the same bed are to be punished as adulterous acts.

It is not necessary for us to examine in detail the ideas of the rest of the *Dharmaśāstras*; for, they all breathe the same spirit and present hardly any differences from the *Manu-smṛiti*. We shall, therefore, proceed now to examine the evidence of the *Śukra-*

33. The detailed description of the administrative system under Chandragupta also bears out this point. Refer Smith: *Early History of India*, pp. 118 ff.

34. *Theory of Government in Ancient India*, p. 96.

35. *Manu*, III, 13; VIII, 418; see also Ch. IX.

36. *Ibid.*, Ch. VIII.

37. *Ibid.*, Ch. VIII, 401, 402.

nīti-śāra on this point, which, according to Dr. Beni Prasad,[38] represents the last summing up of Hindu political thought.

"The king," says the *Śukra-nīti-śāra*,[39] "is the cause of setting on foot the customs, usages and movements, and hence he is the cause or maker of time." The spirit of the age, in other words, is what is created by the king's activities; for, on the due discharge of his duties depends the proper maintenance of the order of the universe. The functions of this office, Śukra summarises into eight: "Punishment of the wicked, charity, protection of the subjects, performance of Rājasūya and other sacrifices, equitable realisation of revenues and extraction of wealth from land."[40] "Protection of the subjects," however, must be understood in a wide sense. It includes such functions as the construction and repair of roads, the maintenance of serais and even the promulgation of laws, requiring the subjects *inter alia* not to be harsh towards slaves, servants, wife or children and never to deal out jokes to parents and other respectable seniors.[41] The wide scope of State activity may also be seen from the fact that according to Śukra, "without the permission of the king the following things should not be done by the subjects:—gambling, drinking, hunting, use of arms, sale and purchase of cows, elephants, horses, camels, buffaloes, men, immovable property, silver, gold, jewels, intoxicants and poisons, distillations of wines, the drawing up of deeds indicating a sale, gift or loan and medical practice."[42] In the same way, "serious cursing, acceptance of pledges, promulgation of new social rules, defamation of castes, receipt of unowned and lost goods, disclosure of State secrets, discussion about the king's demerits, forsaking one's own religion, untruth, adultery, perjury, forgery, secret acceptance of gifts, realisation of more than the fixed revenue, thieving, violence and enterprise against the master," all these are

38. *op. cit.*, p. 245.

39. Ch. I, 43-44.

40. *Śukra*, Ch. I, 245-248.

41. *Ibid.*, 589-600.

42. *Ibid.*, 603-608.

interdicted.[43] The king is enjoined positively to "take such steps as may advance the arts and sciences of the country."[44] Śukra, in fact, draws up a momentous catalogue of the duties of the king, perhaps without considering whether and how these could be discharged in practice.[45]

So far, then, our evidence is unanimous. The Hindu State recognises no limits to its scope. Our ancient sages and thinkers conceived of the office of kingship as the sustainer and preserver of the order of the universe and hence of the social order. Naturally, therefore, they never evince a distrust of governmental action.

Let us now finally consider the evidence of the Buddhist and Jaina works and see if their conception of the sphere of the State is in any way different from the one we have been noting all along.

According to the author of the *Milindapanho*,[46] "the king is one who rules and guides the world; predominating over all other men, making his relatives rejoice and his enemies mourn, he raises aloft the sun-shade of sovereignty; he is held worthy of respect by the multitude of persons who approach him and come into his presence; when pleased with a strenuous servant, he gladdens his heart by bestowing gifts; he censures, fines, and executes the man who transgresses his commands; proclaiming the right and the wrong principles according to instructions laid down in succession by righteous kings of old, and ruling in righteousness (*dhammena*), he becomes dear to his people and by the force of his righteousness establishes his dynasty long in the land." The king's office is evidently conceived of here as the essential sustainer of *Dharma*. The attributes of sovereignty enumerated here agree with the general view of the *Mahābhārata* and the other works noted above. So far, then, as the purpose of the institution of kingship is concerned, the Buddhist author quite agrees with the

43. *Ibid.*, 609-616.

44. *Ibid.*, 740.

45. B. Prasad: *Theory of Government in Ancient India*, p. 259.

46. R. Davids: *The Questions of King Milinda*, Vol. II, pp. 28-30.

Brahmanical authors. And this attitude leaves open no possibility of setting a limit to the sphere of the State.

The Jātaka stories throw some light on the problem of the scope of governmental activities. In the *Buddhist Parables* is reproduced a story of a king who took upon himself the sins and sufferings of his people.[47] In this story, the king is represented as accepting his moral responsibility for the sins and sufferings of the subjects. "If there are any," he says, "in my kingdom that suffer from hunger, it is I that have made them hungry;" "if there are among my people those that suffer from cold, it is I that have stripped them of their clothes." The material and spiritual interests of the realm depend on the king. He admits that on him alone depend the sufferings and enjoyments of the people and refuses to penalise a man who was compelled to steal on account of pressing need. The king is thus the maker of his age, as it is he who sustains *Dharma.* Reviewing the Jātakas as a whole, Dr. Beni Prasad concludes that the king was the motive force of the whole government. "One of his principal duties was the administration of justice...... The king must promote morality...... The people believed that everything depended on the king...... The king did sometimes play the role of a moral teacher."[48] The exhortation of the king to the subjects reproduced by the same author brings out the traditional conception of the sphere of State activity.[49]

Arya Sura enumerates the duties of the king and solemnly advises the king: "Betake yourself to *Dharma.*"[50] He also lays down that the king must make Righteousness the guide of his actions and must direct his mind to securing the salvation of his subjects.[51] The picture of the kingdom ruled according to these precepts, that is given in the text, reminds one of the similar picture in the *Mahābhārata.* The association of kingly office with the concept

---

47. *Buddhist Parables,* translated by E.W. Burlingame, pp. 293 ff.

48. *State in Ancient India,* pp. 138-139.

49. *Ibid.*

50. *Jātakamālā,* XXIII, 64 (translated by Speyer).

51. *Jātakamālā,* Ch. XXIII, 73.

of *Dharma* is so powerful in the mind of the author that he imagines that the proper discharge of kingly duties assures not only the preservation of the social order but also of the order of the physical world.[52]

The description of Suddhodana, given by Asvaghosha also represents him as illuminating his people on every side, showing them the paths they were to follow.[53]

The Edicts of Asoka indicate unmistakably that in the opinion of the emperor, there could be no aspect of life, public or private, beyond the purview of the State. Not only did he assume the role of a moral teacher but he also appointed "censors of the law of Piety" to "promote the establishment of Piety, the increase of Piety," to prevent "wrongful imprisonment or chastisement" and to supervise "the female establishment of my brothers and sisters as well as of other relatives."[54] In the Borderer's Edict, he says: "All men are my children and just as I desire for my children that they may enjoy every kind of prosperity and happiness in both this world and the next, so also do I desire the same for all men."[55] In this view the king should endeavour to secure "every kind of prosperity and happiness" for the subjects not only in this world but also in the next.

The Jaina works seem to have reproduced more or less completely the rules and principles already elaborated by their Brahmanical rivals in the past.[56]

According to the *Ādi Purāṇa*,[57] government becomes necessary because of the decline of virtue and the fall of man from the primitive state of pure happiness. The coercive authority of government is essential for the preservation of order. The function of government is, however, educational in the widest sense of the

52. *Ibid.*, Ch. X, 27-30.

53. *Buddha Karita*, Bk. I, 9-II.

54. Vide V. Smith: *Asoka*, pp. 161-163.

55. *Ibid.*, pp. 177-178.

56. cf. Ghoshal: *Hindu Political Theories*, p. 202.

57. See Beni Prasad: *Theory of Government in Ancient India*, pp. 221 ff.

term. It is to lead people in all that concerns them. The king must possess all virtues and unremittingly give his time, attention and energy to the 'protection' of the people.[58] The *Nītivākyāmṛita* opens with a salutation to the State and refers to it as a source of religion or morality, wealth or success, and the enjoyment of happiness.[59] The king's duty of protection, again, is not to be understood in a negative sense; for, it is his duty to promote the prosperity of the people by regulating agriculture and commerce and by such other means.

To conclude, the sphere of the State in ancient India was taken to be as wide as the concept of *Dharma* itself. The king was the pivot of the constitution and the centre of political life, with all power concentrated in him. He was not only the head of the State but also of society in all its relationships. There never has been, on the part of any of our ancients, an attempt to delimit the sphere of the State: for, the State, as the embodiment of *Dharma*, was the supreme arbiter of all loyalties.[60] Not only is there no idea of artificially limiting the scope of governmental action but there is not even the realisation that the State, by its very nature, cannot touch the inner thoughts and motives of men. The Hindu thinkers, on the other hand, want the State definitely to ally itself with the forces and influences which touch the inner springs of

---

58. *Ibid.*, p. 226.

59. *Ibid.*, p. 230.

60. It is really amazing in the face of this evidence to be told that "India presents the rare and remarkable phenomenon of the State and the society coexisting apart from, and in some degree of independence of each other, as distinct and separate units of entities, as independent centres of national, popular and collective life and activity." The author goes on to say that "both of them were independent organisms with distinct and well-defined structures and functions of their own and laws of growth and evolution." The evidence we have adduced above leaves us in no doubt whatsoever that the author is entirely misled here. Equally sweeping and unwarranted are the further generalisations that "the limits of State interference were so defined and fixed as not to encroach upon the sphere of the activity of the social organisation," and that "a policy of non-interference was regarded as the ideal policy of the State, the functions of which were ordinarily restricted to the irreducible minimum—viz., protection of life and property and realisation of the revenue for the proper execution of that duty...... " (See, Mookerji: *Local Government in Ancient India*, pp. 3-4.)

action.[61] Government, in the eye of a Hindu, is associated with an ultimate spiritual purpose—the realisation of 'moksha.'[62]

There is also another reason why the problem of delimiting the scope of government activities did not present itself to our authors at all. That reason is their failure to develop any adequate conception of liberty at all. The activity of the State did not seem to them to be an encroachment on the legitimate sphere of the individual. The individual's function in life was, according to them, to perform his prescribed duties; he need not at all look beyond them and face the problems arising out of the common life. That is why, as we observed in another connection, the State did not present itself to the Hindu authors as a co-operative endeavour. It seemed to them to be an instrument, operating in subjection to the self-same *Dharma* to which all—by the very law of their being—owed their allegiance. And since the scheme of *Dharma* represented an eternal ordering, not to be touched by the sacrilegious hands of man, no wonder the idea of specifying the limit of governmental action never occurred to them at all.

It has to be recognised that there can really be no limit to the sphere of the State except such as is inherent in its very nature. The increasing activities of the State need not be viewed with alarm, for there is really no antagonism between the State and the individual. Liberty and law are not antithetic terms. The widening of the scope of State action can be perfectly compatible with liberty; for, State action is nothing but the collective action of the community.[63] And the true collective process does not involve the sacrifice of the individual; but rather the proper valuation of his contribution by the process of integration, as Miss Follett has shown. The sphere of the State tends to be limited because the State as such can only secure the performance of external actions.

---

61. Beni Prasad: *op. cit.*, p. 4.

62. N.N. Law: *Aspects of Ancient Indian Polity*, pp. 142-145.

63. cf. "Not only material security, but the perfection of human and social life, is what we aim at in that *organised co-operation of many men's lives and works which is called the State.* I fail to see good warrant of either reason or experience for limiting the co-operative activity of a nation by hard and fast rules"—Sir F. Pollock: *History of the Science of Politics*, p. 134.

It is unable to determine that the action shall be done from the ground or motive which alone would give it value as an element in moral life. This being so, the State has to confine itself to the hindrance of hindrances to the full life.[64] But this should not be construed as a mere negative function. It involves something positive as Barker has rightly pointed out in his criticism of T.H. Green's view of the sphere of the State.[65] Properly interpreted, this means ultimately that the only limitation on State action is that imposed on it by its end or supreme purpose.[66] According to Hindu authors also, the only limitation on the sphere of the State is that imposed on it by its end. But the end itself, viz. the maintenance of *Dharma,* is defective, as we have seen, from various points of view. On account of this imperfect and defective visualisation of the end of the State, State action would be directed only to the perpetuation of those defective conditions.

The end, functions and sphere of the State thus stand in an intimate relation to the concept of *Dharma.* In fact, the ancient Indian Polity, in all its aspects, bears an indelible stamp of *Dharma.* This point has always to be taken into consideration. A superficial study of the end, functions and sphere of the State, in all their comprehensiveness, might lead one to the conclusion that such a State would be an unmitigated absolutism. It must not, however, be forgotten that the king, according to our ancient works, is himself subject to *Dharma.* Therefore, in order to be able to judge adequately whether the State was an autocracy or whether it was

---

64. Bosanquet: *Phil. Theory of the State,* pp. 175-177.

65. *Political Thought in England,* pp. 17-48.

66. Sir Henry Jones: *Principles of Citizenship,* p. 132.

cf. also "We conclude, then, that the function of the State, and its aim in issuing its laws and controlling the lives of its citizens, is to educate them for their own sake, in the sense not of framing their beliefs for them, however true they may be, but of inspiring them with that love of truth which pursues the truth, and fostering their power to form for themselves beliefs which are true. Within the limits of this, the ultimate end of the State, I am not able to see that there is anything which the State may not do, or any department of man's life, however private, into which its entrance would be an invasion and interference. On the other hand, the State that is loyal to this end, will wisely refrain in many ways from 'interfering' with its citizens" (*Ibid.,* pp. 136-137).

a "rule by ministers," (Sachiva tantra) as P.N. Banerjea calls it, the checks and limitations imposed on the king by *Dharma* must be taken into account. We must see, in other words, whether and how far the king could rule according to his own sweet will.

We have seen how the office of kingship is exalted by our Śāstrakāras. The king, as the preserver and sustainer of *Dharma*, wields enormous power. We must now turn our attention to the injunctions laid down for the king, who must rule according to *Dharma*; we must, that is to say, examine the Hindu conception of an ideal monarch.

The heavy responsibilities devolving on the monarch make it essential that he should be thoroughly educated, and trained in the art of government. The high degree of skill and attainment that the Hindu authors expected of the king may be seen from the elaborate scheme suggested by them for the education of the Prince.[67] From his very infancy, he is placed under the care and guidance of competent tutors. After tonsure, which is generally performed in his third year, he is taught the alphabet and arithmetic; and after investiture with the sacred thread in his eleventh year, he commences his higher studies. These include Trayī, Ānvīkshakī, Vārttā and Daṇḍanīti, taught by eminent scholars, superintendents of government departments with thorough practical experience and by practical statesmen. Besides these subjects, he has to hear daily from competent professors the Itihāsa, which includes in its scope Purāṇa, Itivṛitta, Ākhyāyikā, Udāharana, *Dharmaśāstra* and *Arthaśāstra.*[68] He has also to acquire proficiency in the military art, comprising Hastividyā, Aśvavidyā, Ratha vidyā and Praharaṇa vidyā. Having completed this course of study, the prince was probably charged with responsible duties in government departments.[69]

---

67. Dr. N.N. Law: *Aspects of Ancient Indian Polity*, pp. 70-74. The following remarks are based on Dr. Law's conclusions on this point, arrived at from ample evidence as they are.

68. *Ibid.*, p. 152.

69. *Arthaśāstra*, Bk. I, Ch. 18, p. 35.

Such was to be the early training of the king, designed to fit him for his enormous duties. Further, he was expected to have various qualities, intellectual and moral. "The king," says Kauṭilya,[70] "shall ever be wakeful." He also recounts in detail the various qualities the king must possess as the head of the seven elements of sovereignty.[71] The daily time-table laid down for the king, not only in the *Arthaśāstra* but also in the *Manu-smṛiti*, the *Yājñavālkya-smṛiti*, the *Agni Purāṇa* and several other works shows unmistakably that the ideal king would have to devote himself to State-business for the major part of his time. There would be little leisure for him to lead a life of idleness and luxury.

In the *Mahābhārata*, we find, the duty of the king to rule in righteousness is emphasized in a variety of ways. The doctrine of Svadharma makes it imperative that every one should discharge his appointed duties. The reward thereof would be the realisation of the *summum bonum*. It follows that the king, who duly fulfils his Svadharma by keeping the subjects in the path of *Dharma*, attains to the "region of bliss."[72] "The Kshatriya," it is laid down, "who acts thus, following the well-known duties of kings, is sure to reap excellent fruits both in this world and in the next."[73] Pṛithu, the first king, was enjoined by the gods and Rishis to "renounce lust, anger, covetousness and pride." He was also asked to promise that he "would never act capriciously."[74] In order that the king may be able to discharge his duties properly, the *Mahābhārata* enumerates "thirty-six virtues which a king should practise."[75] These thirty-six virtues include some general qualities and some qualities which he must have in view of his duties. A perusal of the list cannot fail to impress upon us the fact that the Hindu thinkers envisaged an exalted ideal of monarchy.[76] The ideal king, according to them,

70. *Arthaśāstra*, Bk. I, Ch. 19, p. 36.

71. *Ibid.*, Bk. VI, Ch. 1.

72. *Śānti Parva*, Ch. XVIII.

73. *Ibid.*, Ch. XXI, 13-16; XXV, 33-35; XXVIII, 57; XXXIV, 48; LXIX, 105.

74. *Ibid.*, Ch. LIX, 104-107.

75. *Ibid.*, Ch. LXX.

76. *Śānti Parva*, Ch. LXX; see also Ch. LVII, 30-44 and CXVIII, 16-27.

must possess certain personal qualities; he must be well-educated and trained for his office; and he must govern the kingdom with a constant eye to *Dharma.* We cannot help feeling that the king's office is not a sinecure. It is not a privilege without duty. On the other hand, there is not the slightest doubt that a king, who really attempted to put into practice the various injunctions laid down in our Śāstras would certainly prove a veritable father to his subjects and a cause of delight to them, as the title Rājan signifies.[77] The life of the king, as sketched by our ancient sages, would be one perpetual act of service to his subjects. However, as we shall presently see, there is no constitutional check on the king. Besides indicating these various qualities which the king must possess and the various rules he must follow, the *Mahābhārata* emphasizes the king's duty never to swerve from the path of righteousness by laying down spiritual penalties for default. Thus, the king who does not protect his subjects, whose passions are not under control, who is full of vanity, who is haughty and malicious is said to incur sin.[78] It is only "the righteous king" who "partakes of the merits which accrue to persons practising the duties of the four modes of life."[79] On the other hand, "the sin a king incurs by neglecting for a single day to protect his subjects is such that his sufferings are not terminated in hell till after a thousand years."[80] From the immediate and practical point of view also the policy of oppressing the subjects is not profitable. It is just like cutting off the udders of a cow to get milk.[81] And finally, there is always the fear of the subjects breaking out into a revolt in the last resort. "That crooked and covetous king who suspects everybody and who imposes heavy taxes on his subjects is soon killed by his own relatives and servants."[82] The *Mahābhārata* has

77. We must not, however, lose sight of the castes, sanctified by *Dharma* itself and sought by the State.

78. *Śānti Parva,* XXIV, 18-20.

79. *Ibid.*, LXV, 14.

80. *Śānti Parva,* LXXI, 28; cf. XXIV, 12; and *Anuśāsana Parva,* LXI, 34-35.

81. *Śānti Parva,* LXXI, 15-16.

82. *Ibid.*, LVII, 27.

no hesitation in advising the subjects to shun like a leaky boat on the sea the king who does not really protect them.[83] Nay, the king who pretends to protect his people but does not actually protect them may even be slain by his subjects like a mad dog afflicted with rabies.[84]

It is easy to see from the above that the only checks on the autocracy of the king are extra-constitutional. The early training of the king and the injunctions of the sacred works may possibly bring home to him the necessity of conforming to the regulations of *Dharma*. The fear of incurring sin, the futility of oppression to yield the desired result and the danger of provoking a rebellion may possibly prove to be motives strong enough to keep the king in the path of duty. If, however, these fail, there is no ostensible remedy for the subjects except to unfurl the standard of revolt. This is always a remote possibility because of the inherent inertia of the people. Hence this so-called "right to tyrannicide" cannot be called a "right" at all inasmuch as it can be exercised only by stepping out of the bounds of legality.

And what is true of the *Mahābhārata* in this respect is also true of the rest of our ancient works. The *Manu-smṛiti*, for instance, expects the king to study the three Vedas, the science of government, and the science of dialectics and to acquire the knowledge of the (supreme) Soul.[85] He must shun all vices which spring from sensuality, greed and wrath. "Day and night he must strenuously exert himself to conquer his senses; for he (alone) who has conquered his own senses, can keep his subjects in obedience." The whole time of the king is spent in looking after the affairs of the State.[86] The imperativeness of these duties for the king lies in the fact that they constitute his Svadharma. There is, indeed, no constitutional machinery to secure the king's compliance to these regulations. The nemesis of misrule is the loss of life and

---

83. *Ibid.*, LVII, 43-44.

84. *Anuśāsana Parva*, LXI, 31-33.

85. *Manu*, VII, 43; cf. *Yāj.*, XIII, 309-311.

86. *Ibid.*, VII, 216-226.

kingdom, probably at the hands of the subjects.[87] As Yājñavālkya picturesquely puts it, "the fire which emanates from the sufferings of the subjects engulfs the king, his fortune and his family."[88]

Śukra depicts the ideal king succinctly. He is constant to his own duty; the protector of his subjects; he performs all the sacrifices and conquers his enemies; he is charitable, forbearing and valorous, has no attachment to the things of enjoyment and is dispassionate. His reward is salvation.[89] Śukrāchārya cites the instances of Nahusha and Vena, who were ruined on account of vice; and he makes a clear distinction between a king who is virtuous and one who is otherwise.[90] He lays stress on discipline as the chief quality of the king.[91] He definitely advises the king to find out his own faults by getting information through spies as to who among the people accuse him and why.[92] The king must study *Ānvīkshakī, Trayī, Vārttā* and *Daṇḍanīti* and must rule in accordance with the injunctions of the *Nīti-śāstras.*[93] The penalties for misrule are evidently extra-constitutional and spiritual. Thus, we are told, "the subjects desert a king, who is uncharitable, who insults men, who practises deceit and uses harsh words and who is severe in punishments."[94] This would mean only that in case of gross misrule, the subjects might desert or repudiate the king. There is no means, however, to avert such a contingency by constitutional means. Besides this danger of rebellion, the other penalty is that of sin and hell.[95]

The Hindu thinkers of old clearly realised that the varied and complex functions of government could not be managed by the

87. *Ibid.*, VII, 111-113.

88. *Yāj.*, XIII, 334-341.

89. *Śukra,* I, 59-62.

90. *Ibid.*, 135-140.

91. *Ibid.*, 181-182, 197-226.

92. Śukra, I, 260-266.

93. *Ibid.*, 301-304.

94. *Ibid.*, 279-280.

95. *Ibid.*, Ch. IV, section V, 16-17, 535-536. I, 239-240.

king alone. To assist him in the work of administration, the king must, therefore, have ministers.[96] These ministers were to be men of blameless private life, with excellent intellectual attainments, a high sense of duty and sound judgment.[97] They may have exercised considerable influence over the king; they may have dominated a weak king. The important position assigned to them as an element in the constitution may be inferred from the fact that the minister was expected to avert a crisis in case of a calamity to the king, by skilfully keeping under control forces, internal and external.[98] It should not be forgotten, however, that the ministers were all loyal servants selected and appointed by the king and holding office during royal pleasure. The king was at liberty to consult any number of councillors he chose to take into confidence. In case of differences of opinion among the councillors, the opinion of the majority may have been followed. The king, however, was not legally bound by it. He was free to exercise his own judgment and adopt any course of action likely to lead to success.[99] In a word, the sovereignty of the king was beyond question; there was no element in the constitution to which he must bow, except as it suited him.[100]

The *Mahābhārata* similarly recognises that a king who has no capable minister cannot govern his kingdom even for three days.[101] But, as in the *Arthaśāstra*, they are merely to offer advice, by constantly consulting his well-qualified ministers and following their advice, the king would ensure his own success, not only in

96. *Artha.*, Bk. I, Ch. VII, p. 12. "Sovereignty (Rājatva) is possible only with assistance. A single wheel can never move. Hence he shall employ ministers and hear their opinion."

97. *Ibid.*, Bk. I, Ch. IX and X.

98. *Ibid.*, Bk. V, Ch. VI.

99. Bandyopadhyaya: *Kauṭilya*, pp. 127-129.

100. P.N. Banerjea, however, says that the council of ministers possessed immense powers and enjoyed a great deal of independence. We fail to see where this independence comes in. The author does not give his grounds here. *Public Admn.*, p. 103.

101. *Śānti Parva*, Ch. VI, II.

the internal management of the kingdom but also in the dealings with other kings.[102]

According to Śukra, the ministers should be bold enough to raise their voice even against the king. "If the king fears them, they are good ministers." "Can there be prosperity in the kingdom," he asks, "if there be ministers whom the ruler does not fear?"[103] This only means that the ministers should offer their advice to the king in all conscience; the king, however, may reject it, though at the risk of inviting difficulties, such as estrangement from the subjects.[104] The ministers were subordinate to the king; they were his advisers; as such they may wield great influence; but the king was free to disregard their advice and to dismiss them, if he liked. As to their indirect "responsibility" to the people, to which P.N. Banerjea refers,[105] it could only mean the duty of the ministers to keep in view the interests of the subjects. It cannot of course mean that the ministers were legally accountable to the people or were removable by them.[106] It is misleading, therefore, to read the principle of "ministerial responsibility" in the general injunctions to ministers to place before the king their view of the good of the subjects.

We may say, then, that the Hindu monarch was, constitutionally speaking, an autocrat. As the head of the State, he owed allegiance to no person or institution within the State. He was the supreme legal authority, the fountain-head of justice and the apex of the whole administrative machinery. We might almost say that he was the determinate authority in the State acting as the ultimate source of power. It may be unjust and immoral for him to oppress his subjects; but there was no constitutional machinery to determine the limits beyond which he may not go.

---

102. *Ibid.*, Ch. XVIII, 7-15.

103. *Śukra,* Ch. II, 163-165.

104. *Ibid.*, Ch. II, 5-8.

105. *op. cit.*, p. 115.

106. Prof. B.K. Sarkar asserts that the ministers were the people's representatives and guardians. (*Positive Background of Hindu Sociology*, pp. 43 ff.) This view is also untenable in the light of what we have said above.

Further, it is sometimes asserted that he was bound to abide by the decisions of a popular assembly of some sort. We are not certain about the nature of the Vedic Sabhā or Samiti. The Vedic Index[107] notices the diversity of opinion on this matter. According to Ludwig, the Sabhā was an assembly not of all the people but of the Brāhmaṇas and Maghavans ("rich patrons"). Zimmer took it to be the meeting-place of the village council, presided over by the Grāmaṇī; while to Bloomfield, it seemed to be a term referring to a house, not to the assembly at all. All that we are certain about is that the king sometimes went to the Samiti. And we must note that Samiti and Sabhā are much the same, the one being the assembly, the other primarily the place of assembly.[108] As to what the function of this assembly was and how far it could be a constitutional check on the king, we are not in a position to say anything definitely. It is, of course, very probable that at no time was the Samiti a place where any or much attention was paid to the views of the common man.[109] Even if the Samiti had any political function, it is certain that it declined in importance as time passed. In the *Mahābhārata*, the assembly is simply a military body for consultation. "Both priests and people are silent in the face of force."[110] It is not correct, therefore, to say with Hopkins that "the epic King is no autocrat,"[111] for there are no constitutional checks to curb) his autocracy. On the other hand, as Hopkins himself recognises, in the Epic itself "each king is represented as doing what seems good to him without advice." The king was without doubt, the most prominent factor of the heroic State and his powers were practically unlimited.[112] And we have already seen how in the Kauṭiliyan State, all power rested ultimately with the king.

107. Vol. II, pp. 426-27.

108. *Vedic Index*, Vol. II, pp. 430-431.

109. *Ibid.*, Vol. II, p. 431.

110. *Camb. History of India*, Vol. I, p. 271.

111. *Ibid.*

112. N.K. Sidhanta: *Heroic Age of India*, pp. 192-193.

On the whole, then, we might safely assert that the government in ancient India cannot be said to be "a limited monarchy," as P.N. Banerjea proposes to call it; for monarchy can be said to be "limited" only if there is some constitutional limitation on it. Neither is it proper to regard it as a "Sachiva Tantra" in view of the fact that the Sachiva was, after all, no more than a servant of the king. The fact that, in practice, the policy of the king may be determined by the ministers or by any other body within the realm does not in the least make any difference, theoretically, in the position of the king. Dr. Beni Prasad is perfectly right when he maintains that "a limited monarchy in which the sovereign is only a dignified part of the constitution would have been incomprehensible to Hindu writers," and that "the monarchy was despotic."[113]

Our observations, it must be noted, do not refer to the nature of power but to the basis of power. When we say that the king was autocratic, we do not mean that he necessarily ruled arbitrarily. With the numerous threats of spiritual penalties and also with the dignity and authority of the Brāhmaṇas and ministers he would have been more than human if he ruled only according to his whims. Most of the writers on Hindu Polity, however, ignore the distinction we are seeking to make here. They fail to note that though the actual exercise of royal authority may not be arbitrary and tyrannical, its basis may nevertheless be autocratic.[114] When we say that the king was, constitutionally speaking, an autocrat, it must be noted that we are not passing a moral judgment on the actual exercise of his power. We must emphasize, however, that the various checks on the arbitrariness of royal power, which we have noted above, are all the necessary concomitants of the

---

113. *Theory of Government in Ancient India*, p. 358. cf. also K.V.R. Aiyangar: *Some Aspects of Ancient Indian Polity*, p. 63.

114. Dikshitar, for instance, maintains that the ancient Indian State was "a democratic monarchy." He speaks of the various checks on the autocracy of the king—checks like open revolt, deposition and choice of another king by the people. With these checks, he says, the king "could not conduct himself as an autocrat in any manner." (See *Hindu Administrative Institutions*, pp. 71-77.) It is evident that he fails to observe the distinction made above.

king's conformity to *Dharma.* It is, thus, misleading to assert that in ancient India the king regarded himself as merely exercising a trust or that there was a cabinet of ministers as an essential part of the administrative machinery, exercising a check on the king. Such statements would imply the direct influence of the people on the foreign policy of the State, the responsibility of the executive to the governed, in short, the control of the administrative machinery not by the will of a single individual but by the will of society.[115] The point to note is that whereas the subjects have above them the king, who punishes any departure from *Dharma* on their part, there is no authority to punish a similar breach on the part of the king. Legally, he is "adaṇḍya," immune from punishment.

Having thus determined the sphere of the Hindu State and the position of the king in the empirical ordering of *Dharma,* we shall now pass on to consider how the existence of various other social institutions affects the position of the monarch. Are these other institutions independent of or co-ordinate with the State? Does the recognition of the place of these institutions in society involve a limitation of the sphere and authority of the State? In other words, can we accept the dictum that "only a pluralistic theory can grasp the Indian phenomena?"[116] How far is it true to speak, as Prof. Radha Kamal Mukerjee does, of the "old and established tradition in political pluralism" with reference to India?

It seems probable that some sorts of guilds and corporations existed in India from early times. The word "Sresthin" occurs in several passages of the *Brāhmaṇas* and may probably mean the "headman" of a guild. "The Vedic evidence is, however, inadequate to afford ground for positive assertion or denial of the existence or organisation of guilds during the Vedic times."[117] Guilds are referred to in the *Dharmasūtras* and they play a considerable part in the Buddhist texts and the Epic. Gautama lays down that justice must be determined in accordance with the precepts of

115. See Prof. Jadunath Sarkar's Article in *Modern Review,* 1917.

116. See Beni Prasad: *op. cit.,* p. 9.

117. *Vedic Index,* Vol. II, pp. 403-404.

the Vedas, Institutes, Aṅgas and the Purāṇas; but the laws of the country, castes and families, when not opposed to these sacred records, are also authoritative. Cultivators, traders, herdsmen, money-lenders, artisans can lay down rules for themselves which the king must consider as authoritative within the limit specified above.[118] Vasishṭha similarly remarks that the king must know "all the laws of the country, castes, and families," and should make the four castes follow their particular duties.[119] Thus, according to the authors of the *Dharmaśāstras*, the laws of these corporations have a validity in so far as they do not conflict with the injunctions of the sacred law.

The *Mahābhārata* lays down that the king should not abolish these special customs of families or old countries.[120] The *Manusmṛiti* requires the king to "establish as law what may have been practised by the virtuous twice-born men devoted to the law," if such practices are "not opposed to the customs of countries, families, and castes (jatis)."[121] There are similar injunctions in other *Dharmaśāstras* also.[122] And the *Śukranīti* is quite in agreement with the earlier texts on this point.[123]

What is exactly the significance of such injunctions? Do they involve a limitation of the king's authority? The answer to these questions can easily be given if we just examine the evidence regarding the relation of the king to such corporations. According to Gautama, the king should ascertain the state of affairs from those who have the authority to speak and then give his decision.[124] The statement indirectly implies that the king has the final authority with him to give the decision regarding the activity of corporations. The Jātakas throw a little light on the question.

---

118. *Gautama,* XI, 20-22.

119. *Vasishṭha,* XIX, 7.

120. *Śānti Parva,* LXXVII, 19.

121. *Manu,* VIII, 46.

122. *Nārada,* X, 3; *Bṛihaspati,* XXVII, 24; *Yāj.,* XIII, 366-368.

123. *Śukra,* Ch. IV, section V, 35-36.

124. *Gautama,* XI, 20-21.

Fick[125] notices in this connection the heredity of occupations, the localisation of the different branches of industry and the institutions of "jetthakas" or aldermen. There were, he thinks, definite organizations of merchants and artisans.

The extent of power wielded by the alderman cannot be definitely ascertained. Nor is it possible to determine to whom the alderman was responsible. There is, however, a reference in one of the Jātakas to a state officer, Bhandagarika, treasurer or Superintendent of Stores, who acted as judge for members of merchant guilds. It would seem, then, that the guilds were not perfectly autonomous. The State was entitled to exercise some sort of supervision over them, particularly in the matter of justice.[126] The initiative of the various associations in society was probably not discouraged. Dr. Majumdar speaks of various corporate activities in ancient India—in matters political, economic, social and religious. The President of such corporations may have exercised a considerable amount of powers but any person punished by the President could appeal to the king[127] and if it would appear that the conduct of the President was not in accordance with prescribed regulations but was simply actuated by personal feelings, the king could veto his resolutions. The various guilds and corporations could not thus have been co-ordinate with the State. Kauṭilya requires the king to see to it that the superintendent of accounts keeps a record of "the history of customs, professions and transactions of countries, villages and corporations."[128] The king is not counselled to leave these alone. He is rather to make them conform to certain rules. For instance, the guilds of workmen should have a grace of seven nights over and above the period agreed upon for fulfilling their engagement.[129] Some of these corporations seem to have been very powerful. Kauṭilya suggests

125. *Social Organization in North-East India in Buddhist Times,* Ch. X.

126. B. Prasad: *Theory of Govt. in Ancient India,* pp. 312-313.

127. cf. *Ibid.*

128. *Artha.,* Bk. II, Ch. 7.

129. *Ibid.,* III, Ch. 14.

ways and means of keeping them on one's side.[130] In some cases, a corporation may have to be put down by arresting its leader or a part of the corporation itself.[131] Kauṭilya is an advocate of a strong, energetic government. He cannot therefore look favourably on organizations which might divide the allegiance of subjects. The acquisition of the help of corporations, he says, is better than the acquisition of an army, a friend or profits. The relation of these to the State is, however, to be one of due subordination to the imperative command of the latter. Those corporations which are opposed to the king must, therefore, be put down by sowing the seeds of dissension among them and by secretly punishing them.[132]

That these organisations could never claim to be independent of, or co-ordinate with, the State, comes out clearly from some of the injunctions of the *Dharmaśāstras.* The *Yājñavālkya-smṛiti* lays down that it is the duty of the king to "discipline" and "set in the right path" the families, castes, the Srenis, the Ganas and the Janapadas, who have deviated from their duty.[133] Nārada, while admitting the necessity of taking into account the traditions and customs of merchants, artisans and the like, clearly realizes that the king should prevent them from undertaking such acts as would either be opposed (to the wishes of the king) or contemptible in their nature, or injurious to his interests.[134]

Clearly, then, the corporations are not beyond the purview of the State; nor can we say with Dr. Mookerji that they are treated "more or less on terms of equality."[135] In the injunctions of the law-givers to the effect that the customs, laws and traditions of various groups should be kept undisturbed so far as they do not conflict with *Dharma,* we have only to notice a particular application of the fundamental maxim that the king must maintain *Dharma.* Just

130. *Ibid.*, VII, Ch. 16.

131. *Ibid.*, VIII, Ch. 4.

132. *Ibid.*, IX, Ch. 1.

133. *Yāj.*, XIII, 361.

134. *Nārada,* X, 2-4.

135. *Vide Local Govt. in Ancient India,* p. 7.

as the maintenance of *Dharma* means the maintenance of the Svadharma of castes and orders, so it involves in this case the maintenance of local customs, usages and practices. While not crushing out the initiative of these groups, the king had certainly the power to see that they kept within the bounds of *Dharma.* The jurisdiction of the courts of the Kulas, Srenis and Ganas was recognised within specified limits and an appeal from them lay to the king himself. The king, says Śukra "is higher than all—the dictator of what should be done and what should not be done."[136] The local usages and customs and the traditions of various corporations have to be honoured as a safe course in actual administration. No limitation on the authority of the king is really implied here. It may be true that "various societies, each representing a different principle or social force operating in society, grew up more or less independently, contemporaneously with the military organisation or at any rate before the military organisation had grown into the homogeneous State."[137] It is well known that the State first enters the field as the interpreter and enforcer of custom rather than as the creator of new rules of conduct.[138] This historical precedence of certain associations does not, however, alter the nature of the relation of the State to these groups. In the earliest *Smṛitis* these societies may have enjoyed a position of independence or rather isolation inasmuch as they were not yet properly integrated into the homogeneous State. So long as the king represented merely the military principle, he evidently did not exercise the power effectively to control the other institutions in society. It is probably this fact which explains why in the earlier *Smṛitis* the duty of the king to regard these societies is imperative, while with Manu and Yājñavālkya, it almost sinks to a recommendation and a matter of grace.[139] The history of Indo-Aryan society after the earliest *Smṛitis* is really the history of the integration of these various principles under a ruling one

136. Ch. IV, section V, 59-62.

137. Sen Gupta: *Law and Society in Ancient India,* p. 19.

138. Willoughby: *The Nature of the State,* p. 147.

139. Sen Gupta: *op. cit.*, pp. 18-20.

and the subordination of all societies to the one representing the ruling idea.[140]

A topic which has obvious affinity with the above problem is the nature of local government in ancient India. It is to the ancient system of local government that the preservation of the integrity, independence and individuality of Indian culture are said to be due.[141] Sir Charles Metcalfe spoke of the village communities in India as "little republics." We have to see how far this characterisation can be said to be true.

From the earliest times, India has been a land of villages. The Vedic Indians lived in villages, which were scattered all over the country, some close together, some far apart. The relation of the villagers as among themselves is difficult to ascertain. It appears, however, that the village was not a unit for legal purposes in early days and it can hardly be said to have been a political unit. At the head of the village was the Grāmaṇī, whose functions were probably both civil and military. His post seems to have been sometimes hereditary and sometimes nominated or elective. What is remarkable, however, is his connection with the royal person. The Grāmaṇī seems to have been an influential person and it is probable that he was a nominee of the king rather than a popularly elected offcer.[142] The early States, however, being small in size, there could hardly be a clear division of Government into central and local. As the State grew larger, the distinction between the two kinds of governmental activity must naturally have become more marked, and in the *Mahābhārata*, the *Manu-smṛiti* and the *Arthaśāstra*, the organisation of local government is discussed at considerable length.

According to the *Mahābhārata*,[143] the administration of the kingdom demands an elaborate organisation of officials for looking after the smaller units as well. The smallest unit for

140. *Ibid.*

141. Mookerji: *op. cit.*, p. 1.

142. See *Vedic Index*, Vol. I, pp. 246 ff.

143. *Śānti Parva*, LXXXVII.

administrative purposes is the village under the management of the headman, selected by the king. The headman must ascertain the characteristics of every person in the village and all crimes which need punishment. Over ten villages there should be placed a superintendent, to whom the headman of every village should report everything about his charge. This Superintendent should report the same to the officer in charge of twenty villages. The latter, again, should report the conduct of all persons within his province to the officer in charge of a hundred villages. Next comes the lord of a thousand villages who also has similar duties. Over them all is the minister who has to supervise the administrative work and the mutual relations of these officers. This minister should employ spies to learn the conduct of those under him. He is to keep constant supervision over them "like some dreadful planet moving above all the asterisms below." The Epic thus provides for a machinery to keep the central government always in touch with the smallest units under its charge. Whatever in practice may be the latitude allowed to the villages in the management of internal affairs, there is no doubt that in theory at least the government is a centralised bureaucracy, seeking effectively to govern the smallest units of administration. And it is probable that the scheme which the *Mahābhārata* prescribes is a reflex of the then existing practice.[144]

The *Manu-smṛiti*[145] reproduces the above plan for local government. Every village must have a headman. The successively higher areas of local government are to be the groups of ten, twenty, a hundred and a thousand villages as in the *Mahābhārata*. Every official in the hierarchy is to keep his superior fully informed of all happenings and all crimes within his jurisdiction. Above them all is to be the minister at the headquarters in charge of the whole sphere of local government. This minister, evidently, is directly responsible to the king and the hierarchical arrangement is thus complete.

---

144. Beni Prasad: *Theory of Government in Ancient India*, p. 50.

145. *Manu*, VII, 113-123.

The Kauṭiliyan arrangement, though not the same in detail, is conceived in the same spirit. Kauṭilya recognises, for instance, the advisability of allowing the "elders of five or ten villages" to adjudicate in cases of boundary disputes.[146] But it is the village headman who is officially the superintendent of the village. There is a reference in the *Arthaśāstra* to his liability to make good the value of merchandise lost or stolen in his village.[147] The village thus continued to form the unit of administration. The whole kingdom was divided into a number of provinces governed by Viceroys. Each province was divided into circles of eight hundred, four hundred, two hundred, one hundred and ten villages, administered by officers in a hierarchy.[148] Above all these officers was the minister in charge of the collection of revenue and the police.[149]

Similar provisions are laid down in the *Vishṇu-smṛiti*[150] and in the *Śukra-nīti-sāra.*[151]

To conclude, it would be misleading to say that the villages in ancient India were autonomous units. Our evidence shows that they were all linked up to the central government by means of an elaborate administrative machinery. All we may say is that the villages were perhaps not subject to vexatious interference from the central government, so far as their internal affairs were concerned. But they formed a part—an integral part—of the great administrative machinery.[152]

We are now in a position to answer the question we proposed to ourselves. A study of the relation of the king to the various associations in society and of the system of local government in ancient India shows clearly that whatever in practice the extent of

146. *Artha.*, Bk. III, Ch. 9.

147. *Artha.*, Bk. IV, Ch. 13.

148. *Ibid.*, Bk. II, Ch. 1 and 25.

149. cf. Bandyopadhyaya: *Kauṭilya*, pp. 250-251 and *Camb. History of India,* Vol. I, p. 487.

150. *Vishṇu*, III, 7-15; also *Gautama*, X, 9-12.

151. Śukra, I, 377-384; V, 162-171.

152. Banerjea: *Public Administration in Ancient India,* pp. 288 ff.

freedom from interference these may have secured for themselves, in theory, no doubt, the king had the right to say the final word. These various associations were in no sense on a level of equality or co-ordinate with the State. It is, indeed, assumed that every guild, corporation, family or caste has its own Svadharma. The end of the State being to maintain *Dharma*, which means Svadharma, the king would certainly be bound not to impose his own will or in fact, any outside will, on these associations. They must be free to follow their Svadharma. In the case of the Varṇas and Aśramas, the Svadharma has been definitely laid down by our Śāstrakāras. In this case, such an attempt would be evidently absurd. It becomes the duty of the king, then, to find out what the Svadharma of a certain corporation is, in case there is a dispute on the point. When the king is called upon to adjudicate in matters of dispute between these associations, his duty evidently would be to consult the people who are acquainted with the matter at first hand, determine the Svadharma of the associations and decide whether and how far a particular association had strayed from its proper limits. So long as these various societies within the body politic kept to their *Dharma*, they would certainly be left unmolested by the king. It is only in this sense that we can speak of the "autonomy" of these groups. The intervention of the king would be justified only when it was meant to uphold *Dharma*. The position of the king is thus peculiar. He is the ultimate authority in the State; in him are concentrated the various principles governing the social institutions. There is thus no limit to the sphere or scope of his activity. At the same time, he is himself subject to *Dharma*. His authority is final because he is the upholder of *Dharma*. And *Dharma* is the principle underlying the moral order of the world. The various castes, orders, families, corporations—in fact, all the institutions in society embodying diverse purposes—are all subject to *Dharma*. *Dharma* is the sovereign principle of the universe. The king is the sustainer of the empirical order of *Dharma*. He does not, therefore, "legislate" for the people. The sources of law are laid down in the Śāstras and these he must abide by. We do, indeed, hear of laws to be promulgated by the king, in the *Śukranīti.*[153] But the presumption probably is that they are no more than declarations of *Dharma.* It is not difficult to see that the injunctions laid down by Asoka in his edicts are also supposed to be the declarations of *Dharma* and not laws as such ordained by the king himself. When this fact is noted, it is not at all surprising that the king should not initiate legislation for other associations in society. The king has to intervene only when *Dharma* is violated; and in this respect, there is no distinction at all as between one institution and another. We cannot, therefore, speak of "decentralisation" as being the policy of the Hindu State; for "decentralisation" can really come after "centralisation." The recognition of the sanctity of the Svadharma of every individual and every group is the fundamental axiom of Hindu thought. The idea of a State so militant and overbearing as to crush all local initiative and to impose its fiat on all institutions in society is thus foreign to Hindu thought. Our ancient thinkers clearly recognised the need of fostering the growth of various associations and institutions in society. In order to secure this, they laid it down as the essential duty of the king to respect and to give due consideration to their customs and traditions. At the same time, they did not favour a kind of development that would weaken the authority of the State. Śukra seems clearly to have recognised this. "There should only be," he says,[154] "one leader in a State, never many, and the king should never leave any situation without a leader." If, again, we look to the actual administrative arrangements, for instance, of Maurya kings we find that the central government, by means of local officers, exercised strict control and maintained close supervision over all classes and castes of the population.[155] The scholars who maintain that we cannot speak of "decentralisation conceded by a central

153. Ch. I, 587 ff.

154. I, 682-683.

155. V.A. Smith: *Early History of India,* p. 127. It is surprising to see that in the face of this evidence Dr. Mookerji maintains that the Mauryan Empire "aimed at an elastic system of federalism or confederation." (See: *Local Government in Ancient India,* pp. 7-10.)

government" with reference to the Indian Polity[156] are right. It is incorrect, however, to rush to the conclusion that the ancient Indian Polity was "federal" in nature. If the king was not entitled to interfere with the working of the associations and corporations except in the interests of *Dharma*, we must bear in mind that these associations were not affiliated to the State by any "conventions and agreements which operate as charters regulating their mutual relations." In short, the recognition of the legitimate activities of the various associations or corporations within the State does not impose a limitation on the authority of the king; for, such limitation is implicit in the end of the State itself.[157]

The Hindu thinkers thus recognise that the State is not merely one among many associations. It is rather the institution of institutions because of its relation to *Dharma*.

It sets the perspective for other institutions in society. It is really the operative criticism of all institutions—the various institutions in society are not ends in themselves. They cannot be of significance except as related to a central spiritual purpose to which alone the loyalty of the individual is really due. The Hindu State is thus not merely "to keep the ring" when the various institutions in societies carry on, as it were, a struggle among themselves for self-assertion and survival in the conflict of a myriad wills. It is actively to maintain and promote *Dharma*, by recognising the diversity of the Svadharmas of the various institutions in society. The State is entitled thus to adjust, to reconcile, to synthesize the claims and obligations of various associations and institutions by referring them to the general scheme of values implicit in the concept of *Dharma*.

This view of the Hindu State involves, it will be noticed, the rejection of the view that it was essentially "pluralistic." We hold, rather, that Hindu political thought recognises "plurality"

---

156. R. Mookerji: *Democracies of the East*, p. xvi. cf. Mookerji: *op. cit.*, p. 317.

157. We have here an instance of what Prof. Dicey calls the "internal limit to the exercise of sovereignty." *The Law of the Constitution*, p. 77.

or diversity because that is the nature of Svadharma. But this is really far from saying that the State is pluralistic.

It is beyond the scope of this Essay to enter into anything like an adequate discussion of the problem of sovereignty in its various aspects. One of the most marked effects of the great war upon social theory has been the profound distrust of the State and various proposals have been made to "discredit" the State and expunge once for all the conception of sovereignty from political theory. The pluralistic theory claims to "place the individual at the centre of things." It regards the State as "only one of the associations" to which the individual belongs. It tries to show that "the monistic theory of the state, making it sovereign and therefore absolute, runs counter to some of the deepest convictions we can possess."[158] The new theory thus seeks to criticise severely the "metaphysical" theory of the State and to dethrone it from its position of pre-eminence. We must be prepared to find out the elements of value in this attack and reformulate the theory of the State in the light of such criticisms. It would be wrong to accept as self-evident the proposition that the pluralistic theory of the State is the whole truth, newly discovered, to which we must transfer our allegiance. We have to inquire into the validity of the various objections raised by the modern critics of the "monistic" theory, before we accept the facile conclusion that the State henceforth "ceases to be unique and sovereignty becomes composite and multiple." And significant attempts have already been made by a few thinkers to meet the objections raised by the pluralistic theory.[159] It will be enough for our purpose, if we just note here only those points which throw light on the problem of sovereignty in the Hindu State.

---

158. Laski: *Studies in the Problem of Sovereignty,* Ch. I.

159. Refer M.P. Tollett: *The New State,* Chs. XXVIII and XXIX and Hsiao: *Political Pluralism.* Hsiao comes to the following conclusion: "Whatever may be the avenue of approach—whether it be through law and legal theory, through the problem of representative government, or lastly through economic and social organization—the final outcome of the pluralistic argument is in every instance not multiplicity as such (as we naturally expect) but some unity that transcends and points beyond mere multiplicity." p. 127.

Much of the misunderstanding about the nature of State-sovereignty has been probably due to the fact that the definition of it given by Austin has been taken to have reference to its ethical basis also. Austin, we must remember, was a jurist; and he attempted merely to analyse the legal conception of sovereignty. As a matter of legal theory, Austin argued that there must be in every State "a definite human superior, not in a habit of obedience to a like superior." The State for him is a legal order in which there is a determinate authority acting as the ultimate source of power. Its authority is unlimited; and law is nothing but the command of the sovereign.

The Austinian theory has been criticised from various points of view. It has been pronounced to be absurd on the historical side; it has been put aside as not really indicating the ultimate source of political authority and it has been regarded as presenting an erroneous conception of law.[160] The only truth about the Austinian theory is in its demonstration that "in a thoroughly developed State there must be some determinate person or persons, with whom, in the last resort, lies the recognised power of imposing laws and enforcing their observance over whom no legal control can be exercised."[161] It is evident, however, that the Austinian conception of sovereignty cannot explain why people obey the sovereign. It is impossible, as Laski observes, to make the legal theory of sovereignty valid for political philosophy.[162] If by sovereign power we mean the real determinant of the habitual obedience of the people, then, it is only the conception of the 'general will' that can explain it. The 'habitual' obedience comes only out of the recognition of the value of the end and attainments of the State. When the conception of sovereignty is related to that of the 'general will,' the sovereignty of the State is no longer antithetic to the liberty of its members.

160. Leacock: *Elements of Political Science*, p. 59. Willoughby: *The Nature of the State*, pp. 163 ff.

161. Green: *Principles of Political Obligation*, p. 97. cf. Mcllwain: "Sovereign power, as distinct from any other power, is the highest legal power in the State." *Economica*, Vol. V, 1926.

162. *Grammar of Politics*, p. 55.

The principle of sovereignty is really the recognition of the personality, whether of one man or of a group or of the State. "Sovereignty," as Dr. Bosanquet observes, "is a feature inherent in a genuine whole."[163] The sovereignty of the State is thus the result of the fact that the State is an embodiment of the 'general will'. There does not really arise a question of imposing the will of the State on the members. Ideally, the State is the individual and the individual is the State. As Plato would put it, the State is the individual writ large, the individual is the State in miniature. The will of the State is the will of the members. The fallacy of the pluralists' argument arises out of their identification of the State with government. Thus, according to Laski, the will of the State is "the decision arrived at by a small number of men to whom is confided the legal power of making decisions."[164] A hiatus is thus created between the State and the citizen, and constant effort becomes necessary to see that somehow the gulf is bridged. If, broadly speaking, this means that the actions of any actual government require close scrutiny, there is certainly nothing to invalidate the statement. But by maintaining this, we are in no way attacking the "monistic" conception. Sovereignty, as we just noted, inheres in the whole. "The State is sovereign inasmuch as it has the power of creating one in which all are."[165] The sovereignty of the State is in no way incompatible with the development of group life. In fact, sovereignty is a moral idea. The individual is really sovereign in so far as he can harmonise his impulses and lead an organised life. A group is similarly sovereign in so far as it can integrate the differences of its members so as to produce a real harmony. The problem, in fact, is how the State can truly be sovereign. In this sense, it is not less but more of sovereignty that we want. The value of the pluralistic criticism lies exactly here.

---

163. *Phil. Theory of the State*, p. XIVIII.

164. *Grammar of Politics*, p. 35. For Prof. Laski, thus, "a theory of the State is essentially a theory of the governmental act." (p. 28.) Similarly, from his point of view, "the sovereign is the person in the State who can get his will accepted, who so dominates his fellows as to blend their wills with his." (*Problem of Sovereignty*, pp. 270, 16-17.)

165. Follett: *The New State*, p. 271.

It is not enough to say that the State is sovereign because of its being an embodiment of the 'real will' of all its members. It is necessary to translate this ideal into practice as far as possible. The real problem for the pluralists, as Dr. Hsiao profoundly observes, "is not to destroy sovereignty but to reorganise it so that political power shall become the true expression of the community."[166] The pluralist contends that the State, as we find it to-day, does not really objectify the totality of social purposes. It is on that account wholly inadequate to give expression to the complete personality of all men in the community. He emphasizes, therefore, the necessity of revivifying group life by a well-planned policy of decentralisation. The organisation of neighbourhood and vocational groups which he advocates is thus meant to be the real basis of the unified and unifying State.

Manifold as the relationships of man in society are, and diverse though his loyalties may be, it is imperative that these must be properly ordered and made coherent by reference to the ideal scheme of values in life. Man has certainly to identify himself with group life in many forms in order to fully develop his humanity. But we must not overlook the fact that none of these group relationships is more than a stage towards a more complete whole within which they all take their places.[167]

The outcome of the whole of our argument may be said to be this: we have discarded the conception of the atomic individual; we must discard also the conception of the particularism of the group as well as of the nation. The individual is in his nature universal and the logic of his nature demands the State. Such a State, however, need not supersede the activities of subordinate groups, for they can be filled into their places "in a larger entirety."[168]

---

166. Hsiao: *Political Pluralism,* p. 140.

167. Follett: *op. cit.,* Introduction by Lord Haldane, p. x.

168. cf. Mac Iver: "Political law keeps its own universality in the small as in the great, in the village, as in the world empire, there is the same need for those other associations, which pursue *on a basis of common order,* the manifold free social purposes of the human spirit." *The Modern State,* p. 21.

We must realise, then, that the conception of sovereignty as inhering in a whole is in no sense incompatible with the recognition of a proper place for all the manifold activities of men in their diverse relationships. "No matter how far we decentralise our social organisation, no matter into how many departments we divide our social life,......so long as we uphold social solidarity as the all-competent principle of social organisation, all these pluralities must finally be ordered and unified by this principle into an absolute system."[169] So, ultimately, sovereignty would mean the principle of solidarity and coherence.

It is thus inaccurate to speak of sovereignty being "composite" and "multiple." It is rather of the essence of sovereignty to be the result of a reconciliation of "composite" and "multiple" loyalties.[170]

Judging from this point of view, the Hindu conception of the sovereignty of the State has valuable elements in it. It involves the assertion, on the one hand, of the supremacy of the one, comprehensive principle of *Dharma* and on the other hand, it attaches due importance to the performance of Svadharma by castes, families, guilds, corporations and all the institutions which express life's manifold purposes. As a result the king is enjoined not to meddle with the normal working of these institutions but only to secure their conformity to *Dharma*, through the instrumentality of Daṇḍa.

To sum up, the sphere of the Hindu State must be regarded as co-extensive and co-terminous with the whole of life, even as the conception of *Dharma*. A limitation of the functions and scope of government is alien to Hindu political thought. This is but natural, when we take into consideration the fact that for Hindu thinkers, the problems of life were undifferentiated. There is no clear distinction between economic, political, social and religious activities. The State is looked upon as the guarantee of the whole social order with its manifold ramifications. There is thus no aspect of human life and human relationship which it may not regulate.

---

169. Hsiao: *op. cit.*, p. 20.

170. Mac Iver admits that sovereign power is an attribute of the common will, made common by community of purpose. *op. cit.*, pp. 14-15.

But this regulation itself is to be organised according to *Dharma*. There is no limit to the scope of governmental authority and to the authority of the king, so far as the empirical ordering of *Dharma* is concerned. This, however, does not mean a "carte blanche" to the king. There are various elements in the polity that he has to reckon with. Spiritual penalties and sacerdotal checks are bound to have an influence on his policy. It is because of these that some of our scholars have been led to speak of the ancient Indian State as a "limited monarchy." In fact, as we have seen, the basis of kingly power was autocratic. The king was the keystone of the constitutional arch, having no constitutional authority above him. The actual exercise of power may not, indeed, have been tyrannical. Our ancient thinkers have laid down the principles of the polity with a view to seeing that the king's authority may be exercised so as to lead to the well-being of the people. While admitting this, we must guard against generalisations that speak of the sphere of governmental activities as being but "the irreducible minimum," and the nature of the kingly authority as a "trust." The only checks on its arbitrariness are those arising from the nature of the polity as determined by *Dharma*. It is necessary, similarly, to bear in mind that the emphasis on giving due recognition to the Svadharmas of castes, families, villages, and other social institutions cannot be regarded as making the State "pluralistic." The State is rather the institution of institutions which gathers up and harmonises the diverse loyalties of its members in the light of *Dharma*. The sovereignty of the State as the embodiment of *Dharma* is not antithetic to the healthy development of group life; for, the Svadharmas of these groups in society have their validity only on account of their relation to the fundamental conception of *Dharma*. In a word, the loyalty of the individual is ultimately to one central unifying principle, though it may manifest itself in diversified and manifold loyalties.

It is clear, thus, that the nature of the Hindu State bears the indelible stamp of the conception of *Dharma*. The functions of the State, the sphere of the State, the limitations on the authority of the State—all these are determined with reference to *Dharma*.

Dharma is the guiding spirit of the polity, to *Dharma* is due the allegiance of the individual. We shall see in the next chapter what political obligation means in the light of this conception and how it was understood by our ancient statesmen and law-givers.

Chapter VIII

Dharma and Political Obligation

"Freedom is the harmonious, unimpeded working of the law of one's own nature. The true nature of every man is found only in the whole. A man is ideally free only so far as he is interpermeated by every other human being; he gains his freedom through a perfect and complete relationship because thereby he achieves his whole nature."

FOLLETT

"The great question is to discover, not what governments prescribe, but what they ought to prescribe; for no prescription is valid against the conscience of mankind. Before God, there is neither Greek nor barbarian, neither rich nor poor, and the slave is as good as his master, for by birth all men are free......"

ACTON

We must now gather up the threads of our discussion and visualise the Hindu view of political obligation as a whole.

The end of the Hindu State is, as we have seen, the maintenance of *Dharma.* The manifold functions of the king are to be understood in the light of *Dharma.* It is *Dharma* that determines the right relation between the State and the individual. The relations of the various groups in society are also regulated in view of *Dharma. Dharma,* thus, is the guiding principle of the Indian Polity and we may well speak of the Hindu ideal of the State as a *Dharma-rājya.*

Dharma, we have noted,[1] is the supreme principle governing the whole universe. It is in obedience to this eternal principle

1. See Chapter V, supra.

that the sun and the moon, the stars, the seasons, the rivers—all these—keep to their appointed course. No phenomenon in the physical or in the social world is beyond the sway of this principle. To our ancients, there is no hiatus between the physical world and the social world, between the world of inanimate matter and the world of living beings. If natural phenomena follow the divine order of *Dharma*, the life of man here must also be lived in obedience to the self-same law.

It is this principle, then, that is said to be the basis of the State. The sanction behind its authority is the sanction of *Dharma*; and the State exists in order to support *Dharma*. Thus, there is a sort of mutualism between them. Or rather, the eternal *Dharma* manifests itself in the empirical world in the ordering of the State.

Political obligation is thus related to this eternal principle. In obeying the State, the individual really renders homage to *Dharma*, which is the true sovereign authority at the back of the king. The Hindu conception of political obligation thus teaches the individual to look beyond the immediate source of authority. Loyalty is due to one central principle in the final analysis. The individual is to observe the rules of the caste or the regulations of the family or of any other institution as a part of his loyalty to *Dharma*. His loyalty to the State does not swallow up other loyalties. On the other hand, it is the necessary condition of the fulfilment of other obligations in various walks of life. Man has his duties in respect of his Varṇa, he has his duties with reference to his Āśrama and he has various duties in general also. For the due discharge of these duties, the loyalty to the State is necessary; because it is the State which makes possible the performance of duties laid down by Svadharma. Thus, on account of its making possible the observance of Svadharma, the State, in the eye of a Hindu, is intimately connected with the ultimate end of life. The State is not merely the necessary instrument to secure material comfort. It is not mere police. Its influence pervades the whole of life. It alone makes possible the pursuit of the threefold Purushārtha—Dharma, Artha and Kāma—and it thereby opens out the way to salvation. "The State," as Dr. Law aptly puts it, "under the direction of the sovereign, leads the people under its protection to the final goal of human existence—emancipation—furnishing at the same time means therefor."[2] It is to this idea of the State that the individual is called upon to be loyal. That is to say, political obligation is not merely political in a narrow sense; because of its association with *Dharma*, it becomes religious or spiritual.

The question is often raised whether the Hindu State could be called a theocracy. This would involve the further question as to the exact connotation of the term "theocracy." We are in a position to say without going into any fine or elaborate distinctions that the conception of *Dharma* at the back of the State does mean a strong religious influence on the State. The State is ultimately connected up with the final goal of existence. This is not so much a social as a religious or spiritual and philosophical conception. But the State is not based on a dogma. Hinduism has never been sectarian in outlook. In the name of the diversity of Svadharma, differences could be tolerated. Nor was the State a purely secular institution. The divinity of the king which we have noted, the importance of Daṇḍa, the maintenance of Varṇa Dharma and Āśrama Dharma, the special privileges for the Brāhmaṇas, the coronation ceremony and the various offerings and sacrifices on that occasion—all these are distinctly religious aspects.[3] In fact, the Hindu mind always delighted in relating the smallest duty to *Dharma*; the most primary functions in life, like eating or bathing even, were thus clothed in a religious garb.

The important point to note is that political obligation is not conceived of as conflicting with other obligations. The State is not placed over against the family or any other institution in society. Man is not, in this view, a creature tormented by competing and conflicting loyalties, swayed now this way and now that by the pressure of the claims of diverse principles upon him. All obligation is traced ultimately from *Dharma*. The Svadharmas of individuals and groups are to be ordered in the light of *Dharma*.

---

2. *Aspects of Ancient Indian Polity*, p. 145.

3. For a discussion of the religious aspects of the Ancient Indian Polity, refer *Ibid.*

Thus each principle in life has its own proper place, a harmony is evolved and well-ordered life becomes possible. It is because of this that a rule of conduct is equally sacred whether relating to. the every-day duties of a householder or to a broad question of the State or to social status. A violation of any such rule would not be a breach of a private duty, leading to certain legal consequences; but it would also be adharma or outrage to *Dharma* with consequences in the hereafter which would have to be redressed no matter whether by Daṇḍa, self-infliction, prāyśchitta or reparation, which are all different ways of *Dharma* adjusting itself.

It must be considered as a great achievement of our ancients that with a bold stroke of intuitive insight, they could realize the fundamental unity of purpose that governs the entire universe. They saw that the world is not a fortuitous concourse of atoms; neither is it a brute collocation of facts. There is one underlying principle which manifests itself in diverse forms. The goal of all endeavour must, therefore, be for man to keep in view before him this eternal verity and to approximate his conduct to it, so as to be in tune with the rhythm of the universe. It is because of this realisation that our ancients thought of the State as an instrument not merely for social well-being, as they understood the term, but also for the maintenance of the moral order of the universe.

The acceptance of this truth does not, however, solve our difficulties. Rather, it is just the beginning of real difficulties. Man must exercise his volition. It is given to him to be able to visualise the consequences of his actions and to mould his life in view of his ideals. His task, therefore, is to discover the real significance of *Dharma* and to translate it in institutional terms. Having realised that the end of the State must be no less than the maintenance of *Dharma*, the problem is how to make our social institutions the concretised expression of that eternal principle. It is a gigantic problem which it is the mission of humanity to solve. No scheme can once for all be laid down to be serviceable for all time. It is rather an eternal quest and in the quest itself lies the progressive realization. The end of the State, therefore, cannot strictly speaking be said to be the maintenance of *Dharma.* It must rather be spoken of as progressive approximation to the order which is *Dharma.*

Our ancient sages visualised the principle of *Dharma* but it seems they could not realise its implications. They felt, however, that *Dharma* must be translated into institutional terms. How was this to be done? They must have been strongly impressed with the need for stability and order in society and in obedience to the natural inclination to regard the existing institutions as necessary and inevitable, they merely identified the "status quo" with *Dharma.*[4] The duty of the State thus came to be regarded as the preservation of the existing order of society. And the existing order was a hierarchical order, determining man's functions in life by the mere fact of birth, perpetuating the privileges of the Brāhmaṇas and heaping up disabilities on the lower classes. Instead of the ideal being actualised, the actual was idealised. The sanction of the divine law was thus attached to the existing institutional arrangements, which came to be regarded as sacrosanct. As a result, we find law-giver after law-giver expounding the principle of the inviolability of the particular scheme of life with the Varṇadharmas and Āśramadharmas and all other implications. And the law of Karma further strengthened the idea of the impossibility of reorganising social institutions so as to make possible a fuller life.

Thus, although the original conception of *Dharma* has a grandeur about it and commands our admiration, the same cannot be said about its actual application to social life. The sanctification of any actual—and necessarily imperfect—social arrangement on the ground that it is really the concretised expression of *Dharma* is evidently fraught with danger.

So far as the problem of political obligation is concerned, one of the dangerous consequences of the sanctification of the "status quo" is that the loyalty of the individual now attaches itself to this defective ideal. One can understand the need for rendering

---

4. See Chapter V, supra.

allegiance to an actual institution in as much as it is a partial manifestation of the ideal and a progressive realization of the ideal. But when the actual itself is taken to be the ideal, political obligation is reduced to mere conformity to the requirements of the "status quo." The healthy questioning spirit which dares to challenge the validity of traditional ideas and institutions gets blighted. If the existing social order is regarded as divinely ordained, as being the embodiment of *Dharma*, then, certainly, to raise a doubt about its validity would be but blasphemy and sin. Faith and implicit obedience would be demanded of the individual and his creative spirit choked under the dead weight of tradition. To deny all need for social readjustment and reconstruction involves, as Mac Iver rightly points out, a denial of the necessity that institutions must change with the times and "involves the yet vaster denial of the liberty wherein the spirit can create."[5]

We shall now see how the various hints as to the proper explanation of political obligation that we get in Hindu works can be interpreted in the light of these remarks.

The theory of the divine right of the king has, as we have seen, an important place in Hindu political thought. Our analysis of the ideas of various thinkers on the subject has led us to conclude that the doctrine of the king's divinity is not a mere metaphor but a theory offered as an explanation—if an explanation it can be called—of political allegiance.[6] The people are called upon to obey the king because he is divine. At the same time, the very exposition of the idea of the king's divinity is so managed that this divinity comes to be associated with the maintenance of *Dharma*. For example, in the *Mahābhārata*, as we have seen, it is said that "no one should obey the king by taking him to be a man, for he is in sooth a great god in human form."[7] This assertion, however, does not stand by itself. It comes at the end of a long discussion, which explains the origin of the office of kingship and brings out the importance of the functions of the king as the guardian of

5. *Community*, p. 190.

6. See Chapter I, supra.

7. *Śānti Parva*, LXXII, 25.

Dharma here. It is not difficult, therefore, to relate the idea of the king's divinity to the conception of *Dharma*. Since *Dharma* is a divine principle, the king's office which is conceived of as being connected with *Dharma* must also be divine. It is in the course of the discharge of his functions as the maintainer of *Dharma* that he has to assume the forms of various gods. The maintenance of *Dharma* is, again, such an important function that the king may well be spoken of as being created by divine will. And the sanction of divine authority that is said to be at the back of the authority of the State is also the result of his being the protector of *Dharma*. In a word, the association of the idea of *Dharma* with the kingly office is, by itself, enough to give us a theory of divine right. It is probably by way of amplifying this idea that our authors go on to point out how the king's divinity could be traced from his creation by the Lord or from a similarity of his functions with those of various gods. The king, then, is divine but this divinity is peculiar; it is divinity as seen in the light of *Dharma*.

We have discussed in an earlier chapter, how far the contractual view of political obligation can be traced in Hindu thought. It is not easy at first sight to see how we can reconcile the conception of the king's divinity with the ideas of Hindu authors suggesting a semblance of a contractual basis for his authority. But such reconciliation is possible. We have discussed fully how we cannot speak of a truly contractual theory of political obligation in Hindu thought.[8] The detailed implications of these suggestions as they occur in different versions by different thinkers have also been already worked out in the same connection. The essence of these may well be stated here. On the one hand, they emphasize the idea that people, without the king, were under the sway of matsyanyāya. On the other hand, they insist on the duty of the king to protect the subjects because he receives taxes. The logical fallacies that inevitably crop up in trying to fit these seemingly unrelated—if not antithetic—ideas into the terminology of a compact are obvious. To put them briefly: starting with individuals in that condition, no conception of society can be arrived at; with such

8. See Chapter II, supra.

men to manage—men naturally prone to evil—the king need not recognise any obligation at all. No system of rights and duties can emerge out of a combination of mutually repelling atoms. Such, however, has not perhaps been meant to be the interpretation of these statements. The doctrine of matsyanyāya is brought in just to inculcate the great importance, the absolute necessity, of the king's office as preserver of *Dharma.* The exaggerated statements of the doctrine are but the necessary result of the tendency of Hindu thinkers to lay all emphasis they can on the particular point they set out to explain. As a consequence, some of their statements cannot be reconciled with the general trend of their whole teaching. It is because of this feature of Hindu political thought that we have to analyse and understand the various strands of thought presented to us in their works and then only arrive at our conclusions.[9] The doctrine of matsyanyāya only serves to emphasize the duty of the subjects to obey the king. This is the only significance it can possibly have; for, as we have already seen, there is no logical connection between this state of nature and the civil society that arises later. The insistence of Hindu thinkers on the duty of the king to "protect" his subjects because he receives taxes from them has to be understood as an exposition of the king's Svadharma. Thus, there is really no compact between the king and the people. The duty of the subjects to obey the king is the result of his being the protector of *Dharma* in its empirical aspect. The subjects, therefore, would do well to look upon the king as divine. The king, on his part, is to rule according to *Dharma.* He is not to run away with the idea that being divine, he is irresponsible. He is sharply reminded of his coronation-oath. He is also told that he has definite duties to perform; he has his Svadharma. The responsibility of the king for the discharge

9. Political thought as distinguished from political theory has always to be interpreted like this. It is, by its very nature, vague and inchoate. The complex of political ideas which we call political thought is often embedded in institutions, from which it must be disengaged. Political thought is as broad and wide as the community itself, and is not, as political theory, the product of individual minds, self-conscious and analytic. See Barker: *Political Science in Relation to Other Cognatic Studies*, p. 26.

of his Svadharma is not to the people but to God, or rather to the principle of *Dharma* which underlies the whole universe. His spiritual well-being, we might say, is bound up with the due discharge of his duties. His Svadharma requires him to protect the people and perhaps to behave as if he were their servant. If the divinity of the king emphasizes one aspect of his office, his Svadharma emphasizes the other aspect. The divinity of the king on the one hand and all his duties on the other hand must therefore be taken together. If *Dharma* results in the king's divinity, it also makes him a servant of the people. The daily time-table that has been laid down for him by Kauṭilya, Manu, Yājñavālkya and others gives us the impression that the king is a hardworking official, "a servant of the people." We must not forget, however, that in practice he could alter it to suit himself, so long as the bounds of expediency were not transgressed. Thus, when the king is referred to as "a servant of the people" his direct responsibility to the people is not inculcated. Political obligation does not rest on a contractual basis in that sense. This being so, the statements referring to him as a servant do not really contradict the theory of the king's divinity.

By thus correlating with *Dharma* the divine right of the king on the one hand and the suggestions which seem on the other hand to inculcate a contractual basis of his relation with the subjects, we can understand their real significance.

The implications of the conception of *Dharma* have to be appraised, if we wish to have a true insight into the relation between the king and the subjects. *Dharma*, as we have seen, comes to mean Svadharma.[10] The king must maintain *Dharma* by keeping his subjects in the performance of Svadharma. In order to be able to do this, he must observe his Svadharma. This would define the principles on which the administration of the State is to be carried on. Rājadharma, thus, makes it obligatory on the king to conduct the affairs of the State with the help of his ministers. These were, indeed, his servants and it would be incorrect, therefore, to maintain that they acted as constitutional

---

10. See Chapter V, supra.

checks on his authority.[11] These injunctions are of the same nature as those advising the king to respect the Brāhmaṇas or to respect as far as possible the usages and customs of castes, families, guilds, etc. These indicate the lines along which the king's authority has to be exercised. The very purpose of the State is so conceived that this course of action is inevitable. These rules and regulations cannot therefore be taken as limitations on the king's authority in a constitutional sense. These are all influences, varied and subtle, which leave a profound impression on the whole polity. Nevertheless, the king could legally set them aside, if he wanted to. Still, we cannot afford to ignore the fact that our ancient thinkers were not content merely with a divine right theory. They did not stop with a mere catalogue of the duties of the subjects. The king was "adandya"—immune from punishment—in so far as he was, constitutionally speaking, the ultimate source of the law of the State, the final authority dispensing justice in accordance with *Dharma.* He could not be subject to this law. As a medieval European theorist would put it, "positive law, whether it be declared by will of the prince, or promulgated by the sovereignty of the people, is plainly the creation of the political power of the State, and as such cannot be regarded as below the State."[12] If, however, we understand "law" in a broader sense, if we take it as "not merely that which is decreed by the State" but as "the system of rational order co-extensive and identical with human reason," if, in a word, we take it as "the objective manifestation of moral rule in the social realm," then, certainly, the State must acknowledge its allegiance to that ideal.[13] The king, according to our śāstrakāras, is "adandya" because there is no element in the State to which he must bow. He is, however, subject to *Dharma,* from which the law of the State ultimately derives its sanction.

We see, thus, that the king's divinity does not involve a defence of arbitrariness. Constitutional checks with which we are to-day familiar were quite alien to the Hindu mind. The Hindu statesmen

11. See Chapter VII, supra.

12. cf. Hsiao: *Political Pluralism,* p. II.

13. Hsiao: *op. cit.,* p. 10.

and law-givers could not, therefore, think of such limitations on the authority of the king. A genuine contractual basis of political obligation would thus be incompatible with the spirit of their teachings. But equally absurd would be the contention that the king ruled on the strength of his right divine, recognising no moral obligations himself. On the other hand, whenever the Hindu authors deify the power and position of the monarch, they do it not because he is a repository of power, but because behind the king's power there is a definite purpose. They would not, therefore, look upon the State as merely the embodiment of power. If the king's authority were apotheosized as mere authority, then, it would be but an apology for tyranny. But here the king's divinity has a significance in the ordering of *Dharma*. As a result, we find that Daṇḍa, which is the principle of authority or power, coercive from the stand-point of the ruler but protective from the stand-point of the subjects, has been correlated to *Dharma*.[14] Further, it is evidently because of this emphasis on *Dharma* as the guiding spirit of the whole polity that though the basis of the king's authority was autocratic, its actual exercise need not have been tyrannical.[15]

The nature of political obligation as visualised by Hindu thinkers cannot, thus, be comprehended within the limits of any one of the theories we have discussed in our earlier chapters. One has to go much deeper into the problem. The king of the *Dharma-rājya* is pictured by our ancients as "delighting his people by means of *Dharma*." The duty of the king to identify his interests with those of his subjects has been repeatedly stressed by them. The detailed injunctions to the king to rule with the help of a particular administrative machinery to mete out justice on a definite principle, to act in a particular way according to time and place and in a word, to follow the policy laid down in the *Nīti-śāstras*—all these—are an unmistakable indication of the intense conviction of our ancient sages that *Dharma* alone must be the guiding spirit of the polity. They tried to express this sometimes

---

14. See Chapter III, supra.

15. See Chapter VII, supra.

by speaking of the king as a servant (Bhṛitya) of the people. Sometimes they expressed it by saying that the king must he a veritable father to his subjects. It is strange and surprising that some of our modern scholars have interpreted this to mean that the king had absolute control over the subjects, like the father has over his children. The correct significance of this paternal attitude, we feel, is otherwise and has well been brought out by the poet, who speaks of the king as the father of the people because of his protecting them, maintaining them and educating them (Kalidasa: *Raghuvamsa*). It is also the self-same motive of emphasizing the king's subjection to *Dharma* that religious merit is regarded as accruing to him if he rules according to *Dharma*—i.e. according to the principles laid down in the sacred works. The nemesis of misrule is also spiritual downfall and sin. By these various means, the Hindu thinkers attempted to translate in institutional terms their vision of the State based on *Dharma*. It is in this light that we have to read the significance of their injunctions regarding the ordering of the State.

Similarly, when the king is spoken of as Daṇḍa-dhara, when Daṇḍa is personified and deified, it would be wrong to say that the State is made to rest on sheer might. For, Daṇḍa is the means by which *Dharma* is to be maintained. It is coercive indeed, but not without a purpose. Daṇḍa is not might or force which the king can make use of to suit his arbitrary whims and fancies. It is a two-sided weapon. If it punishes the subjects, it also punishes the king. The king appears to be wielding Daṇḍa and visiting it on the subjects as he likes, but really, he has to keep himself within the bounds of *Dharma*. Daṇḍa is related to *Dharma*. It is to be utilised by the king to safeguard *Dharma*. This principle, which is to guarantee the performance of their Svadharmas by the subjects, would not be trampled under foot by the king. For, in relation to the king himself, the operation of Daṇḍa is automatic. If the king fails to discharge his duty, Daṇḍa is a principle that exacts penalty automatically. 'Adandya' legally, the king is not morally or spiritually immune. That is why the authority of the State as symbolised by Daṇḍa is not force, pure and simple; it is force backed by a moral principle.

Having thus stated the attitude of Hindu thinkers to the problem of political obligation, we must now turn our attention to some of their errors and shortcomings. Our analysis of the various hints regarding the problem of political obligation brings out clearly that ancient Indian thought generally places too much emphasis on the king's divine right and also exaggerates the part played by force in the management of the State.[16] And here again, it is their extraordinary attachment to stability and order in society that seems to have misled them. Once the social order has been identified with *Dharma* and the king's divinity postulated in view of his protection of *Dharma*, all innovation naturally comes to be distrusted. The authority of the king tends unduly to be exalted, and the inevitable conclusion can hardly be avoided that "even an infant king should not be despised"[17] and that "a king, though worthless, must be constantly worshipped by the subjects."[18] Clearly, such an attitude penalises the questioning spirit. The mere admission of the possibility or even the advisability of abandoning, deposing or killing a king who rules in glaring contravention of *Dharma* does not really make the position of the subjects in any way less intolerable. It is because of this that we have refused to accept the view that "only a righteous king was regarded as divine."[19]

This is one instance of how the identification of the actual social order with *Dharma* has led to the suppression of the claims of individuality. The Hindu view of human nature and the proper function of Daṇḍa has also had similar consequences. We have seen how man is considered by Hindu authors as essentially wicked and as prone to negligence of duty thus requiring some kind of compulsion.[20] The State, to Hindu authors, is not merely the embodiment of brute force. Their idea was rather to order it in such a way that it may be in tune with the eternal harmony of

16. See Chapters I and III, supra.

17. *Manu*, VII, 8.

18. *Nārada*, XVIII, 22.

19. See Chapter I, supra.

20. See Chapter III, supra.

Dharma. But the function of Daṇḍa in the ordering of the State is a denial of the value of human personality. The *Manu-smṛiti*[21] and the *Mahābhārata*[22] even personify Daṇḍa describing him as a monster "of dark complexion and red eyes, having four teeth, four arms, eight legs, and with ears like arrows and hair upright." The fear of punishment is made the motive force behind morality. Thus, the Hindu conceptions of matsyanyāya and Daṇḍa cut at the very root of the idea of obligation; they deny the existence and power of "the still small voice" of conscience and therefore the ultimate sacredness of the innermost convictions which bear the stamp of a distinct personality.

Thus, the exaggerated emphasis on the king's divine right as also on the functions of Daṇḍa have the same effect; viz., of unduly exalting the authority of the king and denying to that extent the right to challenge the existing social order.

The failure to grasp the real nature of individuality is responsible for landing the Hindu authors in such pitfalls. We have seen how the content of *Dharma* in its empirical aspect shows an emphasis on the separateness of the individual, on the autonomy of the self, and does not teach the individual to realise himself in fellowship with others. The quest of human life is not regarded as a co-operative endeavour.[23] Thus, while there is an undue emphasis on the separateness of the individual in the code of social duties laid down by our ancients, we find here that the individual is reduced to an automaton in his relation to the State. The inequalities before law which are sanctified by our śāstrakāras also indicate how the value of human personality as such, apart from membership of caste, was not realised by them. It is on account of this that the organismic metaphor in the Purusha Sukta fails to lead to an organic conception of society.[24] It is thus that

---

21. *Manu,* VII, 14, 17, 22.
22. *Śānti Parva,* Chs. XV and CXXI.
23. See Chapter V, supra.
24. See Chapter IV, supra.

citizenship does not come to be viewed as an ethical function, inspired by the vision of a common good.

To sum up: the real contribution of Hindu thinkers lies in their intuitive perception of the fact that the loyalties of man must ultimately be unified in the light of one supreme principle. Minor loyalties need not be sacrificed; they could all be ordered in accordance with the central unifying principle. And this unifying principle must be sought in the concept of *Dharma*, which underlies the order of the whole universe. Political obligation is thus related to the ultimate obligation to that essential principle which gives man his proper place in the universe, which enables him so to mould his institutions as to attain a harmony with the universe. The function of the State would thus be essentially spiritual. It would be no less than "the adjusting of the requirements and claims of different institutions on him, the resolution of the conflict of his divided obligation and the determination which of these stands for the most fundamental interest to himself and to society,"[25] in the light of *Dharma*. The State would, then, serve, to use Dr. Bosanquet's phrase, as "the operative criticism of all institutions." While the loyalty of the individual would, thus, always be to the ideal, to the actual it would be offered only in so far as it sought to reach up to the ideal.

It must be admitted that it is by no means an easy task to build up institutions that would make possible the realisation of this ideal. Equally difficult it is to arrive at a theory that would synthesize the claims of human personality in the light of such an ideal. The great problem is to relate the conception of *Dharma* to the teleological springs of human life and to develop an adequate theory that would establish the right relation between the State and the individual.[26]

---

25. See Hetherington and Muirhead: *Social Purpose*, pp. 250-252.

26. cf. 'The problem of personality is one of the greatest in philosophy. I am sure that I require and desire enlightenment on it. But I am equally sure that I am not enlightened by being told that my true and ultimate personality lies in my isolation from the world of my fellowmen and of God and that everything else is merely adjectival and accidental.' Muirhead: Article in *Mind*, Vol. XXXIII.

Our ancient thinkers stopped with visualising a principle which would govern the entire universe. When they tried to relate this principle to human life they were baffled. They could hardly have realised the nature of forces that mould society and determine the course of social development. They did not think of a new ideal world-order in which relationship would be organised according to *Dharma*. The law-books, the *Arthaśāstra* works, the *Nīti-śāstras* that they have left us embody the results of an endeavour to systematise life in all its aspects, so as to leave the least possible scope for confusion. It is only in this light that these works have to be appreciated; they are to be approached neither in a spirit of superstitious reverence, nor in a spirit of cynical contempt or derision; they are to be understood with reference to their age.

The defects of the conception of *Dharma* as visualised by them have necessarily to be avoided. We have seen how *Dharma* came to be identified with the actual social order.[27] Stability and order were exalted as supreme ends.

The value of all initiative came to be denied and the claims of human personality were suppressed. Political obligation, thus, came to be identified with unquestioning conformity to the requirements of the "status quo." A good citizen came to mean a person only discharging the duties of his station in life without questioning. An active interest in the affairs of the State was thus made impossible.

It is necessary, therefore, to revisualise our ideal polity. The conception of *Dharma* needs to be reinterpreted. The most important point to note for this purpose is that the relation between the State and the individual must be properly understood. The problem of political theory and of political art is often said

27. It may be pointed out here that in the light of the above remarks it becomes easy to understand how even to-day we are only too prone to look upon the slightest departure from the traditional path as a violation of *Dharma*. *Dharma* has been so completely identified with the actual order that in popular parlance, it is used to indicate all that has the sanctity of tradition behind it. Even the smallest innovation thus comes to be distrusted. It is a welcome sign of the times, however, that this superstitious reverence for the traditional is slowly but surely melting away at the touch of the enlivening spirit of enquiry.

to be to find the real individual. The failure to find the real individual is fraught with danger. It may lead either to uncritical individualism or to equally uncritical collectivism. The question, therefore, is: what is the essential nature of the individual? The fallacies arising from thinking of the individual as in his nature an isolated, independent unit are too obvious to be discussed here. If we start from such a view, "the paradox of self-government" cannot be solved. The liberty of the citizen would, in that case, be measured "not by the nature of the governmental machinery he lives under, whether representative or other, but by the relative paucity of the restraints it imposes on him."[28] How such assumptions "erect the paradox of self-government into an insoluble contradiction" has been demonstrated to us by political philosophers like Green, Bradley and Bosanquet, who summon us back to the glorious vision of Plato. Individuality consists not in the separateness of one man from another; it is not the same thing as eccentricity. True individuality is "the capacity for union" and its true measure is the capacity one has to find one's place in society. "The true nature of every man," it has been said,[29] "is found only in the whole." Man finds the greatest joy of his life not when he thinks of a good that pertains to him as apart from his fellows but when he so orders his life that the fulfilment of his needs enables him to contribute his utmost to the common good. There is thus no antagonism between the individual and the State; for, the end of both is the same—viz., the realisation of the best life. The State, therefore, has well been called a moral whole, through membership of which, every individual can make his unique contribution to the common good and so seek the fulfilment and realisation of his personality.

---

28. cf. Spencer: *Man vs. the State*, p.15.

29. cf. Follett: *The New State*, Ch. VII; Mac Iver: *Community*, pp. 221 and 417. cf. also: "We have to keep in mind that our individuality by its nature is impelled to seek for the universal... The more vigorous our individuality the more does it widen towards the universal. For, the greatness of a personality is not in itself, but in its content, which is universal, just as the depth of a lake is judged not by the size of its cavity but by the depth of its water." Tagore: *Sadhana*, p. 59.

Political obligation has thus its roots in the very nature of human personality. As T.H. Green puts it, to ask why I render allegiance to the State, is to ask why I allow my life to be regulated by that complex of institutions without which I should not have a life to call my own. It is loyalty to one's true self that demands loyalty to the whole which is the State. To speak in terms familiar to our ancient thinkers, this would mean that one's obligation to observe one's Svadharma must rest on the conviction that only by discharging the duties of Svadharma one can develop one's potentialities[30] and so contribute to the better working of social institutions that they may express more and more fully the divine purpose which is *Dharma.*

In order that the individual may thus truly seek the realisation of his self in society, in order that he may identify himself with the end of the State, it is necessary to see that the State represents "the coherence of the whole." The end of the State must be the realisation of the best life that the individual may possibly grow into. This means that the equality of civil and political rights must be guaranteed. Citizenship must be considered as an ethical function transcending the narrower loyalties, so that it may lead to the individual's identifying himself with the good of the whole, which really is the demand of his inner nature. A hierarchical scheme of social classes, involving various disabilities on some and privileges for others, cannot be justified, if we but remember that the State must afford an opportunity for every man to find out his Svadharma by first understanding his Svabhāva. So long as the State seeks merely to protect the privileges of the few, it cannot represent the coherence of the whole. In such a State, there can be only rulers on the one hand and the ruled on the

---

30. Dr. Bosanquet speaking of the Greek citizen says, "...... And to live well meant for him to live that life in which the separate human animal feels and knows himself to have his true being in an 'end'...... an aim or purpose, which is at once in its deepest sense his own and also real and permanent and greater than his separate self, having actual existence in a social group with its sense of community, its spirit and its laws. And such a life is called living well because only in it and not without it, can the nature of a human individual unfold its capacities and become the most and the highest that it has in it to be."—Essay on 'Duties of Citizenship', in *Science and Philosophy and Other Essays*, p. 212.

other hand; for, the interest of those excluded from power are bound to suffer in such an arrangement. It would be futile, so long as such iniquity persists, to expect the development of a healthy citizen spirit, so that every man looks upon his fellow-citizens as essentially on the same quest, aiming at the realisation of the common good.

This means that *Dharma* must be revisualised so as to mean "that perfect order by which all natures and classes do their own business, the right man in the right place, the division and co-operation of all citizens."[31] In other words, we must visualise a functional society, in which each, finding his proper "station," contributes to the harmonious working of the whole. This means, it must be remembered, that there must be an opportunity for every man to determine the place for which he is really fitted. Svadharma, in other words, cannot be a code of duties laid down for all time as obligatory on one by the mere fact of birth. It can only be arrived at, in the light of one's Svabhāva—one's innate aptitude—after a process of trial and error.[32] We must, therefore, visualise the ideal society as one in which every man would get adequate opportunities to discover the requirements of the law of his being, without being hampered by the privileges of birth or power or wealth. Then only should we be able to say that each one duly fulfilling the obligations of Svadharma realises himself and also contributes to the harmonious working of the whole society. It is when Svadharma is thus determined that we can accept the truth of the dictum of the *Bhagavad-gītā* that one's own duty, though inferior from some other point of view, should not be abandoned.

Our study thus shows clearly that Hindu thought has unduly emphasized the maxims and doctrines which inculcate, above all things, the need for the maintenance of the status quo. There are times, indeed, when all change is fraught with danger, when change may mean the destruction of the whole social order and

31. Vide Plato: *Republic*, Introduction by Jowett, p. lxiii.

32. cf. Laski: *Grammar of Politics*, p. 95.

therefore the undoing of the work of generations together. In times of stress, society may be driven to conserving what it already has achieved, instead of adding to its achievements. It is evident, however, that undue emphasis on stability may mean stagnation; and stagnation is death. In the realm of political thought, our ancient thinkers have certainly presented a very defective solution to the problem of political obligation, probably because of their extraordinary attachment to the existing social order.

Further, it is true that Hindu thought does not present a coherent theory of political obligation. We have seen, however, that there is, underlying all the maxims of policy and statecraft that we come across in our ancient works, the idea that all loyalties must be ordered in the light of the conception of *Dharma.* Because of this conception, the sovereignty of the State, as they understood it, was not irreconcilable with the healthy functioning of local groups and the various associations and institutions within the purview of the State. Political obligation—or loyalty to the State—did not, therefore, appear to them as conflicting with the loyalty to other institutions. The State was rather conceived of as the necessary guarantee for the due discharge of these loyalties. We feel that they were thus on the high road to the proper understanding of the problem of political obligation. But when we consider the explanations of political obligation offered by them, it becomes clear that although they are far from justifying or offering an apology for tyranny, there is too much stress laid on the wickedness of human nature and on the divinity of the king. Therefore, instead of being able to relate *Dharma* to the springs of man's moral life, they reduced it to a scheme to be enforced on the individual with the threat of the penalty of Daṇḍa. If only the actual social order had not been identified with the eternal order of *Dharma*, it is likely that the Hindu thinkers would probably have risen to an adequate conception of the nature of individuality. Then, probably, they would have arrived at a theory of political obligation more in accordance with the real nature of human personality.

The greatest need for the present, therefore, is to lay stress on the necessity of ordered change. While recognising the fundamental truth that all loyalties must be ordered and unified in the light of the principle that underlies the universe, we have to emphasize that our social institutions are always imperfect. The conception of *Dharma* ought to be taken to mean that there is an ideal social order which if realised here would not only enable each man to rise to the fullest development he is capable of but would also bring about a harmony all through the universe.

To such an ideal, our ultimate allegiance must be acknowledged. To the actual, loyalty would be due only to the extent to which it attempts to reach up to the ideal. Our loyalty to the ideal may thus demand an unequivocal repudiation on our part of the claim of any actual institution on our loyalty. This involves perpetual vigilance. The good citizen is not one who merely accepts orders. Freedom is not a gift that can be won once and for all. A life of freedom is to be lived every moment. The best institutions would not bring down the millennium, so long as there is no genuine love for freedom in the ordinary citizen. Those people who already have political freedom are not necessarily free, they are merely powerful. In the so-called free countries, it is well-known, the majority of the people are just driven by the minority to a goal which is not even known to them.[33] True citizenship must thus mean a genuine passion for the realisation of freedom. It must mean the readiness to strive after the ideal and to go ever forward at all cost. Creative citizenship involves a close and continuous scrutiny of governmental actions. Here lies the value of the pragmatic attitude. The end of the State may be the realisation of the best life. The actual organisation of the governmental machinery may, however, be such that genuine loyalty to the ideal may make it imperative to withdraw one's loyalty to the actual.[34] Even where it is not necessary to take so drastic a step as this and to declare an open revolt, there is always scope for suggestion and

---

33. Tagore: *Nationalism*, p. 121.

34. cf. Laski: *Grammar of Politics*, pp. 25-27, 96-97.

amendment in any existing institution. Faith in the conception of progress demands that the actual be constantly criticised and hence elevated so as to approximate more and more to the ideal. Not only in their individual capacity, but also in their corporate capacity, men have to "rise on the stepping-stones of their dead selves to higher things." An institution may be good at one stage of society and bad at another. Even "one good custom" may "corrupt the world." Institutions are but instrumental to life. They are not ends in themselves. They have no right divine to claim the loyalty of the individual. Institutions are good or evil according to the ends they serve. Since life means change, our institutions need constant modification and reform, lest instead of offering scope to our creative activity they should overpower us and imprison us within their stonewalls. "We are not fossils," says Miss Follett, "petrified in our social strata. We are alive. That is the first lesson for us to learn."[35] In this sense, it has truly been said, the battle of freedom is never won once for all; we have to win it afresh for ourselves daily. "If history teaches anything at all," observes Mac Iver, "it must surely teach us this, that no community can save itself which regards its institutions as unchangeable, which does not subject them continually to the test of the service of the common weal."[36]

To sum up, finally, the conception of *Dharma* as having the ultimate claim on our loyalty need not be given up. It is a valuable conception that gives us a fair insight into how our diverse loyalties have to be ordered. It teaches that the individual can be true to his real self only by keeping pace with the rhythm of the universe. It is this conception, again, which saves us from the pitfalls of the theory of sovereignty which looks upon the State as a closed institution unrelated to the rest of the world. These are elements of value in our heritage, which we must claim as our own. That is why the conception of *Dharma* should not be surrendered. Only it must be properly interpreted. We look behind only to look forward. The errors of the past have got to be carefully avoided.

---

35. *The New State*, p. 99.

36. Mac Iver: *Community*, p. 165.

While, therefore, we admit that our allegiance is to the ideal social order which is the embodiment of *Dharma* and while we recognise that all our loyalties must be harmonised in the light of that conception, we also lay stress on the fact that this ideal has to be actually translated in institutional terms. The ideal before us is not the ideal of a monarchy, an aristocracy, or of the "counting of heads" democracy. We must emphasize that a monarchy or an aristocracy can no longer appeal to us. It is only in a genuine democracy that the avenues for the expression of the citizen-spirit can be opened out to the individual. This means that the level of the citizen will have to be raised, institutions will have to be created where the various purposes in social life may be realised, opportunities will have to be opened out for the blossoming forth of the latent capacities of the individual. The *Dharma-rājya* of the future cannot be created on the foundation of an iniquitous social order. It is well to build up a great edifice. Organisations have a great value in life. But they sometimes imprison within their dead stone-walls the creative spirit of man. In the State we build up, there shall not be a slave buried alive beneath the foundation. It is obvious that this is a heavy task. But that is the proper field for human endeavour. We have not merely to visualise our ideal polity; we have to live it.

SELECT BIBLIOGRAPHY

Note:—A list of important books consulted is given here. Further references will be found in the Footnotes in the Text.

Acton: *History of Freedom*, Macmillan & Co., Ltd., 1922.

Aiyangar, K.V.R.: *Some Aspects of Ancient Indian Polity*, S.P.C. Press, Madras, 1916.

Arnold, Sir E.: *The Song Celestial*, Kegan Paul, London, 1905.

Bagehot, W.: *Physics and Politics*, Kegan Paul, London.

Bandyopadhyaya: *Kautilya*, R. Cambray & Co.

Banerjea, P.N.: *Public Administration in Ancient India*, Macmillan & Co., Ltd., 1916.

Barker, E.: *Greek Political Theory*, Methuen & Co.

" ": *Political Thought in England*, Thornton Butterworth, London, 1928.

Barnes, H.E.: *Sociology and Political Theory*, Alfred A. Knopf, New York.

Basu, P.C.: *Indo-Aryan Polity*, Pioneer Press.

Bhandarkar, D.R.: *Lectures on the Ancient Indian Polity*, University of Calcutta, 1919.

" ": *Some Aspects of Ancient Indian Polity*, Manindra Chandra Nandy Lectures, 1925.

Blochmann, H.: *Ain-i-Akbari (Tr.)*, Baptist Mission Press, Calcutta, 1875.

Bloomfield, M.: *Religion of the Veda*, Knickerbocker Press, 1908.

Bloomfield: *Hymns of the Atharva Veda (Tr.)*, Clarendon Press, Oxford.

Bluntschli, J.K.: *Theory of the State*, Clarendon Press, Oxford.

Bosanquet, B: *Philosophical Theory of the State*, Macmillan & Co., Ltd., 1925.

" " *Science and Philosophy and Other Essays*, George Allen & Unwin.

Bradley, F.H.: *Ethical Studies*, Clarendon Press, Oxford.

Brinkmann, C.: *Recent Theories of Citizenship in its relation to Government*, Yale Univ. Press.

Bryce, J.: *Modern Democracies.*

Buhler, G. (Tr.): *Sacred Laws of the Aryas*, Clarendon Press, 1886.

" " *Laws of Manu*, Clarendon Press, Oxford.

Burlingame, E.W.: *Buddhist Legends*, Parts: I, II, & IV. Harvard University Press, 1921.

" " *Buddhist Parables.*

Burns, Delisle: *Political Ideals*, Oxford University Press, 1927.

Catlin, G.E.G.: *Science and Method of Politics*, Kegan Paul, French, Treubner & Co., 1927.

Cole, G.D.H.: *Social Theory*, Methuen & Co.

Coulanges, F. De.: *Ancient City*, Lothrof, Lee & Shepherd Co., Boston.

Cowell, E.B. (Tr.): *Buddha-Karita of Asvaghosha*, Clarendon Press, Oxford.

Das, A.C.: *Ṛig-vedic India*, University of Calcutta.

Dasgupta: *History of Indian Philosophy*, University of Cambridge, 1922.

Davids, Rhys: *Buddhist India*, T. Fisher Unwin, London.

" " *Questions of King Milinda*, Clarendon Press, Oxford.

" " *Origin and Growth of Religion*, Williams & Morgate, London, 1906.

" (Mr. and Mrs.): *Dialogues of Buddha, Parts I and II*, Sacred Books of the Buddhists Series.

" (Mrs.) *Buddhism*, H.U.L. Series.

Davidson, W.L.: *Political Thought in England*, H.U.L. Series.

Deussen, Paul: *Philosophy of the Upanishads*, T. & T. Clark, Edinburgh, 1906.

Dickinson, G.L.: *Meaning of Good*, J.M. Dents & Sons, 1921.

" " *Justice and Liberty.*

Dikshitar, V.R.R.: *Hindu Administrative Institutions*, University of Madras.

Duguit, Leon: *Law in the Modern State*, B.W. Huchsch, New York, 1919.

Dunning, W.A.: *History of Political Theories*,
I. Ancient and Medieval.
II. From Luther to Montesquieu.
III. Rousseau to Spencer.
Macmillan & Co., Ltd., New York, 1902, 1905, 1920.

Dutt, M.N. (Tr.): *Agni Purana.*

" " *Mahabharata.*

Dutt, N.K.: *Origin and Growth of Caste in India*, Kegan Paul, London.

Eggeling, J. (Tr.): *Satapatha Brahmana*, Clarendon Press, Oxford.

Fausboll, V.: *Sutta Nipata.*

Fick, R.: *Social Organisation in North-east India in Buddhist Times*, University of Calcutta.

Follett, M.P.: *The New State*, Longmans, Green & Co., Ltd., 1926.

Fowler, W.W.: *The City State of the Greeks and the Romans*, Macmillan & Co., Ltd., London.

Garner: *Introduction to Political Science.*

Gettell, R.G.: *History of Political Thought*, The Century Co., New York and London.

Ghose, Aurobindo: *Essays on the Gita*, Arya Publishing House, Calcutta.

Ghoshal, U.N.: *History of Hindu Political Theories*, Oxford University Press, 1923.

Gierke : *Political Theories of the Middle Ages*, Cambridge University.

Gooch, G.P.: *Political Thought in England*, H.U.L. Series.

Green, T.H.: Principles of Political Obligation, Longmans, Green & Co., Ltd., 1913.

" " *Prolegomena to Ethics*, Clarendon Press, Oxford.

Griffith, R.T.H.: *The Ramayana of Valmiki*, Trubner & Co., London.

" " *Hymns of the Rig-veda*, E.J. Lazarus & Co., Benarus.

" " *Hymns of the Atharva-veda*, E.J. Lazarus & Co., Benarus.

Hadow, W.H.: *Citizenship*, Clarendon Press, Oxford.

Hastings, J.: *Encyclopaedia of Religion and Ethics.*

Havell: *History of Aryan Rule in India*, G.G. Harrap & Co., London.

Hearnshaw, F.J.C.: *Social and Political Ideas of Some Great Medieval Thinkers*, Henry Holt & Co., 1923.

Hetherington & Muirhead: *Social Purpose*, Allen & Unwin, London.

Hobbes, T.: *Leviathan*, J.M. Dent & Sons.

Hobhouse, L.T.: *Metaphysical Theory of the State*, George, Allen & Unwin, London.

" " *Elements of Social Justice*, George, Allen & Unwin, London.

Hocart, A.M.: *Kingship*, Oxford University Press, London.

Hopkins: *Ethics of India*, Yale University Press.

Hsiao, K.C.: *Political Pluralism*, Kegan Paul, London.

Jarrett, H.S. (Tr.): Ain-i-Akbari, Baptist Mission Press, Calcutta.

Jayaswal, K.P.: *Hindu Polity*, Butterworth & Co., Calcutta, 1924.

Joad, C.E.M.: *Introduction to Modern Political Theory*, Clarendon Press, Oxford.

" " *Modern Philosophy*, The World's Manual Series.

Jolly, J. (Tr.): *The Minor Law-Books*, Clarendon Press, Oxford.

" " *The Institutes of Vishnu*, Clarendon Press, Oxford.

" " *Hindu Law and Custom*, Clarendon Press, Oxford.

Jones, H.: *Principles of Citizenship*, Macmillan & Co., Ltd., 1919.

Jowett, B.: *Dialogues of Plato*, Vols. III and V, Clarendon Press, Oxford.

Kamandaka:	*Nitisara.*
Kant, Immanuel:	*Perpetual Peace*, Allen & Unwin.
Keith, A.B.:	*History of Sanskrit Literature*, Clarendon Press, Oxford.
" (Tr.):	*Rig-veda Brahmanas.*
"	*Buddhist Philosophy*, Clarendon Press, Oxford.
Laski, Harold J.:	*Religion and Philosophy of the Veda and Upanishads.*
" "	*Liberty in the Modern State*, Faber & Faber, Ltd., London.
" "	*Political Thought in England*, William & Norgate, Ltd., London, 1927.
" "	*Studies in the Problem of Sovereignty*, Yale University Press, New Haven, 1924.
" "	*Foundations of Sovereignty and other Essays*, George Allen & Unwin, London, 1921.
" "	*Introduction to Politics.*
" "	*Dangers of Obedience and other Essays*, Harper & Brothers, New York, 1930.
" "	*A Grammar of Politics*, George Allen & Unwin, Ltd., London.
" "	*Authority in the Modern State*, Yale University Press.
Law, N.N.:	*Studies in Indian History and Culture*, Luzac & Co.
" "	*Studies in Ancient Hindu Polity*, Longmans, Green & Co., Ltd.
Locke, John:	*On Civil Government*, J.M. Dent & Sons, Ltd.
MacCunn, J.:	*Ethics of Citizenship*, James Maclehose & Sons, Glasgow, 1896.
" "	*The Political Philosophy of Burke*, Edward Arnold & Co., London, 1913.
Macdonell, A.A. & Keith, A.B.:	*Vedic Index of Names and Subjects*, Vols. I and II. John Murray, London, 1912.
Macdonell, A.A.:	*India's Past*, Clarendon Press, Oxford, 1927.
Machiavelli:	*The Prince*, Henry Fowde, London.
Mac'Iver:	*Community*, Macmillan & Co., Ltd., 1920.
" "	*The Modern State*, Clarendon Press, Oxford, 1926.

MacKenzie, J.S.: *Fundamental Problems of Life*, George Allen & Unwin, Ltd., London.

" " *Outlines of Social Philosophy*, George Allen & Unwin, Ltd., London.

McCrindle: *Ancient India*, Calcutta, 1926.

Maine, Sir Henry S.: *Ancient Law*, George Routledge & Sons, Ltd., London.

Maitra, S.K.: *The Ethics of the Hindus*, Calcutta University Press, 1925.

Majumdar, R.C.: *Corporate Life in Ancient India*, Calcutta University, 1922.

Mc'Dougall, William: *National Welfare and National Decay*, Methuen & Co., Ltd., London.

McKechine: *The State and the Individual.*

McKenzie, John: *Hindu Ethics*, Oxford University Press, 1922.

Merriam & Barnes: *Political Theories*, Macmillan & Co., Ltd.

Mill, John Stuart: *On Liberty*, Longmans, Green & Co., Ltd. London.

" " *Utilitarianism*, George Routledge & Sons, Ltd., London.

Monier-Williams: *Buddhism*, John Murray, London, 1889.

Mookerji, R.: *Men and Thought in Ancient India*, Macmillan & Co., Ltd., 1924.

" " *The Fundamental Unity of India*, Longmans, Green & Co., Ltd.

" " *Local Government in Ancient India*, Clarendon Press, Oxford, 1919.

More, Sir Thomas: *The Utopia*, Macmillan & Co., Ltd., 1922.

Mookerjee, R.: *Democracies of the East*, P.S. King & Sons, Ltd., London, 1923.

Max Muller, F.: *Six Systems of Indian Philosophy*, Longmans, Green & Co., Ltd., 1899.

" " *The Upanishads*, Pts. I-II. Clarendon Press, Oxford, 1879.

" " *Selected Essays on Language, Mythology and Religion*, Longmans, Green & Co., Ltd., London, 1881.

" " *Dhammapada*, S.B.E. Vol. X, Part I.

" " *India: What it can teach us*, Longmans, Green & Co., Ltd., 1896.

Muller-Lyer, Dr. F.: *The History of Social Development*, George Allen & Unwin, Ltd., London.

Newman, W.L.: *The Politics of Aristotle*, Clarendon Press, Oxford, 1887.

Pal, Radhabinode: *The Hindu Philosophy of Law*, Bishvabhandar Press, Calcutta.

Pollock, Sir F.: *History of the Science of Politics*, Macmillan & Co., Ltd.; 1912.

Prasad, Beni: *Theory of Government in Ancient India (Post-Vedic)*, The Indian Press, Ltd., Allahabad, 1927.

" ": *The State in Ancient India*, The Indian Press, Ltd., Allahabad, 1927.

Puntambekar, S.V.: *Indian Civilization and Citizenship.*

Radhakrishnan, S.: *Indian Philosophy*, Macmillan & Co., Ltd., 1923.

" ": *The Hindu View of Life*, George Allen & Unwin, Ltd., London.

Rapson, S.J.: *The Cambridge History of India*, Vol. I. University Press, Cambridge, 1922.

Ratzel: *The History of Mankind*, Macmillan & Co., Ltd., 1896.

Risley, Sir H.H.: *The People of India*, Thacker Spink & Co., Simla and Calcutta, 1915.

Ritchie, David G.: *Principles of State Interference*, Swan Sonneschein & Co., Ltd., London, 1902.

Russell, Bertrand: *Political Ideals*, The Century Co., New York, 1917.

" ": *Principles of Social Reconstruction*, George Allen & Unwin, Ltd.

Sachau,Dr. Edward C.: *Alberuni's India*, Kegan Paul, London.

Sarkar, B.K.: *The Positive Background of Hindu Sociology*, Panini Office, Bahadurganj, Allahabad, 1914.

" ": *Sukra-Niti-Sara*, Panini Office, Bahadurganj, Allahabad, 1914.

" ": *The Political Institutions and Theories of the Hindus*, Leipzig, 1922.

Sarkar, Jadunath: *India through the Ages*, 1928.

Sastri, K.S.R.: *Hindu Culture.*

Senart, Emile: *Caste in India*, Methuen & Co., 1930.

Sen Gupta, N.C.: *Sources of Law and Society in Ancient India*, Art Press, Calcutta, 1914.

Seth, James: *Ethical Principles*, William Blackwood & Sons.

Shamsastri, R.: *Kautilya's Arthasastra*, Govt. Press, Bangalore, 1915.

" " *Evolution of Indian Polity*, University of Calcutta, 1920.

Siddhanta, N.K.: *The Heroic Age of India*, Kegan Paul, 1929.

Smith, Vincent A.: *The Early History of India*, Clarendon Press, Oxford, 1914.

" " *The Oxford History of India*, Clarendon Press, Oxford, 1923.

Spencer, Herbert: *The Man Vs. The State*, Watts & Co., London, 1909.

" " *The Principles of Sociology*, Vol. I. Williams & Norgate, 1893.

Speyer, J.S.: *The Jataka-Mala of Arya Sura*, Henry Fowde, London.

Steel, Flora Annie: *India through the Ages*, George Routledge & Sons, Ltd., London.

Tawney, R.A.: *The Acquisitive Society*, Harcourt, Brace & Howe, New York, 1920.

" " *Equality*, 1931.

Telang, K.T. : *The Bhagavadgita, the Sanatsugatiya and the Anugita*, Clarendon Press, Oxford, 1908.

Tiele: *Outlines of the History of Religion*, Trubner & Co.

Tozer: *Rousseau's Social Contact.*

Treitschke, H. Von: *Politics*, Constable & Co., Ltd., London, 1916.

Urwick, E.J.: *A Philosophy of Social Progress*, Methuen & Co., Ltd., London.

" " *The Social Good*, Methuen & Co., Ltd., London.

Venkateswara, S.V.: *Indian Culture through the Ages*, Vol. I. Longmans, Green & Co., Ltd., 1928.

Vaidya, C.V.: *Downfall of Hindu India*, 1926.

Studies in the History of Political Philosophy, Vols. I and II. University Press, Manchester, 1925.

" " *The Political Writings of Jean Jacques Rousseau*, Manchester University, 1915.

Wallas, Graham: *Human Nature in Politics*, Constable & Co., London, 1927.

" " *Our Social Heritage*, George Allen & Unwin, Ltd.

" " *The Great Society*, Macmillan & Co., Ltd., London.

Warren, H.C.: *Buddhism in Translations*.

Weldon, J.E.C.: *The Nicomachaen Ethics of Aristotle*, Macmillan & Co., Ltd., London, 1892.

" " *The Politics of Aristotle*, Macmillan & Co., Ltd., London, 1912.

Wells, H.G.: *The Outlines of History*, Cassell & Co., Ltd., London.

Willoughby: *The Nature of the State*.

Wilson, H.H.: *Rig-Veda Samhita*, Vol. I & VI. Ashtekar & Co., Poona, 1925.

Wolf, Abraham: *Spinoza*.

Vidyarnava, S.C.: *Yajnavalkya Smriti*, Panini Office, Allahabad, 1918.

INDEX